S0-BHX-120

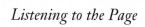

Listening to the Page

Also by Alan Cheuse

FICTION

Candace and Other Stories
The Bohemians
The Grandmothers' Club
The Tennessee Waltz and Other Stories
The Light Possessed
Lost and Old Rivers: Stories

NONFICTION

Fall Out of Heaven

BOOKS EDITED

The Sound of Writing (with Caroline Marshall)
Listening to Ourselves (with Caroline Marshall)
Talking Horse: Bernard Malamud on Life and Work (with Nicholas Delbanco)

Listening to the Page

adventures in reading and writing

Alan Cheuse

columbia university press   new york

LIBRARY
FRANKLIN PIERCE COLLEGE
RINDGE, NH 03461

Columbia University Press
Publishers Since 1893
New York   Chichester, West Sussex

Copyright © 2001 Columbia University Press
All rights reserved

Library of Congress Cataloging-in-Publication Data
Cheuse, Alan.
Listening to the page : adventures in reading and writing / Alan Cheuse.
p. cm.
ISBN 0-231-12270-5 (cloth : alk. paper)
1. Literature, Modern—20th century—History and criticism.
2. Literature, Modern—20th century—Reviews.
3. Books and reading.
I. Title.
✓ PN511 .C423 2001
809'.04—dc21   00-065717

Casebound editions of Columbia University Press books are
printed on permanent and durable acid-free paper.
Designed by Chang Jae Lee
Printed in the United States of America
c 10 9 8 7 6 5 4 3 2 1

For Josh, Emma, Sonya—adventurous readers all

Contents

Part 2. Rereading

Part 3. Writing

Acknowledgments

Thanks to Emma Aprile for her assistance. "Writing It Down for James," "Books in Flames," and "Traces of Light" first appeared in the *Antioch Review*. In "Traces of Light," excerpt from the *Iliad* reprinted with permission from Homer/*The Iliad* translated by Michael Reck, copyright © 1994 by the Estate of Michael Reck, HarperCollins Publishers, New York. "The Lost Books" originally appeared in *Review*. "Hamlet in Haiti" first appeared in *Caribbean Quarterly*. The following pieces appeared in the *Boston Globe Magazine*: "You Can Read Wolfe Again," "Stories of Deep Delight," "Of Steinbeck and Salinas," and "The Return of James Agee." In "Stories of Deep Delight," *Audubon: A Vision* Copyright © 1969 by Robert Penn Warren. *Chief Joseph of the Nez Perce* Copyright © 1983 by Robert Penn Warren. Reprinted by permission of William Morris Agency, Inc. on behalf of the Estate of Robert Penn Warren. Thanks to *Texas Studies in Language and Literature* for permission to reprint "Mario Vargas Llosa and *Conversation in the Cathedral*." Grateful acknowledgment to Elizabeth Tallent for permission to reprint "No One's a Mystery," to Mary Robison for "Yours," and to Amy Hempel for "San Francisco." "Fitzgerald's Christmas Carol" first appeared in *New Essays on F. Scott Fitzgerald's Neglected Stories*, edited by Jackson R. Bryer (Columbia,

Missouri, 1996). Thanks to *Southern Quarterly* for permission to reprint "A Note on Landscape in *All the Pretty Horses*." "Rereading Traven" served as the preface to *The Kidnapped Saint and Other Stories*, by B. Traven (New York, 1991). Grateful acknowledgment to Anne Yeats for permission to reprint "The Indian Upon God," to Random House for permission to reproduce the artwork from *The Sound and the Fury*, and to George Garrett for "Anthologies." Thanks to Andrew Wingfield and the editors of *Pleiades* for permission to reprint "Voices: A Conversation." And thanks to the Squaw Valley Community of Writers, the Texas Center for Writers, the University of Richmond, the Midwest Writers Conference, the Pacific Northwest Writers Conference, the Port Townsend Writers Conference, and the Maryland Institute and College of Art for the opportunity to deliver a number of these essays as lectures.

Listening to the Page

Introduction:
Getting Started; or, Two Thousand Books

In the autumn of 1982, I was living in Knoxville, Tennessee, carefully disguised to myself as a "young" writer. That was a nimble bit of illusion on my part. My fortieth birthday had come and gone. Bennington College, where I had taught literature for nearly a decade, had given me my walking papers, and since my wife at the time—mother of my two daughters—was offered a job teaching English at the University of Tennessee, we moved south.

It was a bit of a shock, though mostly in good ways. After New England, a growing season that began in March and didn't end until November seemed like the climate of Paradise. We bought a small new house in a subdivision just on the edge of the town's western limits, and I learned how to run a gas-powered lawn mower. I also settled into a half-finished basement room, with the desk, an old picnic table, facing a window that looked out under our rear deck to where some redbud trees stood along the line of a small watery ditch, and there I tried, not for the first time, to start writing fiction.

About the only things I knew for certain were that writing was more difficult than learning how to run a gas-powered lawn mower and that before you write you learn the language and you read. Just about everything else was a mystery. Though mystery wasn't bad.

My father was Russian-born, my mother an American whose mother was first-generation New Jersey and whose father was also born in western Russia. Though my mother's family sometimes resorted to what I recall as pidgin Yiddish, my father, except on the rarest of occasions, never spoke Russian in the house because he had no one to speak it with, and so American English was my first language. In the early grades, I learned to read it by working at the ubiquitous "Dick and Jane" textbooks. "See Dick run. See Jane run." I saw them running, but from the start I wanted something more than the flat adventures of these stick figures.

It wasn't long before I was spending many afternoons after school at the local library, where I turned to actual novels for my reading pleasure. I became a promiscuous reader—discovering a true love for sea stories and science fiction while branching out ever more perilously into far-flung territories. I enjoyed popular junk—*A Stone for Danny Fisher*, by Harold Robbins, *Marjorie Morningstar*, by Herman Wouk—and almost by accident I read some serious things—D. H. Lawrence's Mexico novel *The Plumed Serpent*, Mailer's World War II epic *The Naked and the Dead*, and, the circumstances of which I'll explain in a moment, Ralph Ellison's *Invisible Man*. In my first year of high school, I found a copy of James Joyce's *Portrait of the Artist as a Young Man*, which I carried around—unread—like a badge of honor, until one morning my prissy homeroom teacher confiscated it, saying it was too difficult for a boy my age. In my sophomore year, I toted a Faulkner paperback, which a smug study hall monitor, a chemistry teacher, confiscated, saying that it was a dirty book. (I doubt if he had read it.)

That's when I became an official browser, haunting our town's one bookshop, snooping through the narrow aisles, fingering copies of more Lawrence novels and work by Thomas Mann and volumes of science fiction and horror by Alfred Bester and Richard Matheson, and picking up and studying new novels by writers whose names were unfamiliar to me, wondering if I should read them.

(Such bookstores are mostly all gone now, replaced by superstores or bookstore cafés, nice places to frequent that have become in many places real neighborhood centers—though these shops, as wonderful as they are, don't hold much mystery for me the way the old stores did.)

A few years later, when I arrived at Rutgers, I signed up for duty on the literary magazine and published a story in it about a tender moment in a silly non-affair I died through—that's opposed to lived through—while in my last couple of years of high school. It wasn't as bad as the science fiction I was writing, but it was pretty bad. Since no one told me how bad it was, I kept on writing and reading.

A year later I took over the editor's job at the undergraduate literary magazine and became pals with the other would-be writers on campus, some of whom went on to publish, some of whom did not. I enrolled in one writing course. The poet John Ciardi taught it, though that makes it seem awfully well tended. He sat six of us in a room, and one of us would read a story; then, while Ciardi watched, the others went after the writer who presented the story with verbal bowie knives and combat boots.

Ciardi, he of the craggy brow and the mellifluous voice, was then at the top of his form, having published a number of well-received volumes of poetry. He was teaching at Rutgers and writing a column for the *Saturday Review of Literature*, Norman Cousins's then thriving middlebrow magazine. Ciardi also wore the mantle of codirector, along with another of our teachers, the head of the Rutgers University Press, William Sloane, of the Breadloaf Writing Workshops. Came the summer between my junior and senior years and he invited me to Breadloaf to work as a waiter, one of the great honors an undergraduate writer could then achieve.

It was a good time up there in northern Vermont. Work was not difficult. The kitchen staff did most of the heavy lifting and the dishwashing. I fell in love with the odd daughter of a famous literary agent, who eventually dumped me—literally—in a pond. I watched in fascination as a major British poet pursued a slender young waiter from North Carolina, amazed one night to find him drunk and bundled into the fellow's bunk in our cramped waiters' dormitory to wait for his prey. We all smoked a little marijuana. On assignment for *Life* magazine, Alfred Eisenstadt took a photograph of us with Robert Frost in a field across from the Breadloaf Inn. "Children," Frost said, "why are you laughing?" We were too stoned to explain that we were stoned. Later that night, in the big barn, Frost recited for an hour as people called out their favorite poems of his. I wish I could say I was overawed by this, but I callowly assumed that this was the way life was. You drove up to Vermont and you waited on tables and you got stoned, and one of the greatest poets who ever wrote in your language recited his work for you of an evening.

And one of the greatest writers of the period came up to you after a reading and introduced himself.

"Just how heavy are those trays you boys carry around the dining room?" Ralph Ellison said.

I told him about our waiters' drill, and he listened attentively. I knew quite well who he was. I had spent years as an elementary school kid walking past the copy of *Invisible Man* on the Recommended Reading rack of my local library, and one day, at the beginning of eighth grade, thinking that it might be a science fiction novel, actually picked up the book and started to read it. I quickly set it down. And in the next year picked it up again. And set it down. I was a freshman in college before I read the novel all the way through.

Ellison and I talked on and off during the next week, and at a staff party up in the Breadloaf Ski Bowl cabin at the end of the conference, when everyone had drunk quite a bit, mostly beer, and a barrel in the center of the room was heaped high with beer bottles, someone started singing folk songs. And others joined in. When the singers took up "Old Black Joe," yours truly leaped up and in good Dedalian fashion knocked over the barrel, sending empty bottles every which way across the floor and effectively ending the party. I would not let what I took to be a grave insult to Ellison's skin color go unpunished.

Back at Rutgers, in my senior year I set up a little reading series for literature students. Ciardi read for us. Dapper little Oscar Williams, poet and anthologist, read for us. We had a wonderful party for him afterward in a funky student aerie, with cheap wine and Lewis reciting his own poetry and the poetry of others on into the night. Beardless young Richard Yates, a man in his early thirties, took the bus down from Manhattan to read for us. His wonderful novel *Revolutionary Road* had just appeared, to very good notices, but he was more interested in drinking than in boasting about his success.

As an exemplary figure for college writers, Yates was not terrific. But he was a lot of fun for this schoolboy, because he invited me up to visit him in his basement apartment in Greenwich Village and, upon my arrival, instantly poured out a tumblerful of bourbon. (Poor Richard could not bear to be too long in the presence of anyone not drunk.) And then he lit a large electric Madonna and Child, the gift of a drinking buddy of his, a salesman who specialized in religious paraphernalia. By the light of the Mother and Child, we drank ourselves into a gentle stupor and then staggered out onto the street to take a meal of steak and potatoes at Yates's favorite restaurant, the Blue Mill on Cherry Lane, a few doors down from the theater of the same name.

Separated from his wife, mourning his distance from his daughters, Yates lived in terrible emotional pain. And having only one lung—the other was removed after he contracted tuberculosis as an eighteen-year-old while serving with the U.S. Infantry in Europe just after the end of World War II—made his breathing troubled, especially since he smoked several packs of cigarettes a day. In what at the time, in the hubris of my near-twenties, seemed perfectly natural, and now, so many years later, seems like an extraordinary leap of generosity, Yates showed real interest in my own life, such as it was up until then.

After graduation I turned three months' pay as a toll collector on the New Jersey Turnpike into a year in Europe. In Paris and Spain, I had a good time impersonating a young writer, the writer I might have been if I had been prepared to begin writing serious fiction at the time. But I wasn't prepared. I kept a notebook, but wrote little. By the time the year had swung around I was called back to the United States by my local draft board. The war in Vietnam was heating up, and my friends and neighbors wanted to send me there. For better or worse, I flunked the physical examination. (For better, because it kept me alive; for worse, because it deprived me of suffering through the watershed experience of my generation.)

I went to work in New York City at an assortment of jobs, including caseworker for the old New York City Department of Welfare, speechwriter for a successful New York urban planner and landscape artist—fired from that job because, as the office manager explained to

5

me in the men's room, to which he guided me in order to give me the bad news in private, Mr. Planner considered himself a writer and instead of merely changing a few periods and commas in his speech about the future of the New York State park system, I had rewritten entire sentences! I then found a job as a reporter for *Women's Wear Daily*, the garment industry trade publication. After about a year of covering the mink and sealskin auctions at the Manhattan headquarters of the Hudson's Bay Company, I went to work as the managing editor of a small socialist quarterly called *Studies on the Left*.

It was 1963 B.C. (before condominiums), and I was living in a one-bedroom walkup on the sixth floor of a tenement in Little Italy with a bathtub in the kitchen, for which I paid twenty-eight dollars a month. Aside from a few people whom I met at the magazine, my only friends were people I knew from college. And one of them invited me on a cold Saturday evening to a party at her apartment—elevator building, doorman, two bedrooms, bathtub in bathroom—paid for, I suppose, by her parents. There I met my first wife, the enticing red-haired daughter of an Air Force general. She'd been in and out of schools and was currently attending the women's college of my old university, and so was an acquaintance of the girl who was throwing the party.

What does this have to do with books?

Well, you see, dear reader, we married. And one day she came home with a copy of the *Village Voice* and showed me an advertisement. It said WRITERS WANTED. My wife looked at me and said, "You call yourself a writer. Maybe you should answer this ad."

I did. And soon found myself working for a book review service founded in the 1930s by a woman named Virginia Kirkus. Kirkus supplied brief advance reviews of all the new fiction and nonfiction for libraries and movie producers. Working for Kirkus meant reading a book a day and writing a ten-line review for the next morning. Eisenhower's memoirs and a new novel by an obscure Tennessee writer, books on the New Right and fiction about medieval France, it was all one to me—one day, one review. For two years I worked like this, reading nearly eight hundred books and turning in nearly eight hundred (unsigned) reviews, now and then getting things wrong, as in a review about a book of essays by the publisher of the *National Review*, who wrote a letter of complaint about my bias against the conservative point of view, but mostly just digesting these books and spitting out a response—and as a result learning how to read and write on deadline.

This ability served me rather well when a few years later I found myself in graduate school, working toward a degree in comparative literature. Studying with such generous and gifted teachers as Francis Fergusson, John McCormick, Paul Fussell, Glauco Cambon, and David Wilhelm gave me good reason to keep up my reading and essay writing. I said to myself, in effect, You're nearly thirty, and you're supposed to be an adult at that age, so working toward a degree in comp lit that could lead to a university teaching post is not a bad thing. I didn't consciously vow to give up my hopes for writing fiction so much as they became submerged in the daily demands of graduate study and marriage.

Like some long-forgotten deed that returns to haunt the hero of a nineteenth-century English novel, the urge to write resurfaced nearly a decade later, after I had moved to Bennington. "It's not a real college," my mentor Fergusson had said—he had had the experience of founding the drama division in the 1930s when the college had been created by a few rich locals who wanted interesting table talk during the cold Vermont winters—"you'll like teaching there."

And I did. The students were wonderfully attentive, the curriculum was unorthodox, the literature faculty a disparate group of fiction writers, poets, and oddball critics, some of these last among the most brilliant people I had ever met, some of them among the most egotistical and incomprehensible. The fiction writers Bernard Malamud and Nicholas Delbanco became my friends. In fact, I first met Malamud at the Delbanco wedding reception, where we talked a while and he said, after hearing me say that I used to want to write fiction but didn't think much about that anymore, "I think we can be friends, if you never show me anything you write."

A few years later, in circumstances that merit a longer retelling than I have room for here, John Gardner joined the writers among us. I recall a dinner at the Gardner house during that first year he taught with us at which there was a table full of writers. Before the meal Joan

7

Gardner polled everyone about their latest just-published work or work in progress. John went first, debriefing himself at length about the novels and stories and plays he was working on. Malamud went next. Then Delbanco. And a few others. When it came to be my turn, Joan looked at me and smiled. "It's all right, Alan," she said. "Not everyone has to be a writer."

I remember the night that I started to be a writer in earnest. Bennington student housing is divided among a number of large New England clapboard buildings. Mark Strand was giving a reading of his poetry in the living room across from the house where I was living. I left the reading and went to my apartment and wrote the opening of my long story "Candace." It was not that Strand inspired me so much as that at that moment, the way a pregnant woman near term suddenly discovers that her water has broken, my cup began to run over with fiction.

Though my marriage to the general's daughter had foundered, my second marriage had begun (with a ceremony in the Malamud living room in Old Bennington, Vermont, at which we read so much poetry as part of our vows that waggish poet Stephen Sandy, leaning against the wall, cried out, "Is this a wedding or the goddamned *Norton Anthology*?").

Other things had not gone so well. Several of the small-minded critics in the Literature Division were beginning to see a time when they could get rid of me. I was too friendly with the fiction writers and not friendly enough with the critics, was the way the news seeped down to me. A few years later I was told, in effect, that my services would not be required any longer at the small liberal arts college in southwestern Vermont that I had begun to think of as home.

Another story that there is not enough space here at the moment to tell is the way in which Malamud and Gardner rallied around me during the difficult months after I had been given notice. Malamud became my stalwart representative in the many unsatisfying stages of an appeal of the college's decision, the last thing one of the best story writers alive needed to think about. And Gardner, when he first heard the news, put on his purple reading cape and headed for my apartment, where, when I answered the door, he declared that it was war to the death with the administration.

That's how I started moving toward Tennessee, where my second wife took her teaching post and I set up for work as a freelance journalist and began to write fiction as well.

In that half-finished basement of a house in the Fair Oaks subdivision on the then westernmost portion of the Knoxville city limits, in front of a window that looked out under the rear deck of our new house where in the backyard those redbud trees and a willow marked that water-filled ditch at the edge of our lot, I worked on a small manual Wal-Mart typewriter set up on a wooden picnic table—also from Wal-Mart—and completed the story based on the life of Faulkner's Candace Compson.

I sent it out to the *Iowa Review* and received a note back from one of the editors there, a young fiction writer named T. Corraghesan Boyle, who said that he admired the story but it was too long for their purposes. I began my second short story, making a vow to myself that I would publish fiction in a magazine by the time I was forty. This new story was roughly made up out of some scenes from my first marriage. I sent it to the *New Yorker* and, after a revision or three, they sent me a note telling me that they wanted to buy it.

I was home alone when the note arrived. I had to tell someone about my success, and so I left the house and headed next door, where my neighbor Bill Brashears was mowing his lawn. I waved to him, and he waved back over the noise of the mower. Not a great time to talk to him. I crossed the street and knocked on the door of Billy Young, a pharmaceuticals salesman. What he was doing home in the middle of the afternoon I couldn't say, but he answered the door.

"Billy, Billy," I said, scarcely able to get my words out, "I just sold a story to the *New Yorker!*"

Billy took a step out of his doorway, looked up the street and then down.

"Where is he?" he said.

I kept the vow I had made to myself when one month before my fortieth birthday the *New Yorker* with my story in it appeared on the supermarket newsstands in Knoxville, Tennessee.

Meanwhile, my freelance career was beginning to pick up. I wrote essays for the *Boston Globe Magazine* on various literary figures and spent some time in Nashville, three hours away by car on the other side of the Cumberland Plateau, doing research and interviews for articles about the country music business. I was learning fast that as a freelancer I had to work twice as hard as I should in order to earn about half of what I ought to be paid.

One afternoon while driving across town to pick up my daughters at school, I turned to the university FM station and heard a woman named Susan Stamberg interviewing a writer. I can't remember now who that was. But I couldn't forget Susan's voice, the warmth, the brightness, the leisurely intelligence. She turned out to be one of the co-hosts of a new National Public Radio newsmagazine called *All Things Considered*. I sat outside the school for a number of minutes, listening to the show. I had never heard anything like it, and I wanted to hear more and more of it. Later that year, one of the many freelance assignments I came up with was a story for an FM trade journal about this new publicly funded broadcast network called National Public Radio.

I flew up to Washington and spent several days interviewing the people who hosted and produced the morning and afternoon news shows and returned to write my story. Before I finished it, one of the producers of *All Things Considered* called to ask if I might be interested in doing book reviews for them. I hesitated, telling her that I knew a number of people much more in need of work than me. She insisted, and I wrote a review and then recorded it—the subject was a novel whose name I cannot recall—and sent it up to her. She called again with a few suggestions about how to write the script and talk into the tape recorder and asked if I would try another. I tried. And failed again. She called back. My fifth attempt went out on the air.

That was almost twenty years ago. Since then, with the help of a series of smart and literate editors and producers whose commitment to literary culture is unparalleled in American radio, I have broadcast about fifty book pieces a year. That's nearly a thousand reviews, and if you add in the work at Kirkus, that's nearly a thousand more. Add on to that the other freelance work I've done, and I'm shocked myself at the figure; I'm even more amazed at just how many of the books I can recall.

It's been a grand education—an adventure, I have to say. All the places I've traveled to in books, all the people, beautiful and ugly, compelling and repulsive, holy and devilish, that I've met, all the lips I've kissed and dreams I've dreamed and meals I've eaten and wine and beer and well water and salt water and drugs and medicine and ambrosia I've ingested! Horses I've ridden, spaceships I've flown! All the lives I've lived and deaths I've died!

The question I ask myself when such computations are done is whether or not any of this helped me to find my own voice as a writer. Working in radio has certainly helped me to discover my own physical voice. But what have writing and reading aloud all those scripts, and, for that matter, writing essays and articles about modern literature, done for me as a writer in my own right?

I don't know that I can answer that question myself. But I do know that my work would be a diminished thing without all the reading and writing. Writers need to read just as painters have to study paintings and musicians must listen to music. And I have been luckier than most writers I know, in that I have been paid to go to school in contemporary literature and with that money over the years I have been able to furnish my own writer's table. Which, of course, after the bread and the wine, holds mostly other people's books. I suppose I stand with Borges, who, in a poem, said, "I am more proud of the books I've read than I am of the books I've written." That's a good standard for any writer to keep in mind, except for Homer, Shakespeare, and Tolstoy, and a few, rare, others. But most of us readers, whether professional or amateur, find ourselves diving into books for rather simple reasons—as we embark on our quests for news of other minds, other climes, other times, other worlds, news about the way we live, the way we love, the way we work, the way we sing and laugh and weep and mourn.

With such matters in mind, I've arranged the pieces in this book into three groups. "Reading" contains mostly essays and lectures that I wrote from a comparative literature perspective, that is, taking the long view and trying to reveal affinities between sometimes seemingly disparate works of art and make clear the ties between ancient and modern and among various contemporary national literatures. The section also reflects my early interest in the art and motifs of modern Latin American literature.

"Rereading" includes retrospective pieces on modern U.S. literary figures, many of which I wrote for Sunday newspaper supplements in the mid-1980s, and some newer practical critical essays written for literary and academic journals.

"Writing," which I take to be the natural outcome of reading and rereading, is composed of lectures and essays and an interview, with the focus on questions of craft and career and vision of the contemporary writer.

I don't deploy any contemporary literary theories in these pieces, but I do have a vision, one that has haunted me for a long time, ever since I began to read, really, a vision of a world connected across the millennia by works of art and a global present in which all our stories are intertwined in the narratives of our own day.

It is all one story—and we are all the readers of our lives.

part I

reading

I

Writing It Down for James:
Some Thoughts on Reading Toward the Millennium

On a cold, rainy Washington night in December, this traveler drove over to the Congressional Office Building on Capitol Hill to attend the Christmas party of a local literacy council. A group of young professionals, many of them lawyers and college teachers, who serve as tutors for the District's largest adult literacy project—not an official part of either the D.C. or the federal government but rather a non-profit organization that belongs to a national umbrella group that fosters the teaching of reading to adults—served plates of roast turkey and baked ham and many side dishes to a couple of dozen adults and a few teenagers, almost all of them black, who all share the desire to learn how to read.

One of these late bloomers was a fifty-three-year-old truck driver from South Carolina named James. James picked up a newspaper only about a year and a half ago after a lifetime of work and raising a family. He had dropped out of school at the age of six to pick crops at nearby farms and never went back. Though unable to read a word, he'd performed such tasks as stevedore and foreman at a shipping company; for the last two decades he has been working as a teamster, in some instances hauling his load as far away as the Canadian border without knowing how to read the road signs.

When I expressed my astonishment at this feat, James laughed and said, "Hey, once you pass the driver's test, the rest ain't all that hard. It's usually just a matter of counting. Counting the stop signs, things like that. You recognize landmarks in town or out on the road, and you sort of steer by them."

But after a lifetime of living in his own country as though it were a foreign land where he didn't know the language, James decided that since all his children had learned to read and had gone on to good jobs, he could take the time out to learn how to read himself. This he told me over a plate of food, his right leg moving up and down, up and down, his plate shaking on his lap.

"I wanted to learn to read a newspaper, see? I wanted to *read* about life, not just live it. So I can just about do that now. And now I want to read a whole book. I want to read a story. A good story." The desire for a good story—that had been on my own mind ever since I could remember. And over the last three decades reading and writing had become a large part of my daily life. I write, usually, into the early afternoon, and the rest of the day, when I'm not leading a workshop or at the gym or the supermarket or the movies, I give over to reading. Read, read, read, a rage to read. It's an appetite as great as that for sex and food and even for the air we breathe. Death will be a great disappointment if no love or family or friends come with it, but I'd even forgo food in the next life (if there is one) if I could go on reading the good new novels as they come out. In the last decade, I've reviewed hundreds and hundreds of books for National Public Radio's evening newsmagazine *All Things Considered*, and like most people who love narrative, whether fiction or history or politics or science (though fiction is the best narrative of them all), I've read a lot more than those I've reviewed during this past decade, rereading books as I teach them to my writing students (because, as I preach to them, thinking at the same time that if I have to say it to them then perhaps they are already lost, good writers are good readers and great writers are great readers), rereading as I write essays and articles as well as reviews.

But a lifetime—yours, mine—with books has to begin somewhere. And while talking with James over our plates of turkey at the literacy party, I kept on trying to recall exactly when it was I first learned how to read. James could pinpoint his own beginning with the printed word: on a certain night in June, in Washington, at a restaurant where he had first met his tutor. Before that time, printed language was a mystery to him, a cipher used by the rest of the world to keep him constantly on his toes. On the job he devised elaborate formulas to keep up with his work. In the supermarket he often depended on the kindness of strangers to tell him where certain products were located. And as he was talking about his own preliterate life as an adult, I got carried back to one of the few preliterate scenes in my own memory.

Once upon a time a young boy—he must have been about three years old—crawled into bed with his mother and father. It was a Sunday morning, in spring, probably, because even though it was light outside the window, his father still lay in bed rather than having gone to work. While his mother created a space between them where the boy might burrow beneath the covers, his father reached over to the night table and picked up a rectangular object about six by nine inches—it had an orange and sepia cover, an abstract design that suggested not-quite-formed stars and crescents—that he said he had just found in his old trunk from a place he called *Roosh*-a. The boy loved the sound of the word and asked his father to say it again: *Roosh*-a. There was a smell to the object too, this thing made of paper and bound in stiff board, the odor of dust and oranges that had been lying long in the hot sun.

When his father opened the front of it, the boy noticed strange designs stretched out in rows. The only thing he recognized was a drawing, that of a golden rooster-like bird. "*The Tale of the Golden Cockerel*," his father announced as he fixed his eye on the page and began to speak in a strange and incomprehensible fashion, making a series of globlike and skidding sounds, with a lot of *shush*es and ticks and bubblelike slurs and pauses.

The boy was me, of course, and the man was my father, reading to me in Russian, a language I've never learned, from a book of fairy tales that has long ago been lost in the flood of years that rushes through a family's life. And he of course is gone, too, and I'm old enough now to have put aside such fairy tales a while ago and think instead about what novels to give as gifts to my children for Christmas and other occasions. But I still recall the way my father opened to the first page of that now lost volume and began to make those sounds with his mouth and tongue, interpreting the odd designs in front of him as if it were the easiest thing in the world. It was from that day on that I decided, I believe—if "deciding" is what children at the age I was then ever do—that I would learn to read for myself.

I don't actually remember when I first mastered this basic intellectual aptitude. As Roger Shattuck has pointed out in a recent essay, few of us do. "Most minds," he says, "bury those early faltering steps under recollections of later rewards—the fairy tales or comic books on which we perfected our new skill." But some writers have tried to remember. Novelist Nicholas Delbanco describes a wonderful example of this when he writes of a transatlantic crossing, from England to America, at the age of six. On the third day out, he recalls, he received his first pair of long pants and he taught himself to read using a book about boats. Suddenly "the alphabet's tumblers went 'click.' I remember the feel of it, the pride in it, the pleasure, the way the world made sense." Only as a middle-aged adult did he find a copy of a book called *Henry's Green Wagon*, inscribed to him from his kindergarten teacher in London for being "the best reader in Miss Jamaica's Kindergarten Class" in the year before his voyage.

I don't recollect beyond my one tantalizing session with the book of Russian fairy tales that my father ever read to me again. Or my mother. Though I suppose they must have. I certainly hope that my children recall the time that I read to them. If Delbanco can't recall winning his award from Miss Jamaica's kindergarten class, I probably shouldn't expect my son or daughters to keep in mind the hours we spent going over *The Little Engine that Could* or the "Ant and Bee" stories. But if we do teach our children to read we can never forget the first few times that they skate off across the page on their own, a thrill in life something like the first time we sail away on our bikes without the use of training wheels.

An industry now supports this hope-filled activity. The middle class is urged to prep its children in advance of school. IMPROVED READING SKILLS BEGIN AT HOME, say headlines in the "Parent and Child" columns of the *New York Times*. You can buy books, take courses. And you can hook your child up to your computer and plug in such programs as the Disney-made Mickey's ABCs and Follow the Reader. You can learn tips about how to encourage your children to read. And read to them yourself. In a statement about what seems to be the Original Sin of illiteracy, Dr. Michael Pressley, a professor of educational psychology at the University of Maryland, is quoted as saying, "The kids who have the most trouble tend to have parents who didn't read to them when they were younger . . . and didn't see their parents or other people reading and writing."

But just as I have only that single memory of being read to—and in Russian, besides—I don't recall seeing my parents read much at all. I do have the faint recollection of watching my father sit in a small alcove of a second-floor apartment on lower State Street in Perth Amboy, New Jersey, tapping on the keys of a small black typewriter, trying to write stories in English in the manner of the Russian satirists Ilf and Petrov. But I never saw him read anything other than the newspaper or a beat-up old copy of Richard Halliburton's *The Nine Wonders of the World*, the texture of whose cover and quality of photographs— waterfalls, drawings of statues—I recall rather than any text. My mother might have read the front page of the newspaper. I never saw her hold any book in her hand.

But I grew up reading, reading like a bandit. And no fairy tales for me. I went straight to comic books, *Archie Comics* at first, and then the superheroes—*Superman* and *Batman*, *Plastic Man*, *Wonder Woman*— and then on to the horror comics, *EC Stories*, and *The Heap*, building a collection that rivaled just about any in the neighborhood. Of a Saturday you could see us comics fans, pushing baby carriages left over from our younger siblings' infancies filled with our collections on our way to trade-meets at someone's house. After a while a quest for something more than *Archie*, et cetera, sent me onward to better reading, which meant, for me, *Classics Illustrated*. The Western world's greatest poems and stories turned into comic books, from the *Iliad* and the *Odyssey* on through the centuries all the way to Poe—that was my reading for the years of early adolescence.

Some educators these days are encouraging parents to allow their kids to cut their reading teeth on *Classics Illustrated*, then watch them go on to more complicated books. I watched myself graduate to the serialized Christmas story that appeared in our local newspaper each December, then to the sea adventures of C. S. Forester, his Captain Horatio Hornblower series, and to years and years of science fiction novels and short stories. Although we "read" *Silas Marner* in junior high school, I don't remember a thing about it. It was always the adventure stories and the speculative fiction that captured me. Proust's Marcel writes of his afternoons with novels in the fabled Combray:

> On the sort of screen dappled with different states and impressions which my consciousness would simultaneously unfold while I was reading, my innermost impulse, the lever whose incessant movements controlled everything else, was my belief in the philosophic richness and beauty of the book I was reading, and my desire to appropriate them for myself, whatever the book might be. . . . Next to this central belief which, while I was reading, would be constantly reaching out from my inner self to the outer world, towards the discovery of truth, came the emotions roused in me by the action in which I was taking part, for these afternoons were crammed with more dramatic events than occur, often, in a whole lifetime. These were the events taking place in the book I was reading.

How many summer afternoons and long winter evenings this Jersey Marcel, yours truly, spent lost in this fashion! As you all have been lost, discovering and deepening your imaginative life in such a way as to change your ordinary waking physical life forever.

Except for those math geniuses who are probably anomalies when it comes to the quality of their minds, most of us find this period in which we encounter the mental adventures of reading the most important part of our maturation. Though to try and watch it happen is to see nothing. One spring, for example, I spent a few days behind one-way glass observing an eighth-grade reading class at a middle school in Huntsville, Texas. I'm not sure what I expected to find, but this was what I saw: several dozen kids from around ages eleven to thirteen seated at their desks or sprawled on large cushions on the floor holding books open in front of them. They moved their limbs, and their eyes twitched as they might have in sleep. Scarcely any of them did more than change position on the cushions or cross or extend their legs beneath their desks. Yet the internal process in their minds, no more visible than coal changing under pressure into diamond, would change their lives. It would help them to discover the world in a way like no other, to learn of history and philosophy and science and art, to acquire an awareness of God and insects, of water and the nature of life in a mining town in Belgium in 1900, to study Buddhism and physics, or merely to keep boredom at arm's length on an autumn evening in Great Falls, Montana; to become army captains and sales managers and priests and cotton farmers, and to ponder, if they were so inclined, the relation between their hometown and the rest of the state, the country, the continent, the world, the solar system, galaxy, and cosmos.

However, you have only to observe a lower-level reading class in order to be reminded, if you need such an elemental tip, that this skill is not part of what we would call human nature. Kids study the shape of the letters and learn to sound each letter, then groups of letters, then make words. We've sounded letters, vowels and consonants resounding and popping, for our own kids. To watch a whole batch of them at once get this training is like witnessing the first hatch of tree frogs in early spring. The entire air fairly sings and squeaks with the wondering noise of it all. But despite the illusion of the naturalness of reading, this skill is, in the history of Western culture, a relatively new invention. For the majority of humanity in Europe and the West, verbal art was spoken or sung. And what we now call illiteracy was once the normal condition of culture in what we also name the Golden Age of Greece.

The thousand years or more prior to the sixth century B.C. in Athens was the time of the Homeric rhetors or rhapsodes, who chanted and sang the great poems of the culture to devoted audiences. It was only with the faltering of the Homeric tradition, when it seemed as though the transmission of the poems in memory from one generation to the next was in danger of dying out, that Pisistratus, the Greek tyrant, ordered that scribes record the performance of the two great epics, the *Iliad* and the *Odyssey* on papyrus.

Maybe that's when Paradise was truly lost, when it became necessary to read the great songs that had formerly been sung. Is it C. M. Ciorian who describes this transition as the culture's "fall into language"? Before this time no one read, because there was no written language, but a hunger was present—present, it seems, from the beginnings of human culture—the hunger for story, for narrative, for the arrangement of incidents into an action, even an action that might move the listener to feel pity and fear. This craving for order with emotional resonance was satisfied during the preclassical period in the Mediterranean only by oral epic.

Drama arose during the fifth century B.C. and filled, among its other functions, the traditional need for a public gathering at which poetry was performed over an extended period of time. But by the first century A.D. poetry and drama were as often read on papyrus as performed. Prose narratives were composed as well, but these, like the *Satyricon*, seemed to take second place to the more engaging works of history in the mind of an audience looking, apparently, both for a way to restore a certain order to a life from which the formerly awesome power of the old gods had faded and for exciting and interesting stories that spoke to their own daily round.

Between the decline of Greece and Rome and the withering away of Christendom, most Westerners had to settle for one book, the Bible, with its multitudes of stories, as the storehouse of narrative. It wasn't really until the fourteenth century and the creation of *The Decameron* that secular stories came to prominence as literary art— folk narratives were as plentiful as trees—in Europe. As every school kid used to know, the invention of movable type eventually made it possible for the broad dissemination of texts of all varieties, not just the Bible for which the printing press was first widely used. After Luther's revolt against Rome's authority as the prime interpreter of the Holy Book, literacy became a necessity in his part of Europe for the religious man, and soon evolved into a means of power among the rising merchant class, and reading became a sign that a person was wholly civilized.

Consider for a moment what this meant in existential terms for European society. In the great Homeric age of Greece, any citizen of

Athens who could attend the performances of the epics—at four seasonal renderings each year in the great amphitheater of the city—could apprehend them merely by listening attentively. To be a citizen thus meant among other things to be a listener, collectively, with all the other citizens of Athens. You listened and the words of the gods, through the conduit of the poet, went directly to your ears, telling of the great heroes and heroines, gods and goddesses, engaged in the straightening out, or messing up, of epic affairs in heaven, earth, and the underworld.

With the breakup of this oral culture and the rise of scriptural authority, reading became a prized activity, not just for the priesthood but for the elite of the continent's court and fief. The book became a metaphor for the world, and reading emerged as a method for interpreting God's creation. To be illiterate meant one stood several stages removed from a knowledge of sacred reality. The idea that one listened to the words of the epic poet and thus heard the language of the muses directly in one's ears became, in this thousand-year interregnum between the demise of oral poetry and the establishment of a secular reading culture, static and sterile when the priest, rather than the poet, served as middleman between holy work and worshiper. With the secularization of storytelling, from Boccaccio forward, the printed word became even further detached from its sacred origins in oral poetry, telling stories of the death of kings and then barons and then squires, so that by the time of Balzac, readers learned of the lives, loves, and sorrows of the denizens of a great secular city, which is to say, themselves.

As the story evolves—some might want to say descends—from Scripture to tales of middle-class life, the relation of text to reader evolves as well. Christian theology demanded a singular oath from its worshipers, the acceptance of Christ on the part of the individual as his savior. Eighteen hundred years later, the individual picks up a copy of *Tom Jones* and finds that the story illuminates part of his or her daily life, a far cry from any hint of salvation. In fact, quite the opposite, if you consider the distance between the hope of heaven and the worlds in contemporary fiction. To pass one's eyes across the lines of the Holy Writ was an act of prayer. What is it, then, to read modern fiction?

Proust's Marcel has—again—a pretty good way of seeing it. A real person, he asserts, because he is known to us only through our senses, remains opaque:

> If some misfortune comes to him, it is only in one small section of the complete idea we have of him that we are capable of feeling any emotion: indeed it is only in one small section of the complete idea he has of himself that he is capable of feeling any emotion either. The novelist's happy discovery was to think of substituting for those opaque sections, impenetrable to the human soul, their equivalent in immaterial sections, things, that is, which one's soul can assimilate. After which it matters not that the actions, the feelings of this new order of creatures, appear to us in the guise of truth, since we have made them our own, since it is in ourselves that they are happening, that they are holding in thrall, as we feverishly turn over the pages of the book, our quickened breath and staring eyes. And once the novelist has brought us to this state, in which, as in all purely mental states, every emotion is multiplied tenfold, into which his book comes to disturb us as might a dream, but a dream more lucid and more abiding than those which come to us in sleep, why then, for the space of an hour he sets free within us all the joys and sorrows in the world, a few of which only we should have to spend years of our actual life in getting to know, and the most intense of which would never be revealed to us because the slow course of their development prevents us from perceiving them.

So we read for pleasure? and for a glimpse of what a coherent vision of the world might be like? It may well be that putting together in our own minds a lifetime of novel reading is close to knowing what it must be like in the mind of God. From these simple stories, of a foolish hidalgo in search of a phantom lover, of the way the past rises up against the present in an English village called Middlemarch, of a Jewish advertising salesman wandering about Dublin looking for sympathy, of a Mississippi family plagued by alcoholism, madness, and imagined incest, of a woman named Maria who aimlessly drives the L.A. freeways, we make up a cosmos.

Think of reading, then, as an act of praise, of prayer, even, in which individuals reassert their devotion to creation and to the immanent world in which we reside, a world in which every aspect of life, from old tires piled high in a trash heap to the multiform patterns of snowflakes on a day in high winter, from the sickness of murder to the charity of parenthood, all make up part of a larger pattern. And when we read, we reenact that pattern, an activity that may be as close to serious prayer as most of us will get. Or want to. The organized modern religions hold no patent on expressing devotion to the universe. In fact, the pagan poets, the epic Homers of the oldest stories of the western Mediterranean, show a lot more imagination when it comes to creating great characters and overarching plots than the lyricists and lamenters of the Old and New Testaments. Some great poetry in the former, but nothing much in the latter unless you're spiritually bound to the text. Apply the test of narrative coherence and the pagan epics win hands down. And if the response of the reader, the immersion into a story that delights and instructs in the deepest fashion we know, is any test of the presence of godliness, there's no doubt in my mind which stories show the mark of real deity.

If there is such a thing. The great hype about our present epoch is that we've moved into a period of technology with exponential possibility. The computer has become the metaphor for God. Fine with me. I'm an old science fiction fan from way back. Let's fly to Jupiter, let's shine our penlights into black holes. But on those long flights to the outer planets, or even the short hyperspace commuter hops between galaxies, there's going to be a lot of free time. Maybe some techno-hotshots will want to use those hours, or months or years, to play computer games or speak with voice-activated viewer-integrated videos. But most of the crew and/or passengers will probably want to read. And what will we do with our spare time once we move out beyond this current pioneering age of space exploration?

Imagine an engineer lying in his bunk in a space station at the outer reaches of our solar system with a peerless view of stars, to borrow a phrase, like dust. As people such as this have done for—what's the phrase here?—countless eons, he picks up a copy of a book, or punches out the text on his computer screen, and begins to read, or, if you will, scan the text. And what might it be? Anything from the stories of Louis L'Amour to *Paradise Lost* or *Moby Dick*, no doubt. Consider how the poetry of Milton or the ocean scenes of Melville or the cowpokes and bandits of L'Amour would carry him back to Earththemes and Earth-places. Even if he's never set foot on Earth, these are still the stories of his homeplace.

Reading—reading is home itself, the place where we go when we wish to be with ourselves and our own minds and our own hearts. It is an act of the eye that, unlike the viewing of painting or film, has little to do with what the eye perceives before it. Theater and film are the imagination externalized, the created images of the mind or minds of other parties performed objectively before us. While viewing a dance or a play, our eye is captive. Narrative prose or poetry, like music, is a different and, I believe, higher form of representation. The words, like musical notations, are mere potential art, waiting to be performed by the reader on the interior stage of the imagination. And just as nothing could be more public than the performance of a play, nothing could be more private than the reading of a novel or story. As novelist Laura Furman has suggested, reading may in fact be the last private activity of merit in our culture.

Neurologically one can distinguish the act of reading from the perception of other art forms, such as dance and drama, and one can see how it has a social reality distinct from the external performance, and perception, of ancient oral poetry, medieval drama, and all the other theatrical and visual art that has come after. Unlike oral poetry, which presumed the presence of a community ethos and the absence of what we would call individual ego, prose on the page demands individual participation and, ever since the advent of the age of symbolism, individual interpretation. Everyone in the Homeric audience understood the explicit meaning of the poems—there was no implicit meaning—and celebrated these values and beliefs by means of listening. Since the middle of the eighteenth century, readers have pondered the implicit values of a work within the confines of their own imaginations, and sometimes despaired of a world in which such solitariness is the norm and values are determined by the situation of the individual.

It's no wonder then that we all know so many people who never dare venture seriously into the world of reading. For most people a functioning imagination can be a treacherous and even frightening possession, generating such trivial but annoying conditions as hypochondria on the one hand and much more dangerous situations such as jealousy, paranoia, and megalomania on the other. In this regard, we read *Don Quixote*, the first modern novel, as a book about the dangers of taking books literally. Logos detached from its divine origins is a symbol awaiting interpretation by the god within us, which is to say, our imaginative powers. Woe to him—look at poor Quixote—who takes it at face value.

But that woe, the woe of literalism in an age of symbolic inter-pretation, is exactly what many Americans rush to embrace, cheered on by McLuhanite theoreticians of the new media. The flat screen, the so-called interactive game, has become the new repository for the faith of tens of millions, the perfect altar for our neo-Puritanical faith in which efficacy is next to godliness, and poetry (as Auden ironically puts it in his elegy for Yeats) "makes nothing happen," and fiction is relegated to the dustbin of the new age. There seem to be two kinds of citizens in this nation that produced *Moby Dick*, either Ahabs or Ishmaels, and the former appear to be growing in direct proportion to the growth in population, while the latter may be diminishing in number.

The figures on readership in America and the reading aptitude scores seem to suggest that this is so. More Ahabs, fewer Ishmaels. American students are reading less and less and watching more and more television every year. The majority of American students, it seems, read only to get along, most of them having been taken over by the games mentality of the new high-tech sales culture. So-called computer literacy has led to what we can only hope is a temporary rise in a new variety of illiteracy, the willful avoidance of narrative fiction and poetry as a means of knowledge and awareness. For the new exploding ranks of American students it seems to be Gameboy over C. S. Forester, and coming right up behind Gameboy, and as far away from computer games today as they are from pinball, is the burgeoning new industry of virtual reality, or VR. Probably within the next ten years and certainly within the next twenty, VR will become the distraction of choice for the majority of school kids and reading will be demoted even further down the line than where it is now, somewhere between violin lessons and learning a foreign language. In other words, it will become an activity for the few and elite, just as it was in Goethe's Europe after the invention of the printing press.

That's one scenario, anyway, and not an impossible one, considering the current state of popular culture in which trash seems to have driven out the good. From Emerson to Donahue, from Twain to Robert Fulgham, it's been a bad long slide downward. (There are some areas, of course, where we can see actual evolutionary forces at work to good ends, particularly in music. When you consider the way in which jazz has worked its way into the majority consciousness—and radio programming—there's cause for celebration.)

In literary culture, things look bleak. For a century that started out with such wise and valuable critics as Van Wyck Brooks and Edmund Wilson and Suzanne Langer and saw its mid-age in the wonderful company of Alfred Kazin and John W. Aldridge, the prospects for the next century seem less plausible. Great literature demands great critics, and though it may well be that all of us who are writing fiction today truly deserve the company of the myopic—and at the same time megalomaniac—crew of neo-Marxists and post-post-modern academic culture vultures, to have to live with them is not thrilling, to say the least.

On the one hand, they puff up second- and third-rate work because it serves their theses, rather than, as the great critics have always done, discovering their values in the great work of the time. On the other, they ignore entire areas of creation because they do not suit their already-decided-upon values. But more important for the situation of the reader is the fact that none of these critics writes well enough to have much appeal for the layperson. This leaves the playing field to the contest between the reviewers and the publicists. And since many of the best reviewers are novelists (the best of these is John Updike), who put their best efforts—as they should—into writing fiction rather than just writing about it, the formation of public taste is usually worked on full-time only by the publicists.

I don't mean to attack publicists. They do what they're supposed to do, which is bring the books to the public's attention. God help writers these days who don't have a good one working on their behalf. But with hundreds of novels published each year and a limited number of dollars in the pockets of potential readers, someone has to try and do more than merely assert that whatever book they're touting at the moment is the best book of the moment. Yet fewer and fewer voices are speaking with critical authority, style, and intelligence in an effort to help the reading public sort things out.

The results are paradoxical and, for serious readers, not to mention serious writers, somewhat demoralizing. On the one hand we have limited, what we might call "pocket," successes, American versions of the European art novel, that find a small but devoted audience—novels by, say, Joyce Carol Oates or Jayne Anne Phillips. And then there is the work put forward in certain academic circles because it stands as evidence of a particular presentation of American culture (I'm using the word *culture* rather than *life* because this sort of book, for me, at least, never really lives except as part of a larger argument about society), the work of Don DeLillo and Paul Auster coming to mind here. At the other extreme is the big-seller list, which is by and large pretty awful stuff, with Stephen King and Tom Clancy standing at the top of the pile. Now and then a movie tie-in or some ethnic predilection will kick a serious book up on the list, a novel by E. L. Doctorow or Edith Wharton or Amy Tan or Toni Morrison. But for the most part mainstream readers elevate the awful to stardom. It's been that way since the creation of the best-seller list just before World War I, and it will certainly not get better for a while, if at all.

For the past few years, for example, the novels of Mississippi lawyer John Grisham have been all the rage. When I picked up a copy of *The Firm*—having been surrounded at family occasions by relatives urging me to do it—out of a hope for some fast-paced reading pleasure, the kind I used to look for in those sea stories of Forester and in science fiction and for the past few decades have found in a select band of spy novelists and thriller writers from John Le Carré to Thomas

Harris, I was terribly disappointed. But not surprised. The same thing happened years before when I tried out of desperation to fend off the Robert Ludlum crowd. It's all mediocre fare, with no real sense of language or psychology or plot beyond the melodramatic. Danielle Steel and the other romance writers are no better. "He entered her and they made love all night." That sentence of Steel's has stayed with me since I first read it. You can't get much worse and still be writing published fiction. But anything this woman touches turns to money. So that's the good news and the bad news about the American reading public, as John Gardner used to say: "The good news is that in actual numbers more people are reading today than ever before in the history of the planet. The bad news is that they're reading mostly shit."

Commercial publishers don't offer all that much optimism. Even as they produce sales figures slightly above last year's, you notice that the dreck makes up most of the sales. Perhaps it's always been so, but lately it seems more so than usual. As the late publisher Sol Stein once put it so ironically and truly, "It's only those books that transmit the culture from one generation to the next" that are being left off the lists these days. And so-called "midlist" writers, wonderfully entertaining and serious all in one, find themselves driven out of the marketplace for—where? If the trend keeps moving in this direction, an entire generation of gifted but non-best-selling American fiction writers are headed toward oblivion long before death.

"But look at all the book clubs just here in Washington," a friend pointed out to me the other day when I presented him with this portrait of literary culture and readership in chaos. "There are readers all over the place." And it's true. Washington is a city of book clubs, and there are many, many cities like it across the country. And in the schools across the country there's no dearth of bright readers. Those kids lying on cushions in that classroom in Huntsville, Texas, for example. Or the Jane Austen fans at the private girls' school in Troy, New York, where I visited one afternoon to witness a discussion of *Mansfield Park* that was as heated and intense as any gents' squash game. Or the Washington, D.C., public school classes where the PEN/Faulkner Foundation sends visiting fiction writers to discuss their work with interested students.

It's not that we're sliding back into some dark age of total illiteracy. But as we lurch into the new millennium, the news for the future of the American readership is growing exceedingly strange. McLuhanite doomsayers are appearing on all sides. Ivan Illich, for example, argues in his new book (!) *In the Vineyard of the Text* that "the age of the book-ish text seems to be passing." The advent of the personal computer and the electronic era, Illich goes on, has irrevocably undermined the pri-macy of the book and altered our way of pursuing knowledge. Such fad-dish visions make the writer's heart sink.

But it's the reader in me more than the writer that takes the great-est offense. Having grown up in the time of Big Talk About the Death of the Novel and now finding myself on the verge of an epoch in which the Big Talk focuses on the Death of Literature and possibly even the Death of the Book itself, all the Jersey rises up in me and wants to spit on the sneakers of whatever current theologian of culture makes this argument. And there's no help from the academy, either. In exactly that quarter where you'd think you might find people professing their love of literature and the importance, if not the primacy, of the art of fiction and poetry, you meet instead theory-fraught ideologues, wav-ing foreign paradigms about in place of Scripture, telling us of every reason under the sun for spending time with a book except the neces-sary ones.

To know another mind. To know another life. To feel oneself in the heart of another age, in the heart of another human being. To live out the entire trajectory of a human motivation and understand its fullness in time. To move out of ourselves, lifted into another scene, another action, another destiny, so that we might gain a better sense of our own. To warm our spirits by the heat of a fine story, to help us keep the vision (even if illusion) of order in a world constantly on the verge of chaos. Bored theoreticians, losing hold of their own human-ity, turn away from these blessings that the novel offers in order to fur-ther their own pallid fantasies of the modern spirit. And by shirking their responsibility toward the very humanist tradition that spawned them, they show their contempt not only for their own best (now sadly blighted) tendencies as readers but also for the new generations of potential readers who even now in the elementary schools across

America are doing their best to prepare themselves—sounding their vowels, making out their letters, clumping them together into stumbling words on the page—to partake of the riches of our culture from Homer to Virginia Woolf to John Edgar Wideman. And for the potential new readers among our immigrant populations. And for the newly educated adults, born here but not born free enough to learn to read as children, new readers such as James the truck driver, my companion at the literacy council Christmas supper.

"TV gets to you after a while," James said to me as we were finishing up our meal. "And let me tell you, life is tough enough without ever finding out a way to see it a little better. I learned the hard way, by not learning until now. My mama told us good stories when we were children, but she couldn't write them down. I'm missing a good story like in the old days. So when I get good enough with my reading, that's what I'm going to do."

"Write them down?" I said.

James laughed and chewed a bite of food.

"I don't know if I'd ever get that good. But I could like to read one."

"Talking here with you," I told him, "made me remember the first time I ever heard a story, the first time I ever thought about learning how to read."

"Tell me the story," he said.

I explained that I couldn't, because it had been in Russian and all these years I had never found the English version of that tale.

"Well, that's a story by itself," he said. "Remembering it, trying to find it, not finding it. Write that one down. And maybe sometime when I get good enough I'll see it on a page."

So that is what I've done.

Books in Flames:
A View of Latin American Literature

The flat, swampy, low jungle of the Yucatán peninsula is hot enough even in winter for its inhabitants to live without using fires at night for heating purposes. But in the Mayan city of Mani, eighteen kilometers south of Mérida, the state's present capital, in the year 1562, a great fire roared for days outside the walls of a convent newly constructed from the stones of a Mayan temple. Tens of thousands of religious articles and every extant Mayan holy manuscript that the priests, led by Bishop Diego de Landa, could find in the territory fed the flames in a book burning that was much more devastating than those we have seen in films of the Nazi period in Europe. In the age of mechanical reproduction, book burning is a symbolic act. In sixteenth-century Mexico, the priests attempted to destroy an entire culture, the mind of a people, their past, their present, and their future. Nothing was more dangerous to the conquering theologians than the beautiful designs and colors of the Mayan hieroglyphic narratives. For several times a year, as Diego de Landa himself writes in his account of the Mayan culture he worked for decades to destroy,

> the priests would take out the books and extend them on cool
> foliage they had for this purpose . . . while they diluted a bit of

verdigris in a glass with virgin water that they asserted was brought from the mountain where no woman treads, and they would anoint the wooden covers of the books with it . . . and the most learned of the priests would open a book and look at the omens for that year and make them known to those present.

These holy books, with their stately processions and knotted groups of kings and warriors, books of virgin water and succoring foliage, were painted in profound blues, rich golds, deep greens, and earthy reds, on both sides of thin sheets of pounded bark of the indigenous fig tree, and finished with a layer of calcium carbonate obtained from local rocks. Of their actual content, we still know quite little. "Of five apparent distinct varieties of picto-writing, the first treated years and times, the second days and festivals, the third dreams, delusions, vanities, and omens, the fourth baptism and the naming of children, and the fifth rites and ceremonies related to marriage." As the Mexican art historian María Sten describes it, the content of the manuscripts gave the Mayas an entire world.

It was not merely the content of the books that the priests destroyed. To the Mayas, the act of painting the narratives was holy in itself. As the legend has it, Quetzalcoatl, the plumed serpent of the Mexican pantheon, came to the Yucatán in the form of the deity Kukulkan, and before anything else he taught the Mayan people how to create the painted books. In this tropical territory, fire remained secondary in importance to the act of creating narratives. The coolness of an orderly universe stood first in importance. To combat the serpent god's invention, the priests plunged the books into the flames.

The discovery of America was thus not an act of uncovering a continent unknown to cultured human beings. As the Colombian historian Germán Arciñiegas has written, it was not so much an act of des*cubrimiento* as of *cubrimiento*, not a discovery but a covering over, the burial of a great culture by the agents of another. For more than two centuries, the Spanish criollo ruling class bricked over indigenous Indian folkways, supplying the American continent with an imported theology in exchange for a stage on which Spain, undergoing tumultuous social change from within and military and political defeat without, might continue to reenact the tattered glories of its pre-Armada past.

Colonial rule across oceans, however, can work well for the mother country only if the imagination of the colony remains in its thrall. Ironically, the very allegiance to the traditions and mores of Spain that kept Spanish America in harness for several centuries produced the conditions that led to the burgeoning New World revolutionary movements. In the eighteenth century, the Latin American ruling class, true to its sense of itself as a European-oriented group, opened wide its arms to the methods of European science, technology, and education. Rationalism and liberalism took hold among an increasingly enlightened young generation and congress with Spain led to congress with Europe as well, a Rousseau-ist Europe in which man was everywhere throwing off his unnatural bondage to monarchy. In the wake of Bolívar's revolutions there emerged a group of independent Latin nations no longer enslaved by European imperialism. Now, however, they freely chose a way of life that was essentially European in nature. While the Indians toiled on, Madrid and Paris became centers of liberalism and bastions of middle-class power and served as the intellectual capitals of the newly independent American countries ruled by the criollo landowners and professionals.

In his seminal study of Argentine society, *Facundo, or Life in the Days of the Argentinian Tyrants*, nineteenth-century author and statesman Domingo Sarmiento describes the events of his nation's history as a struggle between the forces of civilization and barbarism. This analysis grew out of his understanding of the early period of Argentine post-independence politics and the battles that raged between the educated Creoles of Buenos Aires and the ragged, rugged, uneducated cowboy armies of the countryside, which from time to time threw up a leader to take over the urban seat of national power. Sarmiento boldly shows his sympathy for the European-oriented ruling group of the city. He never doubts the necessity for struggling against the rise of dictators from the pampas such as Facundo Quiroga, the figure who stands in his essay for the forces of misrule, antidemocracy, and the destruction of culture. Barbarism represents for him a return to the murder, rampages, and brutal tyranny that obtained during the short period of Facundo's rule.

Yet it also exerts a powerful attraction for the citified, Europeanized Sarmiento. He reserves his finest prose for the description of life among the barbaric gauchos of the pampas. His passages devoted to the skills and talents of the rough-riding gaucho, such as his abilities as a hunter and tracker, horseman, and singer of ballads, present us with a type reminiscent in its mythic stature of our own nineteenth-century's Natty Bumpo, the Deerslayer of James Fenimore Cooper. The sections dedicated to the evocation of the landscape, the stage upon which these heroic figures ride, strut, sing, and shoot, rival in power and visionary force those of Sarmiento's model, the eighteenth-century French aristocrat Chateaubriand. The vast romantic vista of the pampas becomes a sight worthy of ranking alongside the North American landscapes in *Atalá* and Cooper's Leatherstocking series. The line between earth and sky becomes sublimely blurred as indigenous Homers of the plains wander past, singing of victories over the Indians while herding their great droves of cattle from one hazy horizon to the next. Like the first generation of conquerors, Sarmiento seems to admire what he considers most dangerous in indigenous American culture.

The paradox inherent in Sarmiento's work characterizes the next hundred years and more of Latin American literary production. For while it was not true, as he suggested, that all culture in the New World grew out of the struggle between the forces of civilization and barbarism, it was evident that those who held the power in the Latin American nations behaved as though it were true. Thus brutal dictatorships arose from time to time throughout the continent, more often than not in the name of civilization and the European way of life, and Creole writers produced slavish imitations of European romantic fiction. As Alejo Carpentier has put it, there was an abundance in this period of novels with the names of women, the foremost example being *María* by the Colombian Jorge Isaacs. Poetry turned stale, the fragile tranquillity broken now and then by outcries that at last Venezuela had her Virgil or Brazil her Homer (noises akin to our own nineteenth-century proclamations, such as those made by William

Cullen Bryant that the United States at last had matured to the point where it might make a poetry of its own, with a diction and prosody distinct from that of England). Independence, which came early in the nineteenth century for nations such as Argentina, Venezuela, and Chile, and as late as 1902 for Cuba, did not necessarily mean economic freedom. Certainly it did not mean cultural independence.

For more than a century thereafter, most Latin American novelists applied the techniques of European artists to the materials of their own culture in unashamed imitation. To the ruling practitioners of the time, such models, whether romantic or naturalistic, did not seem "foreign" at all. Since they felt themselves bound to the progress of European culture, these nineteenth-century artists worked as willing slaves to a foreign tradition. The rise of the European regional folkloric novel produced a slight but important turn. Although today most of their works are best left to the specialists, the European writers— Jean Giono, Liam O'Flaherty, Ladislao Raimond—who practiced this subgenre had a great effect on the first generation of twentieth-century Latin American intellectuals. As Alejo Carpentier, born in 1904, has written of his own encounter with these novels, "In the face of an incredible boredom produced by a day of reading a novel about the customs of Alsatians, I asked myself, 'Why not do the same . . . with novels about the customs of Cuban peasants or Gauchos or Yucatecans?'" That day, the Cuban novelist asserts, he became the author of *Ecue-Yamba-O!*, his first novel. Written when he was twenty-five, it grew out of his research into the customs of black Cuban cane-cutters whose lives had been largely ignored by the educated, European-oriented Creoles of the cities and large farms.

In similar fashion across Latin America, writers of the present day looked beyond the romantic imagery of their predecessors to search out in serious, scientific fashion the facts of the daily life of the large masses of the Indian population of the continent, lives that up until then had been "discovered" only to be covered over by the dominant Creoles. The Indians possessed no literature that the curious ethnologists, novelists, poets, and nascent anthropologists might immediately consult. Bishop Diego de Landa had seen to that. But their music, tribal language, work habits, tools, and designs on ceramics or cloth were readily available to the visitors from the urban centers, though most of their ancient cities still lay in vine-covered ruin. This marked the first phase of the true discovery of America by her own inhabitants. Paradoxically, the role of Europe in this major renovation of the Latin American imagination cannot be ignored. To Carpentier, and his Guatemalan contemporary Miguel Angel Asturias, sojourns to the Continent were instrumental in their own personal discoveries of America. What few manuscripts survived the holocaust at Mani in 1552, and the earlier destruction of Montezuma's library in Tenochtitlán when Cortés brought down the pillars of the Aztec empire, could be found only in Paris and Germany. To study the roots of their own culture, these young artists had to study in Europe.

It was in Paris in the 1920s that Carpentier first encountered the manuscripts that would inspire him to return to Cuba and study firsthand the history of his native island. It was in Paris in the 1920s that Asturias first read the *Popol-Vuh*, the sacred book of the Quiché-Maya, whose language and imagery would affect his own fiction for nearly fifty years afterward. But while Europe in the 1920s was a place in which to study, Europe in the 1930s became a place to flee. As Alfonso Reyes, the Mexican essayist, put it, the Continent began to disintegrate before the eyes of the world. The clouds gathering over the concentration camps gave notice that the culture of the conquerors had fallen into a decadence that no Aztec priest, hair smeared with blood of sacrificial victims, could ever have imagined. Europe offered no more idols to worship.

Latin American intellectuals, writers, artists, painters, poets, musicians, suddenly found themselves "exiled" in their own countries. Those who had not already turned their eyes toward the arts and traditions of their own population had no other place to look. In 1945, Carpentier began the composition of his short novel based on the Haitian Revolution led by Toussaint L'Ouverture, *El reino de este mundo* (The Kingdom of This World), which would dramatize the break between Latin American "magical realist" writers and the European surrealist tradition that had nurtured them. In this same period, parallel with the rise of the continent's first indigenous socialist parties, Asturias published *El Señor Presidente*, a ferocious indictment of a

Central American dictator in which he employed linguistic and narrative techniques indigenous to Guatemalan Indian narratives. His
Hombres de maiz (Men of Maize) followed shortly thereafter, signaling
a break with the naturalist tradition in Latin America. Even the anomalous genius Borges, the eternal cosmopolitan, wrote in his unique
"universal" style of city dwellers who dreamed of hand-to-hand combat with murderous gauchos. More than just the rejection of the hegemony of European culture united these men. Like the painters of the
Mexican Revolution, Rivera, Siqueiros, and Orozco, they had finally
uncovered their personal connection to the period of the Conquest
and found themselves on the other side of the Sarmiento paradigm
from civilization in a new world rich with aesthetic possibility and
political adventure.

Four hundred years after the burning of the Mayan scriptures,
Latin America could once again boast of a literature. Before the end of
World War II, the best fiction writers of the continent's first modern
generation of intellectuals (specifically, Borges, Carpentier, Asturias,
the Brazilian João Guimaraes Rosa, and the Uruguayan Juan Carlos
Onetti) had not yet published any of their major work in book form.
But between 1944 and 1952, each of them produced at least one novel
or collection of short stories that brought his name to the attention of
a small but intensely interested national reading public. By the end of
the fifties, a second group of writers had made its debut, including
Julio Cortázar (born in 1914 and thus really a figure who links the two
generations) from Argentina, Juan Rulfo in Mexico, Gabriel García
Márquez in Colombia, Carlos Fuentes, another Mexican, and the
Peruvian Mario Vargas Llosa.

Taken together, this group forms what critic Luis Harss has defin-
itively proclaimed as the "mainstream" of modern Latin American
prose narrative. Although aficionados might wish to add the names of
Peruvian novelist Jose María Arguedas, or the Puerto Rican novelist
Pedro Juan Soto, these nine can be viewed as major artists who leaped
the boundaries of their individual countries and won international
reputation. Asturias, for example, won the Nobel Prize for Literature
in 1967. Carpentier won several major literary prizes in France and
Spain, has been applauded in both Moscow and Peking, and has had

the honor of having his novel *Los pasos perdidos* (The Lost Steps) reissued five years after its initial appearance in New York by the same major American publishing house. *Pedro Paramo*, Juan Rulfo's only novel, a mysterious narrative about life among the dead in a small Mexican village, is currently in print in the same North American edition after twenty years. For a long time, the novels of Carlos Fuentes have rivaled those of Gide and Camus among American college students, but now that the paperback edition of García Márquez's *Cien años de soledad* (A Hundred Years of Solitude) has gone into its eleventh printing, it seems that the Colombian writer has no rival on U.S. campuses, not even our own Vonnegut and Pynchon. Julio Cortázar's novel *Rayuela* (Hopscotch) wins new converts each day. Less well known are Onetti and Vargas Llosa, but the former's best novel, *La vida breve* (A Brief Life), has just been published in translation here after nearly thirty years of life in Spanish. Front-page reviews of Vargas Llosa's *Conversación en la catedral* (Conversation in the Cathedral) and the growing popularity of the paperback edition of his *La casa verde* (The Green House) suggest that these writers may become as widely known as Fuentes and García Márquez. Borges, of course, remains as famous as Kafka.

Every generation has its fads, fiction writers both native and foreign, who mean much more at a special moment in the life of a student than they ever will again, and the "marvelous realities" of García Márquez and Carpentier serve that function, I'm sure, in the imagination of some younger readers. But for others, the current bloom in Latin American writing is no mere fad. It is as much a "discovery" for them as it was a "discovery" for those of us who taught some of the books to them, those of us for whom Spanish was once only one language among many foreign tongues and, for that matter, a lesser one than any one of a number of European languages. We welcomed the tyranny of European culture and called our education complete. We never burned any books—but for a long time we left some important volumes unopened.

Modern Latin American fiction has helped us all to become a bit more civilized and a bit more barbaric. The fruit of an economic system we call "underdeveloped," it instructs us, paradoxically, in the most sophisticated fashion on the root questions of life. Consider, for example, Asturias's masterly *Hombres de maiz*. The story of the war between the small cultivators of native corn in the Guatemalan countryside and the military forces that work on behalf of economic centralization, the narrative employs local dialects and local mythologies in tandem with Spanish prose and Christian imagery. The strife between the old Indian corn farmers and the new technocrats who manipulate the army becomes a battle for reality itself. Pre-Conquest myth challenges Christian ideology for possession of the reader's imagination, and the seemingly loose development of the plot, with its shifts from one time period to another and from one seemingly unrelated group of characters to the next, becomes emblematic of the practice of *nagualismo* or the benevolent lycanthropy indigenous to the beliefs of the region (which allows a postman to turn into a coyote and back into a postman again in order to speed along the mails).

In this fiction, the leader of a peasant revolt rises again and again in the collective imagination of his followers like the shaman, called the "deer of the seventh fire," whom he has supposedly killed. Each time a cornfield goes up in flames, the Indian guerrilla chief rises in rebellion. Though the North American reader of this difficult but rewarding novel may sometimes feel as he makes his way through the alien territory of Asturias's story as though he were trying to track the evanescent coyote-postman himself, he recognizes that he remains in the hands of a narrative master quite unlike any other he has encountered before. The power and the force of the *Popol-Vuh*, the sacred book of the Quiché-Maya, hovers constantly on the horizon of Asturias's modern-day Guatemalan countryside.

The fusion of ancient mysteries and contemporary political struggle occurs within Alejo Carpentier's *El reino de este mundo*, published in the same decade as *Hombres de maiz*. In this short novel, what Carpentier calls "the marvelously real" elements of the Haitian Revolution become metaphors for radical political and social change. The action is presented from the point of view of Ti-Noel, a Haitian of African descent who is first a slave under French rule and then a *houngan* or master of voodoo who struggles against the reactionary mulatto successors in the regime of Toussaint L'Ouverture. Ti-Noel, like

Asturias's coyote-postman, possesses metamorphic powers. Like Mackandal, the leader of the initial rebellion against French rule, he can change from human to animal form in order to further the cause of Haitian independence.

The mode of *El reino* is itself metamorphic, weaving back and forth between, on the one hand, Creole rationalism and, on the other, indigenous belief in magical transformation as though there were no actual distinctions between the two modes of thought. Here, Carpentier's enlistment of surrealist narrative technique in the service of the revolutionary ideal strikes a fresh and pleasing new style quite unlike the social fantasies of European writers from Gogol to Hoffman. Reality in this novel is an amazing realm in which one sees no distinction between what the Haitian revolutionaries believe to be true and what appears to be true.

At the novel's conclusion, we learn that Mackandal and other revolutionaries had disguised themselves as animals,

> to serve man, not to abjure the world of men. It was then that the old man [Ti-Noel], resuming his human form, had a supremely lucid moment. He lived, for the space of a heart beat, the finest moment of his life; he glimpsed once more the heroes who had revealed to him the power and the fullness of his remote African forebears, making him believe in the possible germinations the future held. He felt countless centuries old. A cosmic weariness, as of a planet weighted with stones, fell about his shoulders shrunk by so many blows, sweats, revolts. . . . Now he understood that a man never knows for whom he suffers and hopes. He suffers and hopes and toils for people he will never know, and who, in turn, will suffer and hope and toil for others who will not be happy either, for man always seeks a happiness far beyond that which is meted out to him . . . man finds his greatness, his fullest measure, only in the Kingdom of This World.

Then, as if to suggest the ephemeral nature of such rhetoric, Ti-Noel challenges the new mulatto tyrants to battle and fades away into a

great green wind that blows in from the Caribbean, a Dionysian figure who comes into the world to set things right and then disappears
into the sea, leaving behind nothing but "trails of salt on the flanks of
the mountains."

Other, more recent works by members of this group of writers
further the convention of the "marvelously real" narrative complete
and self-contained within the covers of a book that nevertheless
demands an active and immediate response from its readers. The
person who holds Julio Cortázar's *Rayuela* in his hands is literally
instructed how to play hopscotch back and forth between the scores of
short narrative sequences between its covers, and thus dramatize the
passage, willy-nilly, between European and American culture, the I
and the Other, This Side and the Other Side, inner and outer consciousness, past and present, life and death, passages that the main
character, an Argentinian expatriate named Horacio, attempts to enact
within the formal narrative itself. Because of Cortázar's radical
impressment of the reader in the unfolding of his novel, some critics
have called the work the *Ulysses* of Latin American literature.

The novels of the Peruvian writer Mario Vargas Llosa are long,
difficult, but fascinating works in which the rot and sterility of his
nation's psychic and spiritual life are exposed with Balzacian exacti-
tude. Because of their ties to the European naturalist tradition, they
point up with striking clarity the important transformation of Continental traditions that modern Latin American writers have wrought.
In his first novel, *La ciudad y los perros* (translated as *The Time of the
Hero*), Vargas Llosa employed Joycean interior monologues in a ferocious exposé of social conditions at a Lima military academy. The success of his experiment—the yoking of high-culture, Mandarin literary
technique and naturalist social imperative—may be measured by the
fact that the administrators of the academy he had attended in Lima
bought up all the available copies of the novel and burned them, some
six hundred in number, in the main courtyard of the school. Shades of
Bishop Diego de Landa!

In subsequent novels, Vargas Llosa further refined his use of interior monologue, breaking down the components of the Spanish American sentence itself in order to convey new states of feeling, and apply-

ing Flaubertian finesse to the dramatization of the lives of the near-primitive inhabitants of the Peruvian jungle as well as the cafés and mansions of the Lima middle class. In *La casa verde*, published in 1965, he portrayed the schism between city life and jungle life that is one of the major paradoxes of Peruvian society in such a way as to turn Sarmiento on his head. Further, and perhaps more important, he took apart tense and time, completely reorienting the reader's sense of past and present and thus demonstrating that the rift between regions and subcultures may be seen as a struggle between distinctive conceptions of time itself.

Time, as Georg Lukács wrote, is the single major constitutive element of the novel. Poised between the end of the period of European Conquest and the beginning of a new epoch of individual and political independence, Latin American writers have recognized themselves, in the words of the epigram from Lope de Vega that Carpentier employs at the head of his story collection called *Guerra de tiempo*, as soldiers in the war of time. A number of interesting and innovative younger writers have added their names to this cadre, among them the Chilean José Donoso, the Argentinian Manuel Puig, and the Cuban exile Guillermo Cabrera Infante. But for many North American readers of Latin American literature, the most effective depiction of how this struggle for the invention of a new mode of being in the world may be waged, if not won, can be found in the pages of Gabriel García Márquez's *Cien años de soledad*.

One hundred years, a century, of solitude. The title itself orders time in the same moment that it presents the problem of being in time. This narrative history of the Buendía clan enhances our understanding of this basic contradiction of Latin American society, the opposition of intellect and feeling, rationalism and intuition, and the Apollonian and the Dionysian modes of being. It exposes such paradigms as Sarmiento's as mere rhetorical presentations of situations that can only be understood as living problems, the dialectic made flesh within a clearly defined period of temporal passage. In other words, it is the first major Latin American novel to embrace all of the self-conscious paradoxes of modern Latin American thought in a wholly credible, everyday situation whose nature is entirely unlike any of the major works of Continental fiction.

Many years later, as he faced the firing squad, Colonel Aureliano Buendía was to remember that distant afternoon when his
father took him to discover ice. At that time, Macondo was a
village of twenty adobe homes, built on the bank of a river of
clear water that ran along a bed of polished stones, which were
white and enormous, like prehistoric eggs. The world was so
recent that many things lacked names, and in order to indicate
them it was necessary to point.

The opening lines of the novel mark a good place to conclude this
hurried survey of much more than a hundred years of strife, solitude,
false sentiment, and new solidarity. In the face of impending death,
Aureliano Buendía casts his mind back to a time of origins, childhood,
and the early days of the Colombian village of Macondo, but also,
given the resemblance of the polished stones along the stream bed, to
a pre-historical moment, to an age of ice, a time before language,
before fire. His mental gesture seems highly appropriate to recall the
task of the Latin American writer, which, as Carpentier has written, is
the task of Adam: he must give names to the component parts of the
magical region that he calls home. García Márquez does precisely
that, teaching us how to match language and reality in such a way as to
invent a new world with a fresh history. In the face of the fact that most
of the indigenous New World texts had been burned by the conquerors in the sixteenth century, no labor less than the creation of living narratives from their ashes will do. The result, as Vargas Llosa has
suggested, is a "literature of fire" that illuminates the contradictions of
contemporary Latin America but serves at the same time as its greatest creation. In the ice age of contemporary North American culture,
it serves us well to huddle close to this lifegiving flame.

The Lost Books

Of all the writers whose work has been cast up on U.S. shores as part of the so-called Boom in Latin American fiction in translation, Cuban novelist Alejo Carpentier has yet to win any serious, broad public attention. Carpentier's publishing history in a country that ironically enough was ready, little more than a decade ago, to go to war with the government of his native island is as dismal as one could possibly imagine. Like the main figure in Carpentier's own early short story, "Journey Back to the Source," who at a certain point near death grew younger and younger until he perished into the seed of his own origins, Carpentier's reputation seems to diminish as more of his work comes to be translated here.

The first Carpentier to be translated in the United States was *Los pasos perdidos*, his third novel in order of Spanish publication. Under the title *The Lost Steps*, the late Harriet de Onís's translation came out in the autumn of 1956 as an addition to the distinguished group of European translations published by Alfred A. Knopf. Reviewing the novel in the October 14, 1956, issue of the *New York Times Book Review*, poet and journalist Selden Rodman became the first of a long line of critics and academics who would damn Carpentier with faint praise. At the outset of his essay, Rodman remarks on the novel's eru-

dition, reminding his readers that as U.S. citizens they are traditionally wary of intelligent fiction, and adding that

> despite my awareness of this national limitation—if it is a limi-
> tation—I find myself becoming not a little suspicious, too,
> when I find the protagonist of an adventure story discussing his
> sexual prowess in terms of the Greeks and the Israelites, invok-
> ing Descartes in a dugout canoe, and quoting medieval Latin
> poems in the jungle.

After 250 words devoted to a summary of the plot—in which Rodman
gives a straightforward account of how the unnamed musicologist narrator puts the "hothouse atmosphere of intellectual New York" behind
him and sets out on a quest up the Orinoco for rare primitive musical
instruments, gives over wife and mistress for an Indian woman and the
natural life of the jungle village only to find that his urge to compose
serious music overwhelms him and pushes him back to civilization—
Rodman praises Carpentier for the "suspenseful unfolding" of this
plot and for creating its "brilliantly poetic dialogue and descriptions."
But Rodman admits that he succumbed to what he has already suggested is the national bias against a literature of "ideas" and undercuts
all the positive attention he gives to the novel. "Well," he remarks, "it
doesn't quite come off" because the "hero is so very, very much the
intellectual." Summing up, he complains that *The Lost Steps* is "a book
full of riches—stylistic, sensory, visual—but as a novel it's just a little
cheap."

The translation fared better in the quality magazines. After
declaring inexplicably that he found it a little like the Giraudoux of
"Suzanne and the Pacific," reviewer Ben Ray Redman informed readers of the October 20, 1956, issue of the *Saturday Review of Literature*
that the novel's "jungle pictures" were "masterpieces of evocation" and
that it had "a message of importance" to convey to readers on a subject that he declined to name. A reviewer in the November 1956 issue
of the *Atlantic Monthly* gave his readers a sharper image of the novel's
style and remarked that the publishers were justified in claiming that
"you find in his novel suggestions of Malraux together with sugges-

tions of the W. H. Hudson of *Green Mansions*." *The Lost Steps*, this writer concluded, was in fact "a richly textured and altogether unusual novel which . . . effectively dramatizes pertinent questions about the high price of civilization."

Few readers were ready to pay attention to these messages of importance. Selling less than three thousand copies before it went out of print in 1966 and, after the publisher boldly reissued it in 1967 with a preface by J. B. Priestly, selling fewer than four thousand in its new edition, *The Lost Steps* still has no following among American readers. Like the markers pointing the way toward the hidden village near the headwaters of the Orinoco that were covered over when the river rose in flood, the novel seems destined for obscurity.

When Carpentier's second novel, *El reino de este mundo*, appeared in Harriet de Onís's translation as *The Kingdom of This World*, reviews were initially more encouraging. Mildred Adams, writing in the May 19, 1957, issue of the *New York Times Book Review*, declared that this short narrative was "in substance a handful of heady moments woven together by literary craftsmanship of a high order." Although few other reviewers were able to define the novel's action, they praised the book as energetically as Ms. Adams did. A writer in the June 29, 1957, issue of the *Saturday Review*, for example, raved about the "infectious nature" of Carpentier's "schizophrenic . . . tiny piece of Voodoo gingerbread," though he spent more time describing the dust jacket than he did the plot. A better-informed notice appeared in the August 1957 issue of the *Atlantic Monthly*, in which the reviewer praised the book for its "brilliant, improbable world which has the stylized reality of the great myths." From these reports, it would have been difficult to tell whether much intelligence, if any, lurked within Carpentier's fiction. But praise of Carpentier's "craftsmanship" and style did not encourage any more readers for this novel than for the first one. The book sold 3,032 copies before it went out of print in 1965.

The reviews and sales history of the next two translations follow pretty nearly the same pattern. *El siglo de las luces* appeared in 1963 under the title *Explosion in a Cathedral* and made reviewer Abel Plenn worry in the July 29, 1963, issue of the *New York Times Book Review* that Carpentier's masterful historical novel, with its "lyrical intensity that is breathtaking and beautiful," might yet fail to find much of an audience because of the author's great erudition. Before too long, the novel showed up in remainder bookstores, where it was selling for nineteen cents a copy! When *War of Time*, a collection of shorter works, appeared in 1970, David Gallagher, an Oxford don writing in the July 5, 1970, *New York Times Book Review*, found it quite praiseworthy, as did Anthony West, writing in the *New Yorker* of November 28, 1970. *War of Time* sold 2,450 copies over six years.

The most recent Carpentier to be translated here, the novel *El recurso del método* (first published in Mexico in 1974 and brought out in hardcover by Alfred A. Knopf in May of this year under the title *Reasons of State*) already shows signs of disappearing beneath the obscurity that North America seems to fling over the Cuban novelist's literary productions. Alexander Coleman, writing in the May 2, 1976, issue of the *New York Times Book Review* praised the book for its "breezy panache," but only after complaining that "Carpentier's earlier novels and stories were pretty heavy going, what with their tiresome philosophizing and heavily laid-on historical panoplies." John Leonard, writing in the daily edition of the *New York Times* on June 4, 1976, openly expressed his bias against Carpentier as a stylist, describing the new novel as a mixed bag of interesting set pieces and intolerable lists of objects of culture. My own piece in the June 20, 1976, issue of the *Los Angeles Times Book Review* was much more positive than either Coleman's or Leonard's. The essay by novelist Paul West in *Review* [of fall 1976] is the longest and the most laudatory of any of the responses in English up until this writing. But if the early sales of the novel are any barometer of current public interest in Carpentier's fiction (they stand at a meager 1,511 as of June 1, 1976), *Reasons of State* will do no better than any of its predecessors and possibly even worse.

At this point some readers may have already decided that indeed the reasons for Carpentier's failure to capture an audience here are those same reasons put forth by the earliest reviewers: that his fiction is too "erudite," that he is more a "cultural historian" than a novelist, as both Selden Rodman and Ben Ray Redman have charged, or that he is a "tiresome philosophizer," as Alexander Coleman has suggested. Other critics have added their voices to these accusatory proceedings.

For example, Luis Harss, coauthor of *Into the Mainstream*, the land-mark collection of interviews and critical appraisals of nine major Latin American novelists and poets, complains of the "fake animism" of *The Kingdom of This World*, although he finds it a "teachable" book because of its easily available symbol systems. Harss has less to say for the rest of Carpentier's work, which, with the exception of the novella "El camino de Santiago" (translated as "The Highroad of St. James" in the collection *War of Time*), he labels boring, full of hot air. David Gallagher, after praising *War of Time*, chose to omit a discussion of Carpentier's work from his recent book-length study *Modern Latin American Literature*. Emir Rodríguez Monegal, in his seminal two-volume study *Narradores de nuestra América* (Narrators of Our America), ranks Carpentier's work below that of many other Latin American novelists of this century.

One may quarrel with some of these negative views, but on the question of the absence of a substantial audience for the novelist's work, one flails about like a ghost-fighter, firing at shadows, starting at the slightest sound in the woods. What makes the U.S. reading audi-ence so obligingly ignorant of Cuba's greatest novelist? Perhaps the answer does lie in the books themselves. Certainly *The Lost Steps*, for all its superficial affinities with the variety of romantic fiction that North Americans love to indulge in—from Edgar Rice Burroughs's *Tarzan* to *Gone with the Wind* and the Mandingo novels—presents an odd and strangely formidable face to the U.S. reader. Despite its emphasis on the estrangement of the main character from the life of the modern city and the lushness of its sequences devoted to jungle landscape and its exotic inhabitants, it remains an inherently ironic novel whose bite and tension seem lost in its English translation. Even North American readers of college age require a bit less density in their basic existential texts. They seem to prefer the mindless mur-derer of Camus's *The Stranger* to the culture-burdened narrator of *The Lost Steps*, whose tale is thickly laced with literary, historical, and musi-cal references. When such a masterpiece of irony in native English as Ford Madox Ford's *The Good Soldier* goes begging for customers, per-haps we ought not to expect anything more for the translation of the profoundly ironic Carpentier.

One would think that a better fate might lie in store for *The King-dom of This World*. Its focus on the eighteenth-century insurrection of the Haitian slaves against the French colonial forces in the Caribbean offers fertile reading material for both blacks and whites caught up in the present North American struggle for racial equality and social justice. This fact may explain why this novel is the only Carpentier translation available in an American paperback edition. Its relative brevity may also contribute something to its appeal. These factors, in tandem with its adventurous and exotic subject matter—revolution, magic, the metamorphosis of men into beasts—may yet give it continuing life. Still, in a country whose audiences last century praised Melville for his early sea adventures and dropped him when he published *Moby Dick*, the vagaries of literary taste can hardly be accurately predicted.

A historical novel, *Explosion in a Cathedral* offers the broadest spectrum of any of Carpentier's works in translation. It focuses on a quartet of characters, three young Cubans and an older one, a baker-turned-revolutionary named Victor Hugues (an actual historical figure), who are caught up in the sweep of the French Revolution in the Caribbean. Its style is more vital, catholic, and appealing than that of the other books, and John Sturrock's translation lends Carpentier's pithy amalgam of European and native metaphors and ideas a luster and excitement that some critics have found more appealing than the original Spanish. Carpentier's wedding of fiction and history in these pages stirs the imagination with great force. As the young Cuban named Esteban wades through rowdy scenes of revolution, piracy, and counterinsurrection, or views the baroque underwater creations that crowd the Caribbean sea bottom in mysterious and awesome profusion, the reader may invoke the names of the nineteenth-century masters of the genre in flattering comparison. This novel cannot be accused of either opacity or pretentiousness, two charges that, perhaps, *The Lost Steps* might generate. And yet it goes virtually unread in this country.

War of Time is a collection that brings together in one volume some of the novellas and stories from the original Spanish-language edition *Guerra de tiempo* (minus the novella "El acoso" or "Manhunt," which appeared in Harriet de Onís's translation in *Noonday 1*, a short-lived magazine published by Farrar, Straus in the late sixties) as well as some previously uncollected Carpentier stories brought out in Spain and France. It offers readers in this country the opportunity to see Carpentier at his playful best. In quasi-allegorical short works that toy with the themes of temporal sameness and historical mutability, the Cuban writer rivals in power and execution some of Borges's major enigmatic fictions and shows a face other than that of the dour, heavy-handed historical determinist that some of his critics have made him out to be. The novella "The Highroad of St. James," translated by Frances Partridge, depicts a sixteenth-century pilgrimage to a Spanish shrine that leads to a voyage of discovery, offering the scents and textures of the New World of the Americas as well as a whiff of eternity. It remains one of the most brilliant short novels of the century and yet, among North American readers, as unknown as were the Indies themselves in Europe before the expedition of Columbus. Or less so, since not even legends exist about it in our part of the world.

Reasons of State should appeal at the very least to admirers of such European political and social satire as Alberto Moravia's *The Fancy-Dress Party* or some of the more recent political fiction from Eastern Europe. Because of the rich, thickly lacquered opera bouffe style, its witty, self-parodying recapitulation of many previous Carpentier themes and rhetorical gestures may not be the best or easiest place for readers new to the work of Carpentier to begin. But this account of the fall of a Latin American dictator with a taste for French culture and local rum offers a grab bag of marvelous set pieces (a rebellion here, a massacre there) unparalleled in Latin American "political" novels since the publication of Asturias's masterpiece *El Señor Presidente* in 1949. For all of its allusiveness (and for all the allusions it will stir in its readers), it is an admirably compact work sustained by an uncharacteristic but vigorous sense of humor.

Intelligence and erudition are certainly present in Carpentier's fiction. But so are sex, violence, political uproar, war, revolution, voyages of exploration, naturalist extravaganzas, settings ranging from ancient Greece to contemporary New York City, and characters running the gamut from the simple Haitian protagonist of *The Kingdom of This World* to the worldly wise, word-weary head of state, the dictator of the latest novel, all of this resulting in a complex but highly variegated and appealing fictional matrix. As many elements of the "red-skin" writer as of the "paleface" (to use Philip Rahv's useful terms for the writer of feeling as opposed to the writer of intellect) exist in Carpentier's fiction. Selden Rodman's complaint that the hero of *The Lost Steps* is "so very very much the intellectual" does not hold when applied to the body of the work as a whole. To a certain extent, Rodman's admission that a fiction of ideas puts off American readers is true. But twentieth-century readers have triumphed over this bias to the point where novelists of ideas such as Thomas Mann and Hermann Broch, as well as Musil and Malraux, have a following among university-educated North Americans. In the case of Carpentier, other factors, factors that lie outside the work, must be considered.

First of all, translated writers are always, to some degree, "lost" writers. Their reputations lie at the mercy of translators, publishers, and the professor-critics who serve as the middlemen with respect to foreign imports. As some of the remarks I have quoted earlier would suggest, Carpentier is not the most popular of writers among those who know his work and the literature of the continent in general. But in the case of a Latin American writer, another important extrinsic factor must be considered, that of the traditional cultural bias on the part of North Americans toward Latin American culture.

For a large part of this century, the entire continent suffered from the same enforced obscurity that one finds with respect to the work of Alejo Carpentier. In the great U.S. ideological allegories of the time, Latin America figured as it had for centuries before, as a fecund, barbaric territory composed of large jungles and steamy rivers, sleepy ports, cloud-shrouded plateaus where quaint Indians mingled with llamas, and makeshift cities where the half-breeds constructed comical versions of gringo culture. The same anti-Latin bias that led U.S. citizens to approve of two centuries of imperialist ventures into Spanish-speaking territories did not show any signs of abating until well after the end of World War II, when the combination of Puerto Rican migration to large U.S. cities in the North and Chicano labor organizing in the Southwest forced many Anglo and European Americans to recognize the humanity of Spanish-speaking people of Latin American descent.

Latin American writers suffered from a similar bias. For decade after decade, Anglo-Irish, French, German, and other European writers had a stranglehold on the imagination of the American reading public. Most New York publishers seemed to prefer to ignore the work of first-rate writers from below the Río Bravo while bringing out second-rate European fiction. Only a few brave and forward-looking publishers such as Alfred A. Knopf and Grove Press under the direction of Barney Rosset persisted in adding Latin American translations to their lists. Borges began to challenge Kafka in the minds of many post–Korean War college-age readers. In the wake of the success of the Argentine's work here, publishers reassessed their attitudes toward Latin American fiction. Suddenly writers such as Asturias and Carpentier, who had been publishing major work since the late forties, found their way into hardcovers in translation in the United States. Then with only a few years' lag (in most cases) between publication of the work in Spanish and the American translation, other writers of the Boom began to appear in U.S. editions.

Fuentes, Cortázar, García Márquez, Vargas Llosa—the names are as familiar on U.S. college campuses today as were Gide, Mann, and Camus in previous decades. Donoso and Puig are nearly so. Of the few writers who remain in the shadows as far as this readership is concerned, Carpentier probably stands as the one most destined—again the ephemeral nature of this subject asserts itself—for a large following, which has never seemed to materialize. Perhaps here the fact of his allegiance to the postrevolutionary government in Cuba should be invoked. For while in the eyes of some critics it may well be that he deserves the obscurity in which he dwells, in the eyes of some ideologues it might be well to keep him there. However much a contradiction his elegantly executed and densely packed fictions may seem against the backdrop of sweating cane-cutters swinging machetes in the Caribbean sun, they honor a nation to whose new politics he seems to have pledged his allegiance. How ironic that in the country that made the first American revolution, his work has yet to find the discoverers it so richly deserves!

Hamlet in Haiti:
Style in Carpentier's The Kingdom of This World

Thus conscience does make cowards of us all.

In every cry of every Man,
In every Infant's cry of fear,
In every voice, in every ban,
The mind-forg'd manacles I hear.

Between Hamlet's speech and Blake's lyrical utterance, a great transformation took place in the English mind, centering precisely upon the imagination's relationship to reality. Some archaeologist of words has, no doubt, recorded somewhere all of the uses of the terms *conscience* and *consciousness* between the Elizabethan age and our own, the far side of the Romantic period whose first discoveries were made by Blake and his visionary company. His work would show us that "conscience," that great nay-saying force in Hamlet's mind, has evolved into "consciousness," or the state of self-critical awareness of one's actions in the world (although in Freud's concept of the id, conscience certainly lingers, fixated in the Victorian stage).

As H. Stuart Hughes has suggested, to the generation of European intellectuals of the 1890s consciousness offered the only link between man and the world of society and history. To Croce, the only faith modern man had retained after the fall of Christian belief was his awareness of himself in the world. To Karl Mannheim, consciousness was not simply critical of our actions: it was an action itself in the midst of the world. Thought is praxis; it mediates between things and people just as surely as physical actions mediate. Thus consciousness or self-conscious awareness made cowards of some, fools and heroes of others.

It has gradually become apparent, to the intellectual descendants of Blake, Marx, and Nietzsche, that thought does not merely comprehend the world; by the nature of its comprehension, it changes the world. Even the picture of world as a static place, which we often find in the work of a great number of historians, acts to keep the world as the writer hopes it to remain. "O Lady! we receive but what we give . . . ," Coleridge told us, in his "Dejection" ode, that the human imagination was the most vital element of life in this otherwise "inanimate cold world": "And in our life alone does Nature live." The gods had come to reside, Hegel suggested, in the breast of the human poet. Only the poet could give life to what Wordsworth called "this universe of death." "Thus consciousness does make actors of us all" in the struggle to overthrow the tyranny of "mind-forg'd manacles."

But where in all this lies the Caribbean connection? What's Hamlet to Haiti? Or Haiti to Hamlet? That is difficult to say in one breath. I can't construct a map to indicate the links in time and space that might make you see, as easily as you might the connecting routes between L'Etoile and Nation on a map of the Metro. But the gap that appears to exist between our seemingly European-oriented interests and the matter of the New World, rather than suggesting an absence of landmass, points up the fact that we simply have not charted the territory between.

Haiti, or so the Marcellin brothers, the nation's novelist team, tell us, is a land of myth. For when black people arrived from the west coast of Africa (to have their labor pressed from them like juice from cane), they brought their gods with them. Like pious Aeneas and the Puritans before them, the uprooted Africans of the Yoruba tribe reached the New World with images of their deities in mind. Public life, to the enslaved black people of Haiti, was torturous, and *vodou* offered them the chance to make private life palatable. In Haiti, *vodou* served as both church and Jacobin cell for the Afro-Caribbeans. The French governor viciously suppressed the cult, but this only fostered solidarity among the cultists. To the displaced African coreligionists, the dances of the *vodou* rites conjured up the life of Africa itself, and such a ritual could not be suppressed. It went underground to survive.

As Jahnheinz Jahn has described it, secret *vodou* gatherings "became the cell of the resistance. It needed only an efficient ringleader to drive their angered spirits to rebellion."

Such leaders appeared some fifty years before the French Revolution. Runaway slaves in large numbers took to the hills, formed communities, and amid the territory of the French plantation owners tried to make a free life based upon the mores and economics of old Africa. As they grew in number, they planned desperate guerrilla ventures against the white landowners, hoping to drive them off the island altogether. In 1751, at least three thousand such slaves roamed the mountains. When a leader named Mackandal was thrown up out of their ranks, Haiti witnessed its first massive slave rebellion.

Mackandal, a one-armed man who had lost a limb in a sugarcane press, was a fearless guerrilla leader. In the words of C. L. R. James, he

> was an orator, in the opinion of a white contemporary equal in eloquence to the European orators of the day, and different only in his superior strength and vigour. . . . He had a fortitude of spirit which he knew how to preserve in the midst of the most cruel tortures.

There was a mystical side to him as well, James tells us.

> He claimed to predict the future; like Mohamet he had revelations: he persuaded his followers that he was immortal and exercised such a hold over them that they considered it an honour to serve him on their knees.

Mackandal built up an organization of black slaves throughout Haiti and

> arranged that on a particular day the water of every house in the capital of the province was to be poisoned, and the general attack made on the whites while they were in the convulsions and anguish of death.

But six years of planning came to nothing when Mackandal was betrayed, captured, and burned at the stake in the center square of Port-au-Prince before the eyes of many of his followers. The crowd later reported, however, that he rose out of the flames, that he had transformed himself into a winged beast that flew to safety before it was devoured by the fire. To the blacks of Limbe, his home in northern Haiti, Mackandal had attained a kind of "revolutionary immortality." This "immortality" has its origins in the nature of *vodou* itself. In the *vodou* ritual, the human war chiefs assume the personality of the god of war, Ogou Badaori (or upon occasion Ogou Ferraile, more often the god of the blacksmiths, a fire deity); they dress in red robes or cloths and arm themselves with the ubiquitous and murderous machete. Ogou is martial and boisterous; he smokes cigars and drinks heavily, but most important, he is impervious to physical harm. When the war leader assumes the attributes of Ogou, he is no longer a man but a man "ridden" by the more perfect god. Such beliefs inspired poorly armed black leaders and their followers to overcome enormous odds. (Mackandal, the story goes, was captured only because his "rider" Ogou became helplessly drunk.)

Thus the Afro-Caribbean religion served a serious political function in Haiti, as a revolutionary force that grew yearly as the means by which slaves worked to overthrow the white planters. In spite of all prohibitions, the slaves traveled miles to sing and dance and practice the rites and talk, writes C. L. R. James. After 1789, the cultists used the *vodou* ceremonies as explicitly as any Paris political club of the day. They exchanged political news and laid plans for their political activities.

In 1791 a new leader named Bouckman appeared. He was Jamaican by birth, and a fitting successor to the charismatic Mackandal. A *vodou houngan*, or priest, Bouckman was as gigantic in stature as he was in importance—a tall, strapping figure who served as leader of the slave population of a large Cap Français plantation, and then as revolutionary chief of the twelve thousand slaves (six thousand of them male) who lived in this northern area of Haiti. The goals of the blacks had grown just as their numbers had since the time of Mackandal. They wanted simply to drive out the whites. Bouckman, in the wake of events in France, planned to massacre all those Caucasians who lived in Cap Français.

On the stormy evening of August 22, 1791, anxious to put the plan into action in the face of the growing suspicions of Governor de Blanchelande, Bouckman called leaders from all over the province to a meeting in the forest on the slope of Morne Rouge. Looking down at the peaceful plantations of Le Cap, he administered *vodou* oaths by torchlight and sealed the fate of every Caucasian man, woman, and child on Le Cap. The religion of Africa now directed the destiny of Haiti. Bouckman opened the prayer ceremony by slaughtering a hog and passing its blood around to be drunk. He then charged his fellow slaves to follow the will of their gods:

> The god who created the sun which gives us light, who rouses the waves and rules the storm, though hidden in the clouds, he watches us. He sees all that the white man does. The god of the white man inspires him with crime, but our god calls upon us to do good works. Our god who is good to us orders us to revenge our wrongs. He will direct our arms and aid us. Throw away the symbol of the god of the whites [the cross] who has so often caused us to weep, and listen to the voice of liberty, which speaks in the hearts of us all.

After the ceremony, the blacks descended to Le Cap, where they destroyed nearly all the plantations and executed all whites who lived in the region. Thus began the revolution, which continued for the next twelve years. The leaders to come, Toussaint L'Ouverture, Dessalines, and Henri Christophe among them, were the descendants of the Mackandals and the Bouckmans who first forged the links between the religion of the island and revolutionary action. These commanders inspired in their troops a fervor that European armies had not possessed since the end of the holy wars of the Middle Ages:

> I have seen a solid column [a French officer recalled of the final battle at Le Cap near the end of the twelve-year war] torn by grape-shot, advance without making a retrograde step. The

more they fell, the greater seemed to be the courage of the rest.
... Three times these brave men, arms in hand, advanced without firing a shot, and each time repulsed, only retired after leaving the ground strewn with three-quarters of their troops. One must have seen this bravery to have any conception of it. ... But for many a day that massed square which marched singing to its death, lighted by a magnificent sun, remained in my thoughts, and even today after more than forty years, this majestic and glorious spectacle still lives as vividly in my imagination as in the moments when I saw it.

Our observer neglects to mention that this "spectacle" was the first defeat of the glorious army of Napoleon Bonaparte—more than a decade before its retreat from Moscow! When the French sailed away from Haiti in 1784, their ranks were decimated, and their precious colony became the property, at last, of the people upon whose labor it had been built.

French counterrevolutionary activity had been most harsh. From the first moments of rule, they had sought to divide the Haitian people by means of a system so exact in its cruelty that it designated a ranking system among slaves that included 127 shades of "black." What characteristic element in the social imagination of the slaves produced a solidarity so unbreachable in the face of such force? The answer lies in the nature of the ceremony conducted by Bouckman on that dark night in August 1791. For an

animal sacrificed in the ritual was not only a gift to the *loas*, spirits; its blood bound together those who made the sacrifice; it demanded of each individual who voluntarily entered this ritual group absolute confidence and complete reliability—otherwise the blood of the sacrificial animal would come over him and destroy him. That is, the traditional blood cult of Dahomey [read Africa], which was assimilated to the Voodoo cult and which swore the former slaves to a community that was able, despite being badly armed, to oppose a drilled European army, and which, despite many defeats, repeatedly stirred the rebellion up anew.

Just as to the Greeks of Homer's time the gods acted as part of Nature, the *loas* performed their duties, especially the warrior spirits, within the bounds of everyday reality. Miracles, as Spinoza argued with more than a little irony, are those events that take place outside the natural course of things. By Spinoza's definition, the things that happened on the battlefields of Haiti were not miracles at all but natural occurrences—like those events that took place on the mythical plain of Troy—in which the *loas* came down from their haunts in the rarer air to aid the Haitians in their battle against the French. If in Troy, why not in Limbe? In Ithaca Athena saw that Odysseus had reached the limits of his strength and joined the battle against the imprudent suitors. Why couldn't the *loas* join the attack on the French in Le Cap? While no one "could have guessed the power that was born in them when Bouckman gave the signal for revolt on that stormy August night in 1791," the final battle at Le Cap (which convinced General Rochambeau that it was time for a retreat from the island) was won by a population transformed.

> Oscuro hermano, preserva
> tu memoria de sufrimientos
> y que los héroes passados
> custodien tu mágica espuma,
>
> [Dark brother, preserve
> your memory of your sufferings,
> and may the ancestral heroes
> have your magic sea-foam in their keeping,]

wrote Neruda in his ode to Toussaint L'Ouverture, the great Haitian general. Toussaint was duped by Napoleon's commanders into a meeting that led to his capture and imprisonment, but the idea of freedom lived on in Haiti:

En la Isla arden las penas,
hablan las ramas escondidas,
se transmiten las esperanzas,
surgen los muros del baluarte.

[On the Island the boulders burn,
the hidden branches speak,
hopes are passed on,
the walls of the fortress rise.]

The citadel, fortress and symbol of the power of Henri Christophe, who went from tailor and pastry cook to become Haiti's first dictator, rose, despite Neruda's deliberate oversight in the matter, to proclaim that Haiti's newly won freedom was already in ruins. If you have seen a production of Genet's *The Blacks*, you'll have witnessed a portrait of life at the court of Henri Christophe. As Alejo Carpentier has portrayed it—years before Genet—on a typical afternoon at Sans Souci, the court of Christophe, one might find this mock-bucolic scene:

The little princesses, Athenias and Amethyste, dressed in guipure-trimmed satin . . . playing battledore and shuttlecock. A little farther off, the Queen's chaplain—the one light face in the whole picture— . . . reading Plutarch's *Parallel Lives* to the Crown Prince under the satisfied gaze of Henri Christophe, who was strolling, followed by his ministers, through the Queen's gardens. In passing, his Majesty's hand reached out carelessly to pick a white rose that had just opened amid the boxwood clipped in the shape of a crown and phoenix at the foot of the marble allegories.

But the crown had not risen, phoenixlike, from the flames of Christophe's rule when the then thirty-nine-year-old Alejo Carpentier arrived in Haiti in mid-1943. The synthesis of ornate European grandeur and neo-African civilization that Christophe had tried to effect lay in ruins. To Carpentier, however, the particular nature of these ruins was astonishing.

Long before he had set foot on Haitian soil, his imagination had been arrested by the fantastic vitality behind the seemingly mundane life of the Cuban peasant. In his first novel, *Ecue Yamba O!* ("Save us, O Lord!" in the dialect of the Afro-Cuban *nañigo* cult, the Cuban counterpart of *vodou*), he wrote about the powers of the neo-African forms in Cuba, mainly from the point of view of Menegildo, the somewhat backward son of a sugarcane farmer; it was an exposé of the living conditions of the cane-cutters, at the same time exulting in their way of life—a kind of surrealist *Grapes of Wrath*. In Menegildo's adolescence, his mother, Salomé, "initiated him into the great mysteries, whose dark designs exceeded man's comprehension."

In this world, the visible added up to very little. Creatures lived deceived by a cloud of gross appearances, under the compassionate gaze of superior entities. Oh, Yemayá, Shangó, and Obatalá, spirits of infinite perfection . . . ! But hidden bonds existed between men, a power that could be mobilized through a knowledge of their arcane causes. . . . The space between two buildings, between two sexes, between a she-goat and a girl, showed itself to be full of latent powers, invisible and very fertile, and it was possible to put that space to use in order to attain whatever end. The black cock which pecks an ear of corn is unaware that its head, cut on a moonlit night, and set above a certain number of grains extracted from its maw, can reorganize the realities of the universe. A wooden doll, baptized with Menegildo's name, becomes the dictator of its living double. If there are enemies who would stick a rusty pin in the doll's side, the man would receive the wound in his own flesh. Four hairs belonging to a woman appropriately worked some distance from her hut—the distance does not matter if the sea does not intervene—can "fix" her unfailingly to a lover. The jealous female can securely obtain the happiness of love by the opportune use of the water of her intimate ablutions. . . . Just as the whites have populated the atmosphere with coded messages, symphonic hours and English lessons, men of colour able to perpetuate the great tradition of a body of knowledge delegated over the centuries from father to son, from kings to princes, from initiators to initiates, know that the air is a fabric of seamless filaments which transmits the powers invoked in ceremonies whose role reduces them completely to the condensing of a superior mystery for use against something or on behalf of something. . . . If it is accepted as indisputable truth that an object can be given life, that object will live. The golden chain which contracts will announce danger. The possession of a printed prayer will protect from poisonous bites. . . . The bird foot encountered in the middle of the road is tied precisely to the one who stops in front of it since, out of hundreds, that person alone has been sensitive to its warning. The design was traced by the breath on a plate by virtue of a dark determinism. Law of the face or cross, of star or shield, without any name possible! When the saint deigns to return across the distance to speak through the mouth of a subject in a state of ecstasy, the words are alleviated of all vulgar motive, of conscious ideas, of all false ethic opposed to the expression of its integral meaning. It is possible that in reality the saint never speaks; but the profound exaltation produced by an absolute faith in his presence comes to endow the word with its magical creative power lost since primitive time. The word, a ritual in itself, reflects then a near future which the senses have already perceived, but which reason still grasps for, the better to control it. . . . These practices . . . stirred the deepest and most primordial reflections upon human existence. . . . It is enough to have a conception of the world different from the one generally inculcated in the mind for what seems marvellous to cease being marvellous and place itself within the order of normally verifiable occurrences.

It was clear that neither Menegildo nor Salomé had ever undertaken the arduous task of analyzing primary causes. But they held an atavistic conception of the universe which accepted the possible magical disposition of any creation. And in this took root their confidence in a superior logic and in a power capable of penetrating the difficulties and utilizing the elements of this logic that never showed itself hostile in any way. In the emotional oracles caused by a ceremony of witch-craft, they regained the encounter with the thousand-year-old tradition—old as a dog howling at the moon—which permitted to the man, naked upon an earth which is still in a bad state after its final convulsions, to find in himself an instinctive defense against the ferocity of creation. This man preserved the most lofty knowledge, admitting the existence of things invisible. And if some spells did not give the desired effect obviously the fault lay with the faithful who, searching carefully, always forgot a gesture, an attribute or some essential posture.

Carpentier traveled by Jeep from the coastal area where the earliest uprisings took place to the palace at Sans Souci and the Citadelle La Ferrier.

After having experienced the by-no-means false magic of the land of Haiti, after having encountered magical signs in the red roadways of the Central Plateau, after having heard the drums of Petro and Rada, I have come closer to that marvellous reality the exhausted pretensions of certain European literary movements of the last thirty years tried recently to revive.

How unsuccessful the French surrealists had been in depicting *lo real maravilloso*, the "marvellous reality" of the things of this world. The Compte de Lautréamont (Isadore Ducasse), the Uruguayan ancestor of the French poets, dramatized the metamorphosis of men into animals in the sixth canto of his seminal poem *Les Chants de Maldoror*, but here, in Haiti, such a transformation was a fact of social history. The story of Mackandal was a case in point. And Henri Christophe, to cite another example, was an actual monarch who in word and deed acted far more cruelly than any of the sadistic monarchs of the surrealist narrative verse. The feeble attempts of Europeans to trick meaning from existence by humorous juxtaposition of images paled alongside the effects of everyday existence in Haiti. The surrealists, Carpentier discovered, tried for thirty years to approximate this reality in verse and failed. They were, he concluded, part of the same European decadence that they seemed to decry.

Born in 1904, the son of a Russian mother and a French father, Carpentier had come to Haiti—and these realizations—by a round-about route. He left Cuba at the age of twenty-four, sent into exile by the dictator Gerardo Machado y Morales after having first served nine months in prison for signing a manifesto declaring that Machado was "an ass with claws." When he was released from prison, he befriended the poet Robert Desnos (who was visiting Havana as a journalist) and went to school in the salons of the surrealists in Paris (where he had studied piano at the age of sixteen). He became friendly with André Breton, Louis Aragon, and Benjamin Peret, worked on the Second Surrealist Manifesto, and wrote several ill-fated surrealist tales in French. By 1932 he had come back to writing in his native language, completing the novel he had begun during his imprisonment in Havana (the novel from which I just quoted at length), *Ecue Yamba O!* For all its wealth of ethnological information, *Ecue Yamba O!* was a stiff, willed, decidedly pastoral view of Cuban life, and, as Carpentier himself later admitted, rather mechanical in its production of "automatic" imagery in the surrealist mode. We might add that it lacks a historically interesting plot, tracing as it does Menegildo's progress from birth to death solely in light of his relationship to the *nañigo* (Cuban *vodou*) cult. Nearly ten years had passed since *Ecue*'s publication, and Carpentier had not written much new fiction. On a brief vacation from work on a Communist Party radio station, which he had begun upon his return from a Europe on the verge of World War II, he found himself traveling across this landscape, which had been reproduced only in the imaginative creations of the surrealists and their precursors, a landscape that inspired him to make new considerations about style.

The faith he found among the Haitian people, the faith that produced events such as Mackandal's resurrection from the flames, was not confined to Haiti, he concluded. The history of America, he realized, was full of similar events and figures—the search for the Fountain of Youth, the quest for the city of El Dorado, the flourishing of myth in Central America. The American continent had still not completed its tales of the creation of the universe; its Hesiod had not yet stepped forth to write its *Theogony*. What was the history of America, Carpentier asked himself, but the chronicle of *lo real maravilloso*, a "marvelous reality," a glimpse of which he had caught in his travels across Haiti. And what more inspiration did a novelist need in order to write a book but this recognition?

Carpentier's emphasis on the importance of *place* to the evolution of a new style is itself not a new notion. Bruno Snell has argued that Virgil thousands of years before founded his bucolic style in the Arcadian hills. The broadest nationalistic version of this idea, we know, was put forth by the "German" poets as early as Goethe's time when "Germany" as a political unit had not yet even come into existence. The formation of a specific new style to celebrate and explicate a specific *location* seems to be a particularly Romantic invention. The elevation of the awareness of this problem to an element of culture itself is peculiarly American. When Hawthorne told his readers in the preface to *The Marble Faun* that he found it difficult to create romance in an American setting, he dramatized this new aspect of Western culture. As did Chateaubriand when he painted America as Eden.

The problem of finding a style with which to treat American material was expressed by poets such as Bryant in the nineteenth century when the burden of English rhetoric still lay heavy on their tongues. But not until the end of that century did North American writers—primarily Twain, and James—produce the basic stylistic strategy with headquarters on this side of the Atlantic. One may, for example, look to Faulkner's subsequent view of nature as a link to European Romantic notions of American landscape. Exit Chateaubriand, chased by a Bear. Faulkner conjured up *The Bear* not to serve Christian doctrine but to criticize it. While still pursuing Chateaubriand, we might also recall D. H. Lawrence: Lawrence, in the course of trying to write in an "American" style (by which he tends to mean short, choppy sentences ending with exclamation points), made in his *Studies in Classic American Literature* perhaps the most famous statement of the importance of place in relation to a new national style. (The American "place," according to him, was really a state of *"displacement"* [emphasis mine], ground zero in the quest for a new society. Carpentier's response to the "matter of Haiti" must be viewed in light of this characteristic self-conscious American struggle to develop a style consonant with the new problems attendant upon living in the Americas.

The precursor of this style may be found in the verse of Lautréamont, whose *Les Chants de Maldoror* I mentioned earlier. In that poem, fantastic subject matter is described in a "naturalistic" manner, as though the monsters the poet called forth from the briny deep were as much a part of nature as elm trees and spring rain. But the distinction between Carpentier and his literary ancestors is that he pretends that he is merely describing life rather than interpreting it. He is a literary realist then, rather than a fantasist. As Fernando Alegría has said about his method, Carpentier began to explore Latin American reality as though it possessed "a system of symbols which European culture could only conceive on an abstract, static level." In other words, with regard to Haiti, Carpentier assumed that its reality was more comprehensible and natural because it possessed those qualities that in themselves were usually found in the artificial arrangement of language or forms in art. Here one must make oneself aware of the legacy left to Carpentier not only by those specific poets whom we know he admired but by the Romantic poets in general and, one might even suggest, by the Augustinian tradition.

This sense of "organization" seemed to the Romantics to loom large behind life's seeming chaos. In order to explicate it, Carpentier's kissing cousins in Paris, the surrealist group, had worked up a series of methods—particularly automatic writing and the "shock" treatment of unusual imagery—that might be called, as Erich Auerbach has hinted, an "aestheticist" view of life. Aesthetics was the religion of the Romantics, the substitute for the faith that led early Christian poets and painters to depict the organization of the world clearly and boldly. Now certain Romantics tended to separate themselves from life and dwell among the pillars of an aestheticist temple. ("Poetry makes nothing happen," as Auden tells us.) But others, like Blake, Shelley, Byron, and Keats, found that their aesthetics wedded them to experience to a degree that allowed them to explain the similarities between poetry and life, but not the differences. Poetry linked them to nature; the imagination was a "natural" activity. And yet poetry was more important in the natural round of activities than, say, running a livery stable. It was life, but life intensified. As Byron wrote in *Childe Harold's Pilgrimage*:

> 'Tis to create, and in creating live
> A being more intense, that we endow
> With form our fancy, gaining as we give
> The life we image, even as I do now.

What Carpentier discovered in Haiti was a *life* more intense than poetry, a society whose beliefs synthesized the possibility for faith (now dissipated) that we find embodied in the European tradition and a powerful mythic tradition stemming from the people's African forebears. Myth, the collective belief in myth, and its attendant faith in the reality of local gods, was part of the stuff of everyday Caribbean social reality. Unlike Hawthorne's America, which was a place where European romance could not flourish, Carpentier's America held tales "impossible to situate in Europe." After three months, he returned to his native Cuba to begin the research for such a tale.

The completed narrative was published in Mexico City in 1949—Carpentier called it *El reino de este mundo* (The Kingdom of This World). It recounts the story of the Haitian revolution from its origins in the uprising led by Mackandal and Bouckman up until its dissipation in the imitation European court of Henri Christophe and the mulatto counterrevolution that followed Christophe's death. Throughout, Carpentier draws on the same sources as those consulted by historians of the period, such as C. L. R. James. For example, the rites led by Bouckman (which I mentioned earlier) appear in *El reino*, with Bouckman's concluding sermon following the exact form as the sermon cited by James:

> Suddenly a mighty voice arose in the midst of the congress of shadows, a voice whose ability to pass without intermediate stages from a deep to a shrill register gave a strange emphasis to its words. There was much of invocation and much of spell in that speech filled with angry inflections and shouts. It was

Bouckman, the Jamaican, who was talking . . . he stated that a pact had been sealed between the initiated on this side of the water and the great Loas of Africa to begin the war when the auspices were favorable. And out of the applause that rose about him came this final admonition: "The white men's God orders the crime. Our gods demand vengeance from us. They will guide our arms and give us help. Destroy the image of the white man's God who thirsts for our tears; let us listen to the cry of freedom within ourselves."

The immolation of the captured Mackandal is, as well, portrayed with historical accuracy. It depicts both the awareness of his black followers that he flew out of the flames and escaped and the destruction of his body (of which more later).

The work is, in fact, studded with actual historical personages. Toussaint L'Ouverture, although not a major figure in the narrative, is referred to in passing in an early chapter with particular reference to his pre-revolutionary occupation. He is the cabinetmaker who

had carved the Three Wise Men in wood, but they were too big for the Nativity, and in the end were not set up, mainly because of the terrible whites of Balthazar's eyes, which had been painted with special care, and gave the impression of emerging from a night of ebony with the terrible reproach of a drowned man.

We first hear of Henri Christophe in his capacity as the chef at the Auberge de la Couronne, a Cap Français restaurant, the job he held before joining the colonial artillery. Minor figures, too, have lavish paragraphs bestowed upon them. For example, at the end of chapter 5 of part 2, Ti-Noel, the Haitian slave from whose point of view the action is seen, has gone with his master, Lenormand de Mezy, into exile in Cuba while Napoleon's army attempts to suppress the rebellion in Haiti. In the cathedral in Santiago de Cuba, Ti-Noel discovers the rehearsal of a Christmas cantata directed by a dried-up, loud-voiced, swarthy old man called Don Esteban Salas, the Cuban composer about whom Carpentier had learned much while doing the research for a history of Cuban music in 1945. Ti-Noel finds it, though, impossible to understand why this choirmaster,

> whom everyone seemed to respect notwithstanding, was deter-mined that the singers should enter the chorus one after the other, part of them singing what the others had sung before, and setting up a confusion of voices fit to exasperate anyone. But this was undoubtedly pleasing to the verger, a personage to whom Ti-Noel attributed great ecclesiastical authority because he went armed and wore pants like other men. Despite these discordant symphonies, which Don Esteban Salas enriched with bassoons, horns, and boy sopranos, the Negro found in the Spanish churches a Voodoo warmth which he had never encountered in the Sulpician churches of the Cap.

Other familiar historical figures appear, among them Pauline Bona-parte and her husband, LeClerc, the general whom her brother dis-patched to Haiti to put down the rebellion, and Corneille Breille, the Capuchin confessor to Henri Christophe whom the dictator murdered by bricking him up in the oratory of the Port-au-Prince palace. The his-torical accuracy that lends weight, balance, and an inviting texture to this short novel of only fifty thousand words plays, however, a subsidiary role to the reconstruction of the *fictitious* characters, such as M. Lenor-mand de Mezy, who represents the French presence in the country, and the aforementioned Ti-Noel, whose transformation from young slave to elderly revolutionary forms the central thread of the narrative.

The novelist and critic Mario Vargas Llosa has observed that Car-pentier "the political witness" of the earlier *Ecue Yamba O!* becomes in *El reino de este mundo* "an alchemist, transforming the true events of the Antillan past into myths." But the Cuban's use throughout this narra-tive of the consciousness of Ti-Noel would seem to imply that, rather than forgo the role of political observer, Carpentier recognized that Haitian politics and myth were inextricable. Crucial to the character of Ti-Noel both as a psychological whole and as a figure representa-tive of his class and people is his belief in the *reality* of what are tradi-tionally depicted as Haiti's myths.

The narrative, with the exception of several ironic chapters in which de Mezy's and Pauline Bonaparte's consciousnesses ("Thus she spent her time between siestas and waking, feeling herself part Virginie, part Atalá") give the tone and texture to the scene, presents a world whose epistemological assumptions are that of the devout *vodou* cultist. This becomes clear in the very first scene of the novel, in which we are introduced to Ti-Noel, Lenormand de Mezy's slave, and his adviser on the purchase of a new breeding stallion. Ti-Noel notices a peculiar coincidence of heads. First he sees the pale wax heads in the barbershop, then the pale calves' heads in the butcher shop next door, and then, on the prints hanging from wire by clothespins in the adjacent bookseller's stall, the head of the French king. The logic of this connection is ironically portrayed: "Había abundancia de cabeza aquella mañana" (The morning was full with heads). But the tone here is *not* ironic: when the interchangeability of men and animals is referred to in the next few passages, we can clearly hear lyrical rather than ironic music in the imagery. Consider Ti-Noel's thoughts on the religion of his African homeland, engendered by his catching sight of an engraving depicting an African royal personage receiving a French official. At that moment, the young slave recalled

> those tales Mackandal sing-songed in the sugar mill while the oldest horse on the Lenormand de Mezy plantation turned the cylinders. With deliberately languid tone, the better to secure certain effects, the Mandingue Negro would tell of things that had happened in the great kingdoms of Popo, of Arada, of the Nagos, or the Fulah. He spoke of the great migrations of tribes, of age-long wars, of epic battles in which the animals had been allies of men.

But the lyrical element in the narrative (as well as the definitely ironic texture of the passages devoted to the French characters) forms only a corollary to the major direction of the prose. Irony and lyric are subsumed under the aegis of a larger realistic style. When Mackandal, Ti-Noel's mentor, discovers that lycanthropy is an integral part of nature not only in Africa but in Haiti as well, we're given the first taste of that prose. After losing his arm in a sugar-mill accident, Mackandal spends his time out in the pasture with the cattle. There, in the grass,

> to his surprise he discovered the secret life of strange species given to disguise, confusion, and camouflage, protectors of the little armored beings that avoid the pathways of the ants.

He and Ti-Noel sometimes sneak up into the mountains to listen to the tales of old Maman Loi, which at times were

> of extraordinary animals that had had human offspring. And of men whom certain spells turned into animals. Women had been raped by huge felines, and at night, had substituted roars for words.

The role of the *belief* in lycanthropy, however, becomes secondary to the role that lycanthropy itself plays in the narrative. These "cosas de negros," as Lenormand de Mezy calls them, form the heart of the novel's vision, For,

> as he had the power to take the shape of hoofed animal, bird, fish, or insect, Mackandal continually visited the plantations of the Plaine to watch over his faithful and find out if they still had faith in his return. In one metamorphosis or another, the one-armed man was everywhere, having recovered his corporeal integrity in animal guise. With wings one day, spurs another, galloping or crawling, he had made himself master of the courses of the underground streams, the caverns of the seacoast, and the treetops, and now ruled the whole island. His powers were boundless. He could as easily cover a mare as rest in the cool of a cistern, swing on the swaying branches of a *huisache*, or slip through a keyhole. The dogs did not bark at him; he changed his shadow at will. It was because of him that a Negress gave birth to a child with a wild boar's face. At night he appeared on the roads in the skin of a black goat with fire-tipped horns.

One day he would give the sign for the great uprising, and the Lords of Back There, headed by Damballah, the Master of the Roads, and Ogoun, Master of the Swords, would bring the thunder and lightning and unleash the cyclone that would round out the work of men's hands. In that great hour—said Ti-Noel—the blood of the whites would run into the brooks, and the *Loas*, drunk with joy, would bury their faces in it and drink until their lungs were full.

This power, unlike the alienating metamorphosis of the Old World that one finds, say, in Kafka's work, allows Mackandal, even as he seems to be burning at the stake, to transform himself into a thing with wings, fly out over the crowd in the square and out to sea:

Mackandal was now lashed to the post. The executioner had picked up an ember with the tongs. With a gesture rehearsed the evening before in front of a mirror, the Governor unsheathed his gross sword and gave the order for the sentence to be carried out. The fire began to rise toward the Mandingue, licking his legs. At that moment Mackandal moved the stump of his arm, which they had been unable to tie up, in a threatening gesture which was none the less terrible for being partial, howling unknown spells and violently thrusting his torso forward. The bonds fell off and the body of the black man rose in the air, flying overhead, until it plunged into the black waves of the sea of slaves. A single cry filled the square:

"Mackandal saved!" *[Mackandal sauvé!]*

Pandemonium followed. The guards fell with rifle butts on the howling blacks, who now seemed to overflow the streets, climbing toward the windows. And the noise and screaming and uproar were such that very few saw that Mackandal, held by ten soldiers, had been thrust head first into the fire, and that a flame fed by his burning hair had drowned his last cry. When the slaves were restored to order, the fire was burning normally like any fire of good wood, and the breeze blowing from the sea was lifting the smoke toward the windows where more than one lady who had fainted had recovered consciousness. There was no longer anything more to see.

That afternoon the slaves returned to their plantations laughing all the way. Mackandal had kept his word. He remained in the Kingdom of This World. Once more the whites had been outwitted by the Mighty Powers of the Other Shore.

The prose here is itself lycanthropic, *magically real*, offering up one element of the incident, the historically accurate, and then transmuting it into another, the mythologically accurate, and giving special weight not to either but to both, to each "reality" as it relates to the other. The constituent element of Carpentier's linguistic reality is thus the interplay of these elements.

Neither fantasy nor naturalism, this new style, a self-conscious embodiment of the recognition of the partial truths of both of these modes, offers many possibilities for the literature of the future—some of which is already upon us in the work of Julio Cortázar, Gabriel García Márquez, in Latin America, and in the fiction of Doris Lessing, Bernard Malamud, and John Gardner in our own language, to name some of the main practitioners, conscious and unconscious, of the "magical realist" style. But before going on to some final words about the relationship of this style to our own lives, I would like to backtrack for a moment.

We must all admit that what to European minds was usually taken to be fantasy was regarded in Haiti as an aspect—an important aspect—of reality. The battles that took place in those days between the Haitian irregulars and the French army, those historic engagements in which Napoleon's forces suffered, ten years before the retreat from Moscow, their first major defeat, contained as much "fantasy" as fact. (You will recall the words of the French officer who marveled at the sight of the Haitian irregulars marching toward him.)

The collective reality of the Haitian revolutionaries thus becomes a part of Caribbean history. And as we follow the progress of Ti-Noel from his state as a piece of property on the de Mezy plantation to his final appearance as an old and wise *houngan* of the revolutionary *vodou* rite, his belief that he can transform himself into an animal becomes the objective sign of his consciousness. Ti-Noel turns into a goose, and this belief becomes in these passages the *objective* textual reality. History in this tale is as much an integer of fantasy as fantasy is of history.

Ti-Noel is neither simply the means by which the tale of the revolution is told nor a quaint folkloric figure whose exotic consciousness may have some appeal for American readers. His changing perception of the life and history of Haiti holds meanings more important than these provincial concerns. For while he feels the triumph of the early days of the revolution, in the last part of his life he recognizes that to some Henri Christophe's regime, "this endless return of chains, this rebirth of shackles, this proliferation of suffering," offers proof of "the uselessness of all revolt." Yet his final vision, "a supremely lucid moment," carries him beyond resignation. Even as the mulatto tyrants, the latest rulers in the chain that begins with the ascension of Christophe to the throne, are dividing up the little kingdom Ti-Noel had established for himself and his followers on the ruins of the former de Mezy plantation, he embodies the optimism that Ernst Bloch has called, in his essay of the same name, the Principle of Hope and hurls himself and his followers into the battle against a group of mulatto "surveyors" with renewed force. And in a conclusion that marks, as Carpentier understands it, the end of the first stage of the struggle for Caribbean independence, Ti-Noel, the slave turned revolutionary, like Mackandal before him, fades away into the seascape. The prose turns opaque, eliminating him from its reality. "A great green wind" sweeps across Haiti from the sea, shaking apart the last vestiges of the colonialist epoch by shaking down the few buildings of the old Lenormand de Mezy plantation. Only the salty traces of the Dionysian figure of Ti-Noel—black Dionysus!—fleck the Haitian hillsides.

Thus, by means of the strength of mind-formed liberty, the Haitians snapped their man-forged manacles. Or, perhaps, their gods did it for them, you suggest. The paradox of whether gods create men or men gods seems irresolvable. Carpentier's Haitian drama, however, by convincing us that history holds fantastic and mythical elements within its borders, extends our notion of the possibilities of literary creation and mind-forged social change—there are more things in Heaven and Earth than are dreamed of in *our* philosophy.

Traces of Light:
The Paradoxes of Narrative Painting and Pictorial Fiction

Picture this, as we say: a time in that time before what we usually call history began, when gods and goddesses and human beings mingle together, sometimes even have intercourse, or so the poet shows us, and a gimpy god, a blacksmith, receives a commission from silver-footed Thetis, the water nymph who is the mother of the great aristocratic warrior Achilles, to make a shield for her son so that he might return to the battlefield of Troy and avenge the death of his dear friend Patroclus. So Hephaestus sets to work.

> And on that five-ringed shield Hephaestus made
> many adornments with intricate skill.
> There he fashioned earth and heaven and sea.
> with the tireless sun, a moon at the full.
> and all those constellations of the sky:
> Pleiades, Hyades, strong Orion.
> and the Great Bear, known also as the Wain.
> who circles in her place by Orion
> and alone has no bath in Oceanus.
>
> And there he made two prosperous cities—
> in one marriages and festive banquets. . . .

But two armies in bright armor besieged
the other town—and they stood quarreling
whether to attack or to offer terms
of half the wealth that capital possessed. . . .

And there he set a soft, rich fallow land
on the third plowing, with many farmers
driving their oxen across back and forth. . . .

And there he set an estate, with reapers
holding sharp sickles as they mowed a field.
The grain lay in rows all along the swath
where workers were tying it up with straw. . . .

And there he set a ripening vineyard
of elegant gold, though the grapes were black
and the vines were propped upon silver poles,
round them a ditch of dark-blue enamel
and a tin fence. In led a single path
where villagers came to gather their grapes,
young men and women very merrily
carrying sweet fruit in wicker baskets.
Among them a boy plucked a plangent lyre,
sang the dirge for the departing summer
while the others cried hurrah as they came
leaping and beating the time with their feet. . . .

And there the bent-legged god made a dance floor
like the one built long ago before in Knossos
by Daedalus for fair-haired Ariadne:
lusty young men and graceful young women
danced in a ring, hands on each other's wrists.
The women wore fine linen and the men
elegant tunics gleaming soft with oil—
and the women wore lovely wreaths, the men
daggers of gold that hung from silver slings.

Now they scurried around on skillful feet
with consummate ease, as when a potter
sits by his wheel and sets it a-spinning,
now they hurried toward each other in rows.
A large crowd stood and watched the spectacle
with an intense joy, while two acrobats
whirled among the dancers, giving the beat.

(Trans. Michael Reck)

So in what at first glance might seem a brief if necessary sequence, the smithy of gods artfully constructs Achilles' shield so that the hero can then go into battle fully armed. But as we pass through this sequence we have to notice, if we're watching carefully, that something quite odd and distinctive—from our modern point of view—is taking place with regard to the shield. The heavenly blacksmith does not merely construct a frieze on the front of the piece of armor; he makes a living scene, a little epic that unfolds before our eyes as he creates the piece out of tin and stubborn bronze and precious gold and silver, a sequence of metals that suggests the transition humankind has made through the various levels of refining.

He fashions on the face of the shield two prosperous cities, and we see festivals taking place in their streets with cheering crowds, and then two armies clash before us in a miniature version of the Trojan War, and he shows us how agriculture evolves out of the postwar period, with rich vineyards and high-horned cattle, and finally the poet leads our eye to a peaceful grove with a dance floor where women scurry about and a potter spins his wheel and two acrobats whirl among the dancers. The deity of construction of objects, this blacksmith, has made something miraculous—a static piece of metal with moving scenes within it—and something also quite paradoxical in terms of how we think about space and time in art: a static piece of art that contains a story that evolves over time, a story of the flourishing of two cities, of the wars between them, of the peace that grows after the wars, and, finally, of the bucolic denouement of the unfolding narrative within the face of the shield.

What we see in this object is a work of art that, according to the epochal work of G. E. Lessing, *The New Laocoön*, cannot succeed, because of the two contradictory modalities of art and poetry. Works of art, Lessing tells us, exist in space. Works of poetry exist in time. And as we may surmise, from the work of Werner Heisenberg, we can know only one mode or the other at any given moment. Either we can study space or we can study time, but we cannot study both at once.

But both Lessing and Heisenberg came long after the age of the Homeric Wars and, presumably, Hephaestus and his heavenly crew existed for a much longer period before the Trojan War than we who have come after. Let's imagine that the bent-legged handyman of Olympus had millions of years in which to perfect his craft, while we have had only a few thousand to study ours. So, based on our reading of this sequence in the *Iliad*, it seems plausible to say that in that old time there appeared to be no distinction between spatial art and temporal art, as first discussed by Lessing and subsequently studied by various modern critics (the foremost among them being Joseph Frank, whose essay "Spatial Form in Modern Fiction" is one of the benchmark works of contemporary literary criticism).

When we look at pre-classical Greek vase painting we notice in a spatial art form (pottery) an assumption at work similar to Homer's in the *Iliad*. On many vases we find scenes from various myths, and traditionally we have permitted ourselves to confuse the word *frieze* with the word *freeze*. James Joyce, for example, in his great novella "The Dead," employs this pun in order to convey a certain interior state with regard to his main character, Gabriel Conroy. When we read Keats's "Ode on a Grecian Urn" we notice that the poet regards the scene on the vase as one in which time stands still—"Thou still unravished bride of quietness."

But when we look at the actual Greek friezes as their makers must have seen them—for example, the frieze on the shield of Achilles as "seen" by the Homeric poet as he tells us about it—it becomes apparent that to the Greeks themselves the frieze is just the opposite of something fixed in time. The scenes on the vases depict moments from longer stories, from mythological narratives, that imply both beginnings and endings in themselves. The scenes, rather than being frozen, are flowing, emanating time by their very essence as their makers and their audiences seem to understand it. A sharper reading of Keats's poem suggests the possibility that modern readers might also catch a glimpse of life from this perspective.

Ode on a Grecian Urn

Thou still unravished bride of quietness,
Thou foster-child of silence and slow time,
Sylvan historian, who canst thus express
A flowery tale more sweetly than our rhyme:
What leaf-fringed legend haunts about thy shape
Of deities or mortals, or of both,
In Tempe or the dales of Arcady?
What men or gods are these? What maidens loth?
What mad pursuit? What struggle to escape?
What pipes and timbrels? What wild ecstasy?

Heard melodies are sweet, but those unheard
Are sweeter; therefore, ye soft pipes, play on;
Not to the sensual ear, but, more endeared,
 Pipe to the spirit ditties of no tone:
Fair youth, beneath the trees, thou canst not leave
Thy song, nor ever can those trees be bare;
Bold Lover, never, never canst thou kiss,
Though winning near the goal—yet, do not grieve:
She cannot fade, though thou hast not thy bliss,
Forever wilt thou love, and she be fair!

Ah, happy, happy boughs! that cannot shed
Your leaves, nor ever bid the Spring adieu;
And, happy melodist, unwearièd,
For ever piping songs for ever new;
More happy love! more happy, happy love!
For ever warm and still to be enjoyed,
For ever panting, and forever young;
All breathing human passion far above,

That leaves a heart high-sorrowful and cloyed,
A burning forehead, and a parching tongue.

Who are these coming to the sacrifice?
To what green altar, O mysterious priest,
Lead'st thou that heifer lowing at the skies,
And all her silken flanks with garlands dressed?
What little town by river or sea shore,
Or mountain-built with peaceful citadel,
Is emptied of this folk, this pious morn?
And, little town, thy streets for evermore
Will silent be; and not a soul to tell
Why thou art desolate, can e'er return.

O Attic shape! Fair attitude! with brede
Of marble men and maidens overwrought,
With forest branches and trodden weed;
Thou, silent form, dost tease us out of thought
As doth Eternity: Cold Pastoral!
When old age shall this generation waste,
Thou shalt remain, in midst of other woe
Than ours, a friend to man, to whom thou say'st,
"Beauty is truth, truth beauty,—that is all
Ye know on earth, and all ye need to know."

The poet's view of the images on the vase is beautiful and touching. It is also familiar to us. We agree, and exclaim along with the speaker that the figures are unmoving, that we are viewing along with him an art that stops or freezes time. The beauty of the scene—the innocence of the main figure on the vase—comes in part from that vision of stopped time, from the stillness rather than from turbulence. The essence of the poem, most readers seem to agree, lies in its juxtaposition of the poet's intimations of his own mortality with the permanence of the work of art before him. However, I don't mean to suggest that this is the conventional wisdom. It is the modern wisdom. When we look at the *Iliad* and the marvels of the shield of Achilles, we see another variety of thought at work, a pre-classical vision of the relation of art and time and space that we have put, probably forever, behind us. In the post-*Laocoön* age, we tend to regard experiments with space and time in art with a critical eye. We may applaud Joyce's experiments in *Ulysses* and pay homage to the cubism of Picasso. But for most of us, our taste remains rooted, for better or for worse, in the Romantic vision.

When a great realist like Flaubert incorporates such questions into a work of fiction—the question of the essence of painting as opposed to the essence of writing—the result is a superb and beautiful rendering of the wisdom of the age. For example, in *Madame Bovary* there is a scene in which Emma Bovary, traveling by public conveyance toward the city of Rouen and a rendezvous with her lover, Léon, catches her first glimpse of the city:

> Sloping downward like an amphitheater, drowned in mist, it sprawled out shapelessly beyond its bridges. Then open fields swept upward again in a monotonous curve, merging at the top with the uncertain line of the pale sky. Thus seen from above, the whole landscape had the static quality of a painting: ships at anchor were crowded into one corner, the river traced its curve along the foot of the green hills, and on the water the oblong-shaped islands looked like great black fish stopped in their course. From the factory chimneys poured endless trails of brown smoke, their tips continually dissolving in the wind. The roar of foundries mingled with the clear peal of chimes that came from the churches looming in the fog. The leafless trees along the boulevards were like purple thickets in amongst the houses; and the roofs, all of them shiny with rain, gleamed with particular brilliance in the upper reaches of the town. Now and again a gust of wind blew the clouds toward the hill of Sainte-Catherine, like aerial waves breaking soundlessly against a cliff.
>
> (Trans. Francis Steegmuller)

This is a brilliant example of what I would call "pictorial" fiction. The only thing that seems to be moving in the passage is Emma Bovary's eye, the surrogate for our own. Although technically, while we have to point out that within the fiction Emma is enjoying the "static" view of the city while looking out from a moving coach, the assumption is that her position is basically static along with the view of the city. The entire passage, by Flaubert's own definition, is a "landscape," in this case a pastoral form that conveys an urban scene. Though there is some activity within the passage—the trails of smoke from the foundry chimneys, the clouds blown by gusts of wind—the landscape or cityscape is essentially without motion. Those movements are contained within the overall stasis of Emma's hastily constructed canvas. Unlike the evolving action in the various quadrants of Achilles' shield, the smoke and wind go nowhere beyond the immediate boundaries of the view.

Flaubert's use of detail in his scene-making in *Madame Bovary* is something that we might regard as an implicit "painterly" practice. When we read Proust, we see a writer lavishing a great deal of explicit attention on painting and painters and quite often employing images from painting in his metaphors. This tendency is certainly overt in the opening sentence of the "Combray" section of *Swann's Way:*

> Combray at a distance, from a twenty-mile radius, as we used to see it from the railway when we arrived there in the week before Easter, was no more than a church epitomizing a town, representing it, speaking of it and for it to the horizon, and as one drew near, gathering close about its long, dark cloak, sheltering from the wind, on the open plain, as a shepherdess gathers her sheep, the wooly grey backs of its huddled houses, which the remains of its medieval ramparts enclosed, here and there, in an outline as scrupulously circular as that of a little town in a primitive painting.

The novelist's attentiveness to the art of painting shows through in the narrator's visual attentiveness to nature, and to flowers in particular, both real flowers and those he creates in metaphors. In a passage such as the one in which he encounters the hawthorn blossoms on the altar of the church in Combray, Proust's narrator links the visual to the other senses—in this case, the fragrance of the flowers calls his attention to the sight of the blossoms themselves: " And then I noticed," Marcel tells us, "on the flowers themselves little patches of a creamier color, beneath which I imagined that this fragrance must lie concealed, as the taste of an almond cake lay beneath the burned parts." He then goes on to explore this sensual encounter further:

> Despite the motionless silence of the hawthorns, these gusts of fragrance came to me like the murmuring of an intense organic life, with which the whole altar was quivering like a hedgerow explored by living antennae, of which I was reminded by seeing some stamens, almost red in color, which seemed to have kept the springtime virulence, the irritant power of stinging insects now transmuted into flowers.

This last phrase alludes powerfully to how technique translates from one art form to another, and how this translation illuminates the larger work. In this passage, Marcel moves from the attraction of the fragrance to consider the possibilities of the outer appearance of the flowers and then goes on to accentuate the color of the stamens. The stamens recall to him the season in which the hawthorn bush was pollinated—and the way that the irritating possibility of bee stings becomes transformed into the beauty of the blossoms. This natural transformation thus serves as an emblem of the transforming potential of art. From bee sting to blossom signals the possibility of moving from pain to pleasure, from difficulty to beauty.

Many other allusions to art and its relation to nature occur in the rich and beautiful pages of *Swann's Way*. But none is more striking than Proust's use of perspective. We see this first in the Combray section, when Marcel, describing various errands that his family runs after mass, refers to the church in a specific way. "Even when our errands lay in places behind the church," he tells us, "from which it could not be seen, the view seemed always to have been composed with reference to the steeple, which would loom up here and there among the houses, and was perhaps even more affecting when it appeared thus without the church." Marcel next delivers more than a page of elegiac observations on the centrality of the steeple in French towns he has lived in, and he concludes by dubbing the steeple the "Finger of God" that stands out as a directional guide for wandering human beings.

When we next see that "finger," it points us in the direction of a major connection between Proust's use of painting and his understanding of the nature of prose narrative. This occurs toward the end of one of Marcel's famous ambles along the Guermantes Way, when Dr. Percepied drives up in his carriage and stops for him. The doctor must first make a call at the neighboring village of Martinville-le-Sec and as they ride in that direction, Marcel catches sight of the twin steeples of Martinville, "bathed in the setting sun and constantly changing their position with the movement of the carriage and the windings of the road, and then of a third steeple, that of Vieuxvicq, which, although separated from them by a hill and a valley, and rising from rather higher ground in the distance, appeared none the less to be standing by their side."

The steeples seem to speak to Marcel "of something more than their configuration, something which they seemed at once to contain and to conceal." The sight of them moves him to borrow pencil and paper from the doctor and compose a description—one of the first prose pieces that he would write—of the scene he has just encountered, a description that focuses on the nature of perspective as illustrated by his view of the steeples and their effect on his understanding of time:

> Alone, rising from the level of the plain, and seemingly lost in that expanse of open country, the twin steeples of Martinville rose towards the sky. Presently we saw three: springing into position in front of them with a bold leap, a third, dilatory steeple, that of Vieuxvicq, had come to join them. The minutes passed, we were traveling fast, and yet the three steeples were always a long way ahead of us, like three birds perched upon the plain, motionless and conspicuous in the sunlight. Then the steeple of Vieuxvicq drew aside, took its proper distance, and the steeples of Martinville remained alone, gilded by the light of the setting sun which, even at that distance, I could see play-

ing and smiling upon their sloping sides. We had been so long in approaching them that I was thinking of the time that must still elapse before we could reach them when, of a sudden, the carriage turned a corner and set us down at their feet; and they had flung themselves so abruptly in our path that we had barely time to stop before being dashed against the porch.

Marcel had wondered if perhaps "something more" lay behind the "mobility" and "luminosity" of the vision of the steeples, "something which they seemed at once to contain and to conceal." With the inclusion of his little sketch, what secrets they represent become quite clear. Moving young Marcel to create his first salvageable impression in prose, the vision of the steeples evokes rather dramatically the radical role of perspective in the writer's life and work. Moving through the landscape of his novels, the reader views characters, scenes, historical moments, in ways similar to Marcel's regard of the steeples. The novelist creates a temporal passage analogous to the carriage trip toward Martinville. The landscape here is time.

The realistic writer's representation of the visible world (including the world of time) serves as the very template against which we can pose all modern descriptive narrative. The characters look out upon the world, and their creator reports to us on what they see. The writer's eye and the character's eye seem to fuse, and we read the results of the optical activity, as in, say, a passage from a story of my own—"The Seals"—in which a man in his forties out on a trail near the beach at the Año Nuevo Reserve south of San Francisco discovers "two young elephant seal bulls splashing about in the surf, playing or fighting—it couldn't be said clearly which, at least not by an ignorant observer." They are "towering grey-black creatures with glistening hides and teeth like fence pickets sticking from their hideous elongated snouts." My character sees this, and thus you see it. The equation seems simple. The eye is a camera? Yes, and no. A camera is a camera in the making of fiction films, and the set decorator and the director and the costume designer and the location man and the lighting crew, among others, determine beforehand what the camera sees. In the making of fiction, the writer's eye behaves with much more sophistication than a motion-picture camera, performing all of the operations of the movie production as well as creating out of nothing-ness the very scene it seems to "record." So the writer's eye is not a camera. The writer's eye is more like the eye and the hand of the painter taken together—the writer's eye is a magic instrument of invention, not a mere recording device.

What we call realistic fiction is thus a lot more complicated than it seems at first, incorporating all that I have just described, plus, in constructing character, all of the calibrations of vision ranging from, say, the simple box camera to the X ray and the MRI and sometimes even the electron microscope. If a total energy field is available to the writer in every epoch and age, then we might say that although realis-tic writers working today no longer possess the vision that allowed the Homeric poet to see the action within the static as witnessed by the lit-tle epic that unfolds on the front of Achilles' shield, it is possible for the modern writer to range deep and wide in the emotional and psy-chological realm, something completely unknown to the Homeric poet. Realism means something more than depicting the world as we see it. Realism means depicting the world as we see it, taste it, hear it, and feel it in all of the various levels and regions of mind and heart and spirit.

Is there a corresponding tendency in painting? We can all recog-nize in certain painters the same straining against the boundaries of convention—the urge to make work that exists in both space and time—that we see in the great writers, the urge to make work that is all-embracing, all-encompassing, work that is world-creating, as the Homeric poems are world-creating. We see this in the work of Michelangelo, for example, and in the work of Poussin, two artists who begin with assumptions based in theology or mythology or both. The story-scenes they paint resonate for us with the already present truth of belief. But without the conventions of a religion or a great mythology the task of having a painting tell a story is inestimably dif-ficult, just as difficult as it is, say, for a writer to conjure up the pres-ence of light by means of his prose.

The difficulty in practical terms we may explain easily. To use the elements of narrative in painting is not the same as creating a narrative effect. To invoke the language that creates images alluding to light in fiction is not the same as making us see such light. I learned this myself from having spent several years writing a novel about an American woman painter living out her late years in the Southwest. In this book, *The Light Possessed*, I attempted to use light and landscape in an amalgam of realism and lyrical expression. One character, for example, after a long drive in a truck records that she stops and looks about. "Out of the cab, stretch toward the sky, blink at the odd sun, a strangely white, nearly translucent brightness. . . . Odd odors on the air, a slight resin tang, dusty scent of native light, no sound, smell of oily wind." Or, to watch another writer at work on this problem, we can skip back seventy-some years to the pages of E. M. Forster's *A Passage to India* and hear that Mr. Fielding found Egypt charming—"he re-embarked at Alexandria—bright blue sky, constant wind, clean low coast-line, as against the intricacies of Bombay."

In both passages the quality of light and landscape are reported to us, either by a first-person speaker or note-taker, or by the narrator reporting what the character sees. In each instance we are treated to the results of scrutiny of a landscape by an eye for which there is always a corresponding I, a first-person narrator reporting on what he or she has seen, or a third-person narrator reporting on what the character has seen. The eye in fiction thus always belongs to a subject, to an ego within the fictive reality of the work itself. In early realism the assumption of writer and reader is naive. What we see is what is there.

In certain accentuated moments in twentieth-century realistic novels, or in novels avowedly more lyrical, as in, say, Virginia Woolf's *To the Lighthouse*, things become more complicated as the writer tries to conjure up a feeling that conveys the effect of vision rather than vision itself, a style analogous to impressionism. Woolf's technique— the description of the feeling of vision rather than the realistic reportage of the object of vision itself—seems awfully close to what the French painters were doing with light. But this is an analogy only. Writers can say—I can say—light, more light! And point fingers toward the bright descending orb of the evening sun as it lowers into the heaving horizon of the Pacific. But the language, if literal, still alludes by analogy only to the facts of optics and astronomy and oceanography. If the language is impressionistic, then the combination of nouns and verbs—the red sun descending into the Pacific—may possibly call to the reader's mind something quite other than the realistic scene. Impressionistic prose refers back to the feeling of the writer as much as to any scene under scrutiny in the middle distance between writer and reader.

The difficulty—purists might even say the futility—of trying to evoke light in language seems equaled by the difficulty of trying to make a story in space. Where writers have tried this in recent times we may notice straining and distortion, a pulling away in rhetoric from the normal rhythms of realistic description. In painting we may find a corresponding obscurity of object and reference, evoking mystery rather than demonstrating clarity, for it seems that only a deep affinity with an overarching religion or mythology will make it possible for the painter—and the viewer—to make connections between images or objects in a single spatial realm. And even in the case of those artists who might possess this attribute, as in, say, the case of a Catholic painter or a Jewish painter or a Communist painter, the viewer may not possess the corresponding awareness that will allow him to put together the pieces of the story shown on the face of the canvas or construction.

Where an artist directly wrestles with such difficulty we may see fascinating work emerge, as is the case in *The Sound and the Fury*, the watershed novel of modern American literary style. Its first section is devoted to the point of view of the Compson family idiot, Benjy. Here Faulkner attempts to expunge time as a factor in order to be true to his understanding of Benjy's unique consciousness—a mind in which time and space fuse into a single entity. But Faulkner can indicate the places where Benjy shifts back and forth between what we would call the past and the present only by shifting from regular typeface to italics (his original idea, which the publisher rejected, was to depict the sections devoted to Benjy's past in an ink of a color different from that of the present). The narrative itself proceeds, as all narrative does, in linear fashion across the page, taking our eye with it.

The second section shifts back to the year 1910, when Quentin Compson commits suicide by jumping into the Charles River, and it introduces us to the possibility of another way of seeing time gone by—through the eyes of the dead Quentin, who narrates the story of his own suicide up to the moment when he drowns. There are, we begin to notice, other sets of eyes that appear in this section, from the eye of the sparrow that lands on the ledge of Quentin's Harvard dormitory room and seems to have control over the nature of time on through the jeweler's eye worn by the Harvard Square watch-repair man, suggesting once again the relation of the eye—vision—and the transformation of time, on through the eyes of the waif whom the time-addled Quentin befriends in a bakery—we hear at once that she has eyes "like a toy bear's" and then a moment or so later that she observes the salesgirl setting out two freshly baked buns on the counter with "still and unwinking eyes like two currants floating motionless in a cup of weak coffee."

The third section takes us back to Easter weekend, 1928, where we began with the mentally defective but ironically Christ-like Benjy; now we listen to the oldest Compson son, Jason, a literal-minded barbarian for whom the world is completely flat and composed of nothing but money and linear time. There are scores of I's in his chapter—of the first-person-singular sort, beginning with his pronouncement in the opening sentence about his runaway sister, "Once a bitch always a bitch, what I say." If we listen to the line, it sounds like "what eye say." And vision becomes equal to speech, with a saying or speaking eye rising to the level of vision-creating power. This seems absolutely fitting for the world of Jason, who sees nothing beyond the surface of things.

The fourth and final section of this masterwork of vision reveals to us the apotheosis of the eye in terms of both content and technique. Presented in the third-person past tense, it opens for us on Easter morning, 1928, with the advent of the enduring house servant Dilsey in the subdued light of dawn, "a moving wall of gray light out of the northeast which, instead of dissolving into moisture, seemed to disintegrate into minute and venomous particles, like dust that, when Dilsey opened the door of the cabin and emerged, needled laterally into her flesh, precipitating not so much moisture as a substance partaking of the quality of thin, not quite congealed oil." Dilsey, we have already discovered in earlier sections, has the remarkable ability to hold the Compson family together in the face of alcoholism, chicanery, madness, and moral decay.

In this last sequence we learn that she also has the gift for ordering time. When the broken clock in the Compson kitchen strikes at odd moments, Dilsey relates the correct hour. And in her shamanic incarnation she also announces that she has made visionary witness of the time beyond normal human time—"Ise seed de first and de last," she declares, as black peasant syntax and the cunning of native speech come together to form a declaration with eschatological implications as well as an astonishing pun on the nature of vision, time, and the organic essence of temporal order: eyes seed the first and the last. Sight and time have become inextricably intertwined.

It surprises me each time I see it, in a passage toward the very end of this fourth and final section: Faulkner, in a virtuoso gesture, allows the reader entry into a new dimension in which the eye and vision and time come together on the page. This occurs when Jason, having discovered that his niece Quentin has run off with his cash, and suffering from a migraine that seems to come directly from the fist of God, rushes madly about the countryside in pursuit of the runaway girl. He throws himself into a meaningless brawl with a stranger and, bleeding from a head wound, finds himself at an empty railroad siding "where," we're shown, "grass grew rigidly in a plot bordered with rigid flowers and a sign in electric lights: Keep your 👁 on Mottson, the gap filled by a human eye with an electric pupil."

The reader momentarily fixes an eye on the image of that human eye. Thus the reader's eye and the reality of the world within the fiction join for an instant, eye to 👁 in a new cognitive dimension, releasing the story from the conventional restraints of time and space. In the blink of an eye—or should I say, in the eye's unblinking gaze?—Faulkner carries us back to an older form of reading, to the tradition of hieroglyphics, cuneiform writing, and the old pictographic Mayan books painted on tree bark. But only for an instant. With the next line we fall back into the third-person narrative flow of the final section, bound—or, if you will, sentenced—to the mechanics of the rest of the novel, which, though in themselves quite extraordinary in comparison to any other novel in our modern American canon, nonetheless remain within the realm of our given world.

Faulkner's experiments with space and time in fiction—which we can also see at work in the geometric design of *As I Lay Dying*—have a counterpart in modern painting in the work of Picasso, whose cubist canvases show us the traces of a genius wrestling in his own medium against the constraints of single-dimensionality. With such huge giants testing these conventions we have to admit that this quest for extradimensionality in prose and paint constitutes one of the most salient signatures of the modernist movement.

"Strike through the mask!" Ahab urges in *Moby Dick*, an important precursor to the twentieth-century struggle to find meaning in and yet somehow beyond the things of this world. The will to break through the veil of illusion, to write one's way through it, to paint one's way through it—what a story that is to tell, whatever our means for telling it!

6

Truth as Fiction:
Or, the Tail of the Monstrous Peacock

There is an early lyric by William Butler Yeats that I have admired
since the first time I read it, when I was a boy at school.

The Indian Upon God

I passed along the water's edge below the humid trees,
My spirit rocked in evening light, the rushes round my knees,
My spirit rocked in sleep and sighs; and saw the moorfowl pace
All dripping on a grassy slope, and saw them cease to chase
Each other round in circles and heard the eldest speak:
Who holds the world between His bill and made us strong or weak
Is an undying moorfowl, and He lives beyond the sky.
The rains are from His dripping wing, the moonbeams from His eye.
I passed a little further on and heard a lotus talk:
Who made the world and ruleth it, He hangeth on a stalk,
For I am in His image made, and all this tinkling tide
Is but a sliding drop of rain between His petals wide.
A little way within the gloom a roebuck raised his eyes
Brimful of starlight, and he said: *The Stamper of the Skies,*
He is a gentle roebuck; for how else, I pray, could He

Conceive a thing so sad and soft, a gentle thing like me?
I passed a little further on and heard a peacock say:
Who made the grass and made the worms and made my feathers gay,
He is a monstrous peacock, and He waveth all the night
His languid tail above us, lit with myriad spots of light.

There is no more beautiful statement of the multiplicity of point of view and the relative nature of truth in our time—of what we might call the perspectivalism of our time—than this poem. Here Yeats make music out of the idea that truth lies in the mind of the beholder even as he sings the news that truth is a difficult and sometimes dangerous question.

If, for example, we trace the idea of historical truth back down nearly to its origins, we begin to see just how much of a thicket and muddle has surrounded this concept. Herodotus in his monumental narrative on the origins of the Graeco-Persian War outlines his particular method for us, with some indebtedness, as he tells us, to his teacher Hecataeus. Eyewitness accounts and primary documents serve as the first line of truth for Herodotus. Next comes accounts of eyewitness accounts and secondary documents, or markers, such as the monument to the Greek soldiers at Thermopylae, designating the place where they made their stand against the encroaching Persian armies. When, for example, the Greek historian writes about the flooding of the Nile, midway through his account he says that up to this point "I have confined what I have written to the results of my own direct observation and research, and the views I have formed from them; but from now on the basis of my story will be the accounts given to me by the Egyptians themselves—though here, too, I shall put in one or two things which I have seen with my own eyes."

When evidence is lacking or merely hearsay, Herodotus alerts us to this situation. After all, he is attempting to write a work that itself will stand for thousands of years, that itself will serve as the verbal counterpart to a marked stone in place on one of the many important battlefields.

His battle scenes are epic in scope, as in his depiction of the Battle of Marathon:

The struggle at Marathon was long drawn out. In the centre, held by the Persians themselves and the Sacae, the advantage was with the foreigners, who were so far successful as to break the Greek line and pursue the fugitives inland from the sea; but the Athenians on one wing and the Plataeans on the other were both victorious. Having got the upper hand, they left the defeated enemy to make their escape, and then, drawing the two wings together into a single unit, they turned their attention to the Persians who had broken through the centre. Here again they were triumphant, chasing the routed enemy, and cutting them down until they came to the sea, and men were calling for fire and taking hold of the ships.

But it's in peace, not war, that Herodotus is at his most entertaining on the question of historical truth. In his long and wonderful tour of the exotic Near East he writes as an antique ethnologist, introducing us to a number of strange and interesting tribes and cultures. Commenting, for example, on the various tribes who live along the Libyan coast, he tells us of the fabulous Atarantes,

> the only people in the world, so far as our knowledge goes, to do without names. Atarantes is the collective name—but individually they have none. . . . Once more at a distance of ten days' journey there is a salt-hill, a spring, and a tract of inhabited country, and adjoining it rises Mt. Atlas. In shape the mountain is a slender cone, and it is so high that according to reports the top cannot be seen, because summer and winter it is never free of cloud. The natives (who are known as Atlantes, after the mountain) call it the Pillar of the Sky. They are said to eat no living creature, and never to dream. . . . [B]eyond this point my knowledge fails.

He also demonstrates a sly sense of humor, as when he introduces what he calls the "shameful" practice of temple prostitution in Assyria. "Every woman who is a native of the country," he writes, must once in her life go and sit in the temple of Aphrodite and there give herself to a strange man. Many of the rich women, who are too proud to mix with the rest, drive to the temple in covered carriages with a whole host of servants following behind, and there wait; most, however, sit in the precinct of the temple with a band of plaited string round their heads—and a great crowd they are, what with some sitting there, others arriving, others going away—and through them all gangways are marked off running in every direction for the men to pass along and make their choice. Once a woman has taken her seat she is not allowed to go home until a man has thrown a silver coin into her lap and taken her outside to lie with her. . . . Tall, handsome women soon manage to get home again, but the ugly ones stay a long time . . . some of them, indeed, as much as three or four years.

When it comes to heroes and deities, the truth seems a bit more complicated. Herodotus reports, for example, that Leonidas, the king of Sparta, traces his descent "directly back to Heracles, through Anaxandrides and Leon (his father and grandfather), Eurycratides, Anaxander, Eurycrates, Polydorus, Alcamenes, Telechles, Archelaus, Agesilaus, Doryssus, Leobotas, Echestratus, Agis, Eurysthenes, Aristodemus, Aristomachus, Cleodaeus—and so to Hyllus, who was Heracles' son." The writer seems to be presenting the hero Heracles as a historical figure and a hero—that is, a figure who belongs to an indeterminate group between gods and men. Most heroes had at least one divine parent, and some, like Heracles, were divinized.

At the same time, he gives us the result of his research into the origins of some Greek divinities (or in the case of Heracles, half-gods) and argues that the Greek hero was Egyptian in origin, a god with the same name who appeared "from time immemorial." After sifting through the evidence about the dual nature of Heracles, man and god, he suggests that the wisest course is taken by those Greeks "who maintain a double cult of this deity, with two temples, in one of which they worship him as an Olympian and divine, and in the other pay him such honour as is due a hero."

One culture's religion is thus another's mythology. We're certainly familiar with the way that Christianity reduced the pagan gods to mere legends and put forward the figure of Jesus as a historical rather than a scriptural—which is to say, literary—version of the myth of Dionysus, the god who comes into the world to ensure fertility, only to be torn apart and killed by his once devoted followers. Both the Old and the New Testaments refer to many authentic archaelogical sites in the Holy Land, but the characters who populate the sites are taken to be real more on faith than on evidence.

Most of what we understand as historical truth in Europe is enlivened by being represented in some literary form or other—the factionalism of Dante's Florence, for example, coming alive in his great poem. And the chronicles of certain English kings as we find enumerated in Hollingshead live vividly in the history plays of Shakespeare.

The work of Shakespeare is in fact the culminating legacy of thousands of years of European history, the last point in the progress of the Continent's cultural life when religious belief and major aesthetic creation are fused, the one unable to exist without the other. This synthesis of vision (the justification of God's ways to man) has been imitated, as we see in Milton, but never duplicated.

After Milton, historical truth and aesthetic truth, once seen as a single pathway, begin to diverge. Artists arise in the aftermath—I'm thinking of Stendhal, for example, and Flaubert, and Tolstoy, who include the details of history in their work, in fact making history a fundamental element in the creation of a realistic style. But they write of ordinary middle-class people, for the most part, whose lives are affected by history, not the so-called history makers themselves, the kings and queens, and, later, parliamentarians and prime ministers.

With the rise of bourgeois democracy in Western Europe, the nature of history (which is to say our perception of history) changed utterly. Whereas once it was the story of the events that follow from the decision of kings, history refers to the adventures, marriages, projects, politics, and foibles of the bourgeois European. The truth of history comes more and more to include the habits and dreams and desires of the middle class and less and less the depiction of God's ways at work in the world of men and women. Or, to borrow an image from W. H. Auden's elegy on Herman Melville, "The godhead is broken like bread, we are the pieces."

Compare, for example, the description of battles in Herodotus and this fragment of a scene from Stendhal's *Charterhouse of Parma* when the hero, young Fabrizio del Dongo, stumbles through the battlefield at Waterloo.

> Suddenly everyone galloped off. A few moments later Fabrizio saw, twenty paces ahead, a ploughed field that seemed to be strange in motion; the furrows were filled with water, and the wet ground that formed their crests was exploding into tiny black fragments flung three or four feet into the air. Fabrizio noticed this odd effect as he passed. . . . He heard a sharp cry beside him: two hussars had fallen, riddled by bullets; and when he turned to look at them, they were already twenty paces behind the escort. What seemed horrible to him was a blood-covered horse struggling in the furrows and trying to follow the others: blood was flowing into the mire.
>
> "Aha! Now we're under fire at last! I've seen action!" he kept telling himself, with a certain satisfaction. "Now I'm a true soldier." At this moment . . . our hero realized that these were bullets tearing up the earth. Though he tried to see where they were coming from, there was nothing but white smoke from the battery a great ways off, and amid the continuous roaring of cannon-fire he seemed to hear explosions much closer to him; he could make nothing of it.
>
> (Trans. Richard Howard)

The truth that Stendhal presents is the truth of individual experience in the world of historical events, quite unlike Herodotus's portrait of phalanxes of brave warriors falling in battle for the ideals of their city-states. Each representation is, of course, convincing for its own time, and to embrace Stendhal's truth is not to reject Herodotus's. Each version employs elements that are both real and what we usually take to be imaginary, Herodotus using references to mythology (which, of course, he understood to be part of natural religion) and history, and Stendhal employing historical awareness in a subjective fashion in order to focus on the experience of his invented hero.

The culmination of the nineteenth-century literary mode of historical realism lies in the fiction of Tolstoy (even though, at the end of his life, caught in the grip of an older vision—that of Christianity—he disavowed his work). But with the rise of early-twentieth-century modernism, as opposed to the just merely modern, we find the historical style trumped by a new way of looking at reality in which history is only one of a number of perspectives from which to view the world of men and women, along with mythology, psychology, aesthetics, and economics. The modernist work of art is self-aware of its own untruth (that is, it is based on the premise of its own unrealistic nature) and self-reflexive, referring to its own segments and scenes and action as verification of its wholeness. This makes for a more overtly complex poetry and fiction.

Joyce, for example, fuses both the classical and the modern, the allegorical and the symbolic, in portraying Dedalus, Bloom, and Molly Bloom, as avatars of the old Homeric figures of Telemachus, Odysseus himself, and Penelope. He's writing a novel, of course, the epic of a fallen world, as the Hungarian critic Georg Lukács once described the genre.

The fabled cohesion of Homeric epic links the middle world of the characters to the upper world of the gods and the lower world of the dead, both inside the poem and in the minds of the audience. As Lukács argues, the novel offers the *illusion* of cohesion over the time in which we read it, and when we emerge once again into a world of confusion and incoherence we have at least a metaphor for what wholeness might be like.

By definition all our twentieth-century writers are modern, but not all are modernist. On the one hand we have the realists and naturalists, who attempt to make a seamless story out of the whole cloth of everyday life; on the other hand are the modernists, who insist on calling our attention to the artifice of the work of art in order to have us focus on the essential irony of representing modern reality. You can enjoy the fine twentieth-century realists, Theodore Dreiser and Wallace Stegner and James Jones, to name a few. But the greatest writers of our time, from Hemingway to García Márquez, are those who employ modernist technique in the service of realistic depiction.

For all of these writers, truth, as Hegel would explain it, is situationally determined. Rather than supposing an eternal, Platonic truth, modernists and most other writers derive their values from a dialectic with life and in the case of the full-blown modernists from a dialectical play of values within the works themselves.

In modern times, the best art remains divorced from any serious overarching worldview. When it carries a message, as in, say, the work of socialist-realists and other didactic writers, the results are terribly flawed. If you want a message, as Hemingway once remarked, go to Western Union.

Lukács was a Marxist who, ironically, regarded irony as the watermark of all serious modern art. Because of the nature of his interests, he paid more attention to the flawed greatness of bourgeois art, to Flaubert and to Thomas Mann, than to the shallow correctness of socialist realism.

One important modern American writer who tries to engage himself with the problems of social art, with spectacular aesthetic success, is James Agee. With a personal fusion of Episcopalian Christianity and Marxist convictions, Agee, in his experimental work of nonfiction *Let Us Now Praise Famous Men*, attempted to lay bare the real "truth" about three Alabama sharecropper families. In 1938 he had set out on this quest as an assignment for *Fortune* magazine, along with photographer Walker Evans. The manuscript soon blossomed into a book-length essay, and as Agee saw it, the piece was both a rebuke and a refutation of conventional journalism.

"Who, what, where, when and why (or how) is the primal cliché and complacency of journalism," he writes while in the middle of his sharecropper story.

> But . . . I have never yet seen a piece of journalism which conveyed more than the slightest fraction of what any even moderately reflective and sensitive person would mean and intend by those inachievable words, and that fraction itself I have

never seen clean of one or another degree of patent, to say
nothing of essential, falsehood. . . . The very blood and semen
of journalism . . . is a broad and successful form of lying.
Remove that form of lying and you no longer have journalism.

But it's not just the journalistic approach that, in Agee's eyes, is
flawed:

> Words like all else are limited by certain laws. . . . Words can-
> not embody; they can only describe. . . . Most young writers
> and artists roll around in description like honeymooners on a
> bed. It comes easier to them than anything else. . . . But I . . .
> suspect that the lust for describing, and that lust in action, is
> not necessarily a vice. Plain objects and atmospheres have a suf-
> ficient intrinsic beauty and stature that it might be well if the
> describer became more rather than less shameless.

Foreshadowing much of the fine nonfiction work of Norman
Mailer and Joan Didion, to name a few contemporaries working this
vein, Agee argues that the writer must admit just how much his own perception is part of the story. This, of course, is relativism. But, Agee says,

> name me one truth within human range that is not relative and
> I will feel a shade more apologetic of that . . . I would do just as
> badly to simplify or eliminate myself from this picture as to
> simplify or invent character, places or atmospheres. A chain of
> truths did actually weave itself and run through: it is their tex-
> ture that I want to represent, not betray, not pretty up into art.

In this way, the modernist sensibility insinuated itself into twentieth-century reportage, and set a standard for all subsequent works of
serious nonfiction narrative.

About fifteen years earlier, we see this happening to fiction—as
Gertrude Stein teaches the young Ernest Hemingway a new "truth."
When she suggests that language, as it is used in the making of fiction,
is different from the truth of everyday language, and fiction is a mal-

leable art, the writer shaping language as the sculptor shapes stone, we become witness to a technical revolution in American prose.

Hemingway's signature prose rhythm, the repetitive phrases that he has so often been parodied for, signals a new recognition—a modernist technique—among American story writers that shaping language in specific ways can communicate the emotion of the events described.

Here are some examples from Hemingway's great story "Big Two-Hearted River." When Nick Adams first arrives in the woods of northern Michigan on his solitary fishing trip, he spies from the railroad bridge some trout and watches them "holding themselves with their noses into the current, many trout in deep, fast moving water, slightly distorted as he watched far down through the glassy convex surface of the pool, its surface pushing and swelling smooth against the resistance of the log-driven piles of the bridge." The accuracy of Hemingway's depiction of that "slightly distorted" view of an aboveground object beneath the water should alert us both to the technical accuracy of this master's prose and to the distinctive point of view with which he delivers all of his work. He reinforces this a moment later when as a kingfisher flies up the stream,

> a big trout shot upstream in a long angle, only his shadow marking the angle, then lost his shadow as he came through the surface of the water, caught the sun, and then, as he went back into the stream under the surface, his shadow seemed to float down the stream with the current, unresisting, to his post under the bridge where he tightened facing up into the current.

Further evidence of Hemingway's modernist "distortion" of the ideal comes a page later when Nick notices the grasshoppers he will collect for bait. One of the insects climbs up onto his woolen sock.

> The grasshopper was black. As he had walked along the road, climbing, he had started many grasshoppers from the dust. They were all black. They were not the big grasshoppers with yellow and black or red and black wings whirring out from

their black wing sheathing as they fly up. These were just ordinary hoppers, but all a sooty black in color.

Of course these survivors of what Nick thinks of as "the burned-over country," this stretch of land in the wake of fire, would indeed be black. But the repetition of the word alerts us to the character's appreciation of their tenacity in the face of such a bleak and disastrous event.

Later, after reaching his destination and doing the hard work of clearing the ground so he can set up his tent, Nick crawls inside. In there, it

smelled pleasantly of canvas. Already there was something mysterious and homelike. Nick was happy as he crawled inside the tent. He had not been unhappy all day. This was different though. Now things were done. There had been this to do. Now it was done. It had been a hard trip. He was very tired. That was done. He had made his camp. He was settled. Nothing could touch him. It was a good place to camp. He was there, in the good place. He was in his home where he had made it.

His home here, where he has made it, is the expressive—and protective—shelter of his language. Truth, for Nick Adams, and for a multitude of modernist protagonists who come after, is the truth of experience, expressed by the particular distortion of their creators' language.

Faulkner's modernism suggests that this is so, even though it is both more and less visible, often obscured (in the best way) by his language and his subject matter. The understated use of stream-of-consciousness technique in the opening, "Benjy," section, of *The Sound and the Fury*, the shifting of time in the second section back and forth within the confines of suicidal Quentin Compson's last day on earth (his "death day," as opposed to his birthday, as Jean-Paul Sartre once eloquently described this sequence), the self-conscious deployment of signs in the third section, devoted to Jason Compson, and the multidimensional portrait of Dilsey, the Compson retainer, including her ability to tell time by means of a broken timepiece, completes this Cubist-like portrait of a modern Southern American family in despair and decline.

As it happens, there are few American writers who manage to create something approaching greatness while working outside the modernist studio. Dreiser is one. Willa Cather is another; Steinbeck, another. Creating deeply felt realistic portraits of representative characters is only the beginning of the truth of any period, and the realistic novel remains one of the best ways to record the feel and heft of life at any given moment in our memory span. But a realistic novel, once you read it, subsides from reading experience to datum pretty quickly. There are dozens of writers in any period in modern times who have the skill and talent for the depiction of interesting characters. But only a few, such as Cather and Steinbeck, have the genius to cast their characters against a constantly changing historical background and at the same time elevate them to symbolic status.

(A few writers keep one foot in each camp, as in, say, the work of Richard Wright, a realist for most of his life whose late work, the collection of stories titled *Eight Men*, demonstrates the author's familiarity and affinity for existential philosophy—the modernist philosophy, one might call it.)

We can see, from a recent spate of highly publicized memoirs, that some talented contemporary writers purport to portray the truth of their lives, even as they employ the techniques of the fiction in the presentation of their experience. Frank Conroy's *Stop-Time*, published some thirty years ago, may be the benchmark work of this variety of memoir. Turning his childhood and early manhood into a carefully designed narrative that has the effect of poetry and the force of truth was no easy task. When we look at late-twentieth-century memoirs, such as Mary Karr's *The Liar's Club* or Gore Vidal's *Palimpsest*, we can see that a great proximity to the truth of the subject matter—in these cases, the life of the very writer who is writing that life—still requires the writer to employ all sorts of narrative devices borrowed from the novel, beginning with the point of view, character creation, tone, and most important of all, narrative order. Clearly the best memoirs make the case that having lived a life is only one of the prerequisites for writing about it. The best of memoirs give the impression of truth precisely because, paradoxically, the writer has been as cunning as the successful fiction writer in presenting that truth.

There is only one law of life, says the narrator of Robert Musil's unfinished four-volume novel *The Man Without Qualities*, and that is the law of narrative order. Musil's insight is both exhilarating and frightening, frightening because it allows for callow relativism. But if we have callow relativism on the one hand, we've got bold inventive genius on the other. If the highest truths are created by the human imagination, we are indeed creatures ranking just below the angels. In a world that abounds with Hitlers and Stalins and Saddam Husseins and Hutu and Tutsi slaughter and Serbian militias run amuck, it's somehow reassuring to have Tolstoy and Thomas Mann and Doris Lessing on our side, the side of aesthetic values and humane sanity, truths made known to us only in art.

What is the truth of an epoch completely vanished such as preclassical Mediterranean Greece if not the truth contained in the *Iliad* and the *Odyssey*? What remains of the emotional life of nineteenth-century Europe outside of the lyrics of the great poets, the painting and sculpture of the time, and the music of the great composers? What is the truth of our American nineteenth century if not the images of it synthesized by Hawthorne, Melville, and Twain?

"I have shored these fragments against my ruins," Eliot says in the last part of *The Wasteland*. What are ancient warriors or barques or kingdoms once embracing entire continents—kings called Ozymandias, as Shelley names them—or cutlery or railroad trains or rockets but rumors, legends, or artifacts in a museum, without the narrative to bring them to life?

Reality waits for us on the page, like musical composition, ready to be performed by our imaginations. And once we begin this activity we notice that outside of biology and physics, there are many truths. If we hold to just one, it becomes, as Yeats's Indian noticed, either an undying moorfowl whose eyes drip moonbeams or a giant lotus or a heavenly deer—or a monstrous peacock, waving its languid tail above us all the night.

7

The Consolation of Art

Spring, Leningrad, 1942—"though the word 'spring,'" writes Russian literary critic Lidiya Ginsburg in her memoir, *Blockade Diary*, "had an odd ring to it. The bread ration had been increased, trams made their diffident way along frozen streets. The Germans had halted the bombing raids, but were shelling the city several times each day. The strongest and most vital people had already died—or had survived. The feeble went on belatedly dying. The word 'spring' had an odd ring to it."

As she tells us in this slender but powerful volume, though "the thirst for information was fearful," with people crowding around street-corner loudspeakers several times a day, the besieged Russians of Leningrad longed for other sorts of "information." Ginsburg writes:

> During the war years, people used to read *War and Peace* avidly, comparing their own behaviour with it (not the other way round—no one doubted the adequacy of Tolstoy's response to life). The reader would say to himself . . . So then, this is how it should be. Whoever had the energy enough to read, used to read *War and Peace* avidly in besieged Leningrad. . . .

Tolstoy had said the last word as regards courage, about people doing their bit in a people's war. He also spoke of how those caught up in this common round continued playing their part involuntarily, while ostensibly busy solving problems affecting their own lives. The people of besieged Leningrad worked (while they could) and saved (if they could) both themselves and their loved ones from dying of hunger.

And in the final reckoning that was also essential to the war effort, because a living city barred the path of an enemy who wanted to kill it.

This is a rather astonishing portrait that Ginsburg makes of one of the most tortured times in the second half of our century, the nine-hundred-day siege of one of Russia's major cities—and all the more astonishing because of the equation of satisfying elemental physical hunger and the sating of spiritual hunger by means of reading great literature, in this case, the greatest novelist Russia has ever known. People ate to live—and people *read* to live, in order to keep the city a vital entity so that it would not fall to the invading German army.

The implications of this for the consoling power of great art are enormous, not just for those who are unfortunate enough to be under siege but for all of us alive in the modern Western world today, in the best of times, in the worst of times, where life at its most peaceful seems always to contain elements of shelling and battery. And where do people turn for solace and consolation?

Some go to holy scripture, to the Bible or to the Koran. Others turn to fiction—reading it, writing it, for the consolatory power of art. To be consoled: to have your sorrow or grief allayed, to be comforted in bad times, shored up in the worst of moments and hours.

Tolstoy seems right for a readership fearful of death by bombs and artillery shells, and from the starvation caused by the blockade of the city. At the most dire moments in our existence, who wouldn't want to have the company of the most strongly felt and sharply portrayed and the most broadly constructed work of art? As a reader, I don't want more than that company and comfort. As a writer, I begin to speculate as to just what it may be about the elements of great art that have this powerful effect on the observer—the power to console in the worst of times.

The first element that we have to notice in great fiction is *the consolation of language*, the way that certain combinations of sentences and paragraphs sound in our mind's ear to produce this consolatory effect.

Next is *the consolation of psychology*—the creation of characters, as in Lidiya Ginsburg's reading of Tolstoy, which, because of the writer's keen insight into the working of the human mind and its powers of decision making and imaginings, gives us some kind of solace as we read about them.

Then comes *the consolation of form*, the effect created by the overarching action of a work and the overall impression it creates in our minds.

Last in this list, though certainly not in last place, is what I call *the consolation of the underlying natural rhythms and mythological patterns* of the novel or story in question.

First of all, it seems almost too obvious to say, without the language, nothing. It is by means of the bricks and mortar of sentences and paragraphs that we make our initial contact with the work. Unlike paintings or sculpture, narrative exists not just in time but over the course of a certain amount of time, and to know the story as a whole we must make it up out of the individual sentences. When we look at a painting, our method of knowing comes primarily through the eye. We see the work in its entirety. It may take minutes or weeks or even years before we fully comprehend the relations within the boundaries of the canvas—form and color and line—but it is always all there. When we read a sentence, our method of knowing moves beyond the eye into the mind, with sentences and paragraphs that we immediately translate—in this distinctive neurological way that we have of behaving—into meaning in our minds. But now think of music as opposed to painting, and you can make out the difference in easy fashion. We listen, comprehend, admire, get swept up by the music in time. Fiction is a temporal art form, unfolding in our minds in time, story music.

The successful writer, the writer who moves us in heart as well as mind, consoles us by the sound and rhythm of his creation as well as by the truth about the sensual world that the sentence delivers. Language in the largest sense, though, does not merely convey the world to us—it is the world as we know to express it. Thus, at its best, it offers both emotion and idea in one.

> Soon now they would enter the Delta. The sensation was familiar to him. It had been renewed like this each week in November for more than fifty years—the last hill, at the foot of which the rich unbroken alluvial flatness began as the sea began at the base of its cliffs, dissolving away beneath the unhurried November rain as the sea itself would dissolve away.

The opening of Faulkner's "Delta Autumn" stands as a fine example of the fusion of lyric and descriptive sentence, particularly in the phrases following the dash, phrases that, paradoxically, offer more description even as the rhythm enhances the lyrical aspect of the line.

Or consider the striking prose poem prologue to James Agee's novel *A Death in the Family*, the set piece titled "Knoxville, Summer, 1915," in which the recollective medium, the first-person speaker looking back on his childhood summer twilights on the lawn beside his family's house, becomes not just the vehicle of the recollection but the meaning of the recollection itself:

> We are talking now of summer evenings in Knoxville, Tennessee, in the time that I lived there so successfully disguised to myself as a child. . . . People go by; things go by. A horse, drawing a buggy, breaking his hollow iron music on the asphalt; a loud auto; a quiet auto . . . a street car raising its iron moan; stopping, belling and starting; stertorous; raising and rousing again its iron increasing moan;
> . . .
> Now is the night one blue dew, my father has drained, he has coiled the hose.
> Low on the length of lawns, a frailing of fire who breathes.
> Content, silver, like peeps of light, each cricket makes his comment over and over in the drowned grass.

The next element is the consolation of psychology, the danger-ous but always valuable awareness of how other beings behave. If the fiction writer's understanding of human action is sharp and advanced, the story can seem as real to us as our own experience, or even more real.

Think, say, of the weight of conscience in the story of a figure such as Conrad's Lord Jim. Or the scarcely utterable pain of alienation in the words and actions of Melville's Bartleby the Scrivener. Or in, for another example, the stark awareness of the character of Aunt Geor-giana in Willa Cather's poignant portrait of a plains wife visiting in Boston in the story "A Wagner Matinee."

Georgiana had once been a music teacher at the Boston Conser-vatory. She then married a Vermont boy, with whom she moved west to a life of thirty years on the Nebraska prairie—a life whose first habi-tation was a dugout in a red hillside, their water hauled from lagoons where the buffalo drank, their provisions always at the mercy of bands of roving Indians—a life of cooking three meals a day, the first of which had to be on the table by six in the morning, raising six children, and never going more than fifty miles from the homestead. When a trip to settle an inheritance takes her back to Boston, her nephew, for-merly a farm boy but now a resident of New England, finds her tem-porary lodging and invites her to a concert, an all-Wagner program that begins with the prelude to *Tristan and Isolde* and ends with the funeral march from *The Ring*. After the music stops the people file out of the hall. Aunt Georgiana remains seated while the narrator, her nephew Clark, tells us that "the men of the orchestra went out one by one, leaving the stage to the chairs and music stands, empty as a win-ter cornfield." Clark speaks to her about leaving, and she bursts into tears.

"I don't want to, Clark," she says as she sobs. "I don't want to go!" And the story ends with a one-paragraph coda in which the narrator tells us:

> I understood. For her, just outside the concert hall, lay the
> black pond with the cattle-tracked bluffs; the tall, unpainted
> house, with weather-curled boards, naked as a tower; the

crook-backed ash seedlings where the dish-cloths hung to dry; the gaunt, moulting turkeys picking up refuse about the kitchen door.

This is a highly compact story of a single incident that, as Bernard Malamud has written about the effect of the short-story form, "predicates a life." Aunt Georgiana has worked in pain and isolation for thirty years, almost all of her adult life, but she has not been able to express that pain until this moment after the concert when she realizes that she does not want to return to the prairie. The irony of her entrapment is made all the more intense by the fact that her story is told by the farm boy nephew who has somehow managed to escape Nebraska and make a life for himself in Boston. He is free to remain in the territory of music and culture while she must return to the prairie. He alone remains to tell her story.

The way in which he does so makes the difference between anecdote and short fiction. The narrator, the former farm boy, doesn't merely recount his aunt's visit. He tells of it in such a way that all of her pain and suffering becomes apparent, because he himself understands completely what she has lost by putting New England behind her, and what she faces when she faces the return to Nebraska. Her vision at the end is his vision also, except that he is saved and she is lost. Thus the irony of the telling of this story. Cather's understanding of these two variants of prairie homesteaders, the young fellow and the immigrant aunt, deepen and augment the spare forward line of the tale.

Above all else, the writer's talent for realistic psychological portraiture lends us insight into other minds. To know another mind, to see another human being in situations that require courage, moral awareness, kindness, love, to see someone employ the gift of maneuvering through the tight spaces of life and the ability to broaden insight, to use wit and affection—that is what we witness in good fiction. In great fiction we live through it, suffering when the characters suffer, gaining when they gain.

What else is it about good fiction that consoles us? Form consoles us by showing us the long rhythms of life, by helping us to picture in our minds over time the rise and fall of the arc of an incident, a scene, or a day, or a lifetime. Form requires an act of the imagination, or a combination of imagination and memory, so that we can hold in the mind the evolving architecture of a novel. And because form is intimately related to the matter of time, it becomes all the more difficult to capture it in any single given moment. The form of the work is made up of all of the moments in every scene and every chapter of the overall narrative.

What else does fiction do for us? It consoles in other ways besides those of language, psychology, and form. We know that. We feel it as we read. We can sense this certain inexplicable event taking place as we read. Using form as a springboard, fiction carries us out of the realm of time altogether, though not without first having imprinted on our minds the possibility of an overarching design that carries the story along through years, decades, sometimes even centuries. Moving from the naturalistic realm of time, the greatest books transport us into the region of mystery, faith, and mythology, those largest of patterns that emerge from novel-length fiction and become part of our way of living in the world.

It may be a bit too schematic to single out this one aspect, the sense we gain in reading novels—the sense that is impressed on us by the design and architecture of the work itself, by the behavior of the characters, and by the language that conveys all of this to us—that there is more to life than the life that we have known thus far. Sometimes we know this by a feeling only, sometimes the novelist gives us a sign, as the rainbow (in D. H. Lawrence's novel of the same name), as seen by Ursula Brangwen at the end of the book.

In one place it gleamed fiercely, and, her heart anguished with hope, she sought the shadow of iris where the bow should be. Steadily the colour gathered, mysteriously, from nowhere, it took presence upon itself, there was a faint, vast rainbow. The arc bended and strengthed itself till it arched indomitable, making great architecture of light and colour and the space of heaven.

Sometimes the vision is both internal and external, joining the subjective understanding of the main character with the practical world of nature, as in the justly lauded and moving conclusion to Joyce's novella "The Dead." Gabriel Conroy stands at the window of his hotel room, his wife, Gretta, having fallen asleep. Minutes before she has rejected his advances and made clear to him that she is mourning this particular night the death of a young fellow out of her past who courted her and whom she deeply loved before he died at an early age. Sympathetic tears fill the eyes of this smart and heretofore egotistical and rather priggish modern Irishman as he understands the grief of another for the first time. He has a vision of the dead boy standing out in the rain under a dripping tree. But time is coming to an end—the evening, his own youth, the lives of his maiden aunts who host the annual dance they have just attended—and the season is winter now, and the rain of the past vision has turned to present snow, and Gabriel, standing at the window, apprehends the proximity of other "forms" of the dead.

> His soul had approached that region where dwell the vast hosts of the dead. He was conscious of, but could not apprehend, their wayward and flickering existence. His own identity was fading out into a grey impalpable world: the solid world itself which these dead had one time reared and lived in was dissolving and dwindling.

It begins to snow, and the wind blows the snow against the window. And Gabriel watches this demonstration of the tyrannical power of the natural world, the snow

> falling on every part of the dark central plain, on the treeless hills, falling softly upon the Bog of Allen and, farther westward, softly falling into the dark mutinous Shannon waves. It was falling, too, upon every part of the lonely churchyard on the hill where Michael Furey lay buried. It lay thickly drifted on the crooked crosses and headstones, on the spears of the little gate, on the barren thorns. His soul swooned slowly as he heard the snow falling faintly through the universe and faintly falling, like the descent of their last end, upon all the living and the dead.

What's the consolation here? None of us has written this. But we have *read* it. And it has, in its fusion of language, psychology, form, and myth, will have, will always have, I think, the power to allay our fears and relieve a certain amount of suffering. This story—and you can add your other favorite art form here as well—this story, this poem, this symphony, this dance, this painting, this sculpture, this play—it may tell us about how we all must pass inevitably from this world, but it was made by one of us. And that is the best news I know.

part 2

rereading

8

You Can Read Wolfe Again

When *Look Homeward, Angel* first appeared, in the autumn of 1929, it wasn't immediately apparent that success was a problem that Thomas Wolfe would have to contend with. It was a first novel by an unknown Southern writer, delivered to the bookshops in the midst of the Crash. Who would have predicted its survival? But it flourished, selling tens of thousands of copies.

Wolfe became the third new writer to soar to romantic fame and success under the guiding hand of the best literary editor of the day, Maxwell Perkins, of Charles Scribner's Sons. Perkins's two star authors, Hemingway and Fitzgerald, welcomed Wolfe to the club. Sinclair Lewis, the reigning elder statesman of contemporary fiction of the day, went so far as to praise Wolfe's novel in his Nobel Prize acceptance speech. Wolfe was so grateful for this kindness that he included a worshipful portrait of Lewis as Lloyd McHarg in *You Can't Go Home Again*.

The market crashed, but Wolfe's stock secured. And split, like the manuscript of his second novel, which Perkins and Wolfe eventually wrestled into shape and published under the title *Of Time and the River*. The French have a term for the novel that expands into a series: *roman fleuve*. Wolfe's *fleuve* always surged at flood crest—and washed away just about all critical response. The only reviewer who raised a negative voice was Bernard De Voto in the *Saturday Review*, in which he suggested that the Perkins–Wolfe collaboration demonstrated the novelist's inability to control the tidal force of his own words. Privately, Hemingway, probably as much out of jealousy as critical acumen, remarked to Perkins that the novel was "sixty percent pure shit."

A book of his stories that came out between the two novels did not sell well, but the longer fiction did. Wolfe became a best-seller, a literary personage, a legend in his time, with his (self-proclaimed) Gulliver-like body and soul parading around New York and America, like Swift's hero in the land of the Lilliputians.

His last two novels, *The Web and the Rock* and *You Can't Go Home Again* appeared posthumously, carved out of the pile of manuscript several feet high that Wolfe left behind at his death in 1938 from galloping tuberculosis of the brain. Both books were praised and acquired a good readership.

Next came critical assessment.

"Hungry Gulliver" is what English novelist Pamela Hansford Johnson called her approving academic treatment of Wolfe, which appeared in 1948. "The Rhetoric and the Agony" was the title of the mixed chapter that Alfred Kazin devoted to Wolfe in his epochal study of the American novel, *On Native Grounds*.

By the fifties, Wolfe's reputation was wavering among academics hot in the thrall of the close-reading techniques of the New Criticism, but it was still high among perennially new generations of sensitive young men (and some sensitive young women). When Wolfe strode the pavements of Manhattan, New York was the mecca of all provincials, whether from Tulsa or Hartford, Seneca Falls or Asheville, and his novels cried out about cities to be found as well as childhoods that had been lost. Even as undergraduates in the late fifties thumbed their way through copies of Kerouac's *On the Road*, Wolfe's hegira from Asheville to the nation's largest and most exciting city remained compatible somehow with the lust to take to the road for anywhere.

Scribner's did its part to try and make Wolfe's work academically respectable, reprinting the Johnson essay in softcover under the title *The Art of Thomas Wolfe*. Occasional ripples of interest passed through the educated public, as when a stage adaptation of *Look Homeward, Angel* appeared in 1961, and again after the publication of the late Andrew Turnbull's biography of Wolfe in 1967.

But sometime in the sixties readers in their late teens and early twenties stopped coming home to and leaving home with Thomas Wolfe. Eugene Gant packing his valise and taking the train north to New York and Boston became archaic to the young. The new ideal was to strap on a pack and thumb westward in the hope of finding a place more inspiring than the stagnant small town and the rotten Big Apple.

So even though Wolfe went out looking for America

(the place of the howling winds, the hurrying of the leaves in old October, the hard clean falling to the earth of acorns. The place of the storm-tossed moaning of the wintry mountain side, where the young men cry out in their throats and feel the savage vigor, the rude strong energies; the place where the trains cross rivers. . . . A fabulous country, the only fabulous country . . . the one place where miracles not only happen, but where they happen all the time)

Wolfe's reputation became one of the casualties of the sixties. We are now a nation whose hundreds of thousands of Wolfe readers have given way to a generation in whose minds the only title that lights up when that name is mentioned is "The Kandy-Coated, Tangerine Flaked etc. etc." *People* magazine, whose goal each week seems to be that of bidding its page-turners to empty their heads in order to have their cups filled yet again, referred to the author in a rather blatant puff of the CBS production of *You Can't Go Home Again* as "Tom Wolfe (the elder)." Tom Wolfe (the younger), one hears, at least has the grace to refer to him as "my namesake."

Clearly the years and change of taste (or lack of it) have cut this Gulliver down to size. And until recently nothing has really been able to lift Wolfe back even halfway up toward the heights that he enjoyed just before his death.

As C. Hugh Holman, Kenan Professor of Literature at the University of North Carolina at Chapel Hill, Wolfe's alma mater, says,

"There is no Wolfe 'industry' among literature scholars." Unlike Faulkner, who is second only to Shakespeare in the number of doctoral theses written about him, Wolfe has not only lost his large national readership, he is also lost to the world of academe.

Aside from the publication that goes by the name of the *Thomas Wolfe Newsletter*, a respectable little academic operation (edited out of the University of Akron by Professor John Phillipson), which is a one-note toot against the swelling sounds of the Faulkner, Hemingway, and Fitzgerald thousand-horn marching bands, the only cry of Wolfe these days seems to echo below the Mason-Dixon line. Out of hundreds of seminars scheduled for next December's meetings of the Modern Language Association in San Francisco, only one will be devoted to the work of the favorite son of Asheville, North Carolina.

Occasionally, he finds his way into undergraduate courses, but on most campuses today, you can buy Wolfe stock cheap.

Sitting high above Fifth Avenue watching what Wolfe called "the great man-swarm of the city" buzz by below us, Charles Scribner III, grandson of the Scribner who first published Wolfe, admitted that of Perkins's three geniuses, Wolfe now runs a poor, poor third in sales. We talked in the office where Max Perkins wrestled Wolfe and the flood-crest manuscript of *Of Time and the River* into submission, and the figures convey the pathos of Wolfe's standing. *Look Homeward, Angel* in the Scribner's paper edition sells about twenty-five thousand copies each year. That may seem like a respectable figure in itself—but it is less than a tenth of the sales of *The Great Gatsby* and *The Old Man and the Sea*, and thus quite pathetic.

(Harper & Row acquired the rights to the last two novels when Wolfe, enraged and embarrassed by the De Voto attack on his supposed inability to work without Perkins, broke with his mentor and with Scribner's. The publisher refused to issue sales figures, but we can imagine what they are, since *The Web and the Rock* and *You Can't Go Home Again* are not exactly staples in most libraries.)

Scribner knows all of the lore that goes with his office. And he has some stories that A. Scott Berg didn't include in his recent biography of Perkins (with its wonderfully ambiguous subtitle, *Editor of Genius*).

For example, he learned from talking to Wolfe's grandmother that when she and her husband invited him out for dinner the novelist spent most of the time composing fiction on the napkins. A lean blond fellow under the age of thirty, with an ebullient air and a patent leather smile, Scribner might himself be a figure out of *Gatsby*. Handing over the sheaf of Perkins–Wolfe memorabilia, he makes me feel like a professor who has just given him a quiz in the period. He has a Ph.D. from Princeton in art history, and a visible love of music. He's moved a piano into the space where Hemingway decked *Masses* editor Max Eastman. (The novelist happened to walk in on a conference between Eastman and Perkins and challenged Eastman to repeat some crack he had made about his manhood.)

The office isn't large at all—there's hardly room enough for two men, a desk, a bookcase, and the piano. It's hard to imagine that the two literary geniuses hurt each other much once they got to wrestling on the floor.

For elbow room we have to leave the office and cross the hall to the Scribner library, where even the Gulliver-size Wolfe (who stood nearly seven feet tall and weighed almost three hundred pounds) had the space to stretch out full length after late-night sessions with Perkins.

Scribner proudly points to the rug.

American literature slept here.

He was born in Asheville in 1900 in October, the youngest child in a large lower-middle-class family. The father, W. O., was a stonecutter who owned a monument shop on Park Square in Asheville, where he had settled with his third wife, Julia, after spending his youth in Pennsylvania and his young manhood wandering his way south.

Thomas Wolfe suffered a childhood suffused with passion and blown over by the winds of appetite for love, life, and the need to know all things material and spiritual. At fifteen, when he entered the University of North Carolina, he suffered further. When he headed north to Harvard to take George Pierce Baker's famous playwriting workshop, he suffered more. He was a big bruiser of a man, but his soul bruised easily. After leaving Cambridge he took up work at New York

University in the English department and tried to sell his plays. After two years of painful teaching and unsuccessful playwriting, he sailed for Europe, where he wrote a novel called *O Lost*. Thanks to the efforts of Wolfe's mistress, set designer Aline Bernstein, a married woman nearly twice his age whom he had met on a boat returning to America, Maxwell Perkins read *O Lost*, helped the young novelist edit it down to workable length, and encouraged him to select a better title.

Thus *Look Homeward, Angel* (after lines from Milton's *Lycidas*) reached the bookstores. And Wolfe reached the heights of fame. He spent four years writing the pages that became *Of Time and the River* (in between naps in the Scribner library). And he wandered about the world enjoying his fame and suffering publicly and privately from the sting of the De Voto review. Aboard a steamer in Puget Sound he drank whiskey from a bottle that just before had known the lips of a drunk with a cold.

Wolfe took sick, came down with pneumonia, and after weeks of passing in and out of fevers and rages, calms and storms, succumbed to the ravages of an old tubercular nodule that the present illness had stirred to angry life. He died in Johns Hopkins Medical Center in September 1938 (the same hospital where his father, W. O., had died sixteen years before).

But someone must own those twenty-five thousand copies that Scribner's sells each year.

Where do they hide out?

Below the Mason-Dixon line, mainly.

Save your maps of Asheville, boys, cause Wolfe may rise again!

He may, this wind-grieved ghost of a gargantuan and overgrown and sometimes overblown legend of how a famous writer ought to live and work and die, he may just rise again. There are some signs that he may.

This past April, sixteen million viewers watched the CBS movie based on *You Can't Go Home Again*. (It was not well done, but that it was done at all was a mark of new interest in Wolfe.) Sixteen million! In honor of the occasion, the nationally syndicated Sunday supplement *Parade* ran an item about Wolfe and Aline Bernstein as though the archaic pair of lovers were as trendy as Warren Beatty and Diane

Keaton. Thousands of others may have been educated by a biography of Aline Bernstein (*Aline*, by Carol Klein, Harper & Row), Wolfe's middle-aged Jewish muse.

And this coming October, students may again be carrying copies of *Look Homeward, Angel*. October will mark the fiftieth anniversary of the novel's publication. There'll be a lot more noise and fireworks about Wolfe. It was hearing about that imminent occasion that impelled me to reach for my own copy from the shelf where it had gathered dust. I started rereading, and rereading. Having just returned from this much neglected section of our literary landscape, I will now debrief myself in the hope of offering some intelligence on the subject for those who may want to try the tour.

Look Homeward, Angel is still in many ways Wolfe's finest book, with its carefully detailed story of the education from infancy to college age of the sensitive son of the stonecutter from Altamont, Old Catawba (read: North Carolina), making it perhaps the best book about growing up in America between *Huckleberry Finn* and *Catcher in the Rye*. What surprised me most upon rereading it was this ever-present facticity, its close and immediate attention to the details of everyday life. As I recollected it, through the mist of my own adolescence, the novel spoke in a vague, syrupy voice about every boy's dreams. But with its reproduction of Eugene's rooms and days, with its catalogs of furniture and food, its sometimes hysterical lyricism never veers far over the line into the purple. And its refrain—"O Lost, and by the wind grieved, ghost, come back again!"—established a rhythm for the bulky, immanent, and ubiquitous material world in which the keenly observant and deeply sensitive protagonist lives his youth.

At nine hundred pages, *Of Time and the River* weighs in as one of the longest novels in our literary history. The story of Eugene Gant after he leaves Altamont for the Harvard Drama School, New York, and Europe, it is one of the most flawed and imperfect pieces of work by a writer of genius that you can imagine. Wolfe worked on it for more than four years in Europe and in his apartment in "the huge and rusty jungle of South Brooklyn," as he calls it in *You Can't Go Home Again*. One night Perkins appeared at his door and told him to pack it up because he had completed it. Completed it? You heard me, Perkins told him. You have finished your novel. For the next six months of nights, Perkins and Wolfe edited the thousands of pages of narrative that waxed and waned as Wolfe cut and then, when asked by Perkins to write new pages to hemstitch sections together, produced tens of thousands of new words to replace the discarded scenes. (As Dreiser once wrote to his editor, Horace Liveright, who had cut 50,000 words from the manuscript of *An American Tragedy*, "What's 50,000 words between friends?")

Reading *Of Time and the River* is ultimately frustrating because of the uneven quality of its scenes, but it is never boring. Unless Whitman bores you and early Joyce bores you. But even if what Hemingway said to Perkins after he read the novel is true, 40 percent of it is still pure gold. For this reason, writers ought to study it. And readers ought to read it, slowly and swiftly by turns depending upon whether the scenes (such as the death of old man Gant, one of the most stupefying deathbed scenes in our literature) offer the distance from his subject that Wolfe managed in his first novel, or the oppressive sense of infantile egoism that swells the sections devoted to his education at Harvard.

The later novels are less chancy. The first few hundred pages of *The Web and the Rock* contain first-rate narrative about the young boyhood of George Webber on Libya Hill (the transmutation of Eugene Gant of Altamont), and it's always three o'clock in the afternoon in Libya Hill. Among other things there's a fascinating ghost story, and a fierce tale about the lynching of a berserk black sniper.

The "web" is Webber past, his family, his hometown, his origins. The "rock" is New York City, where he romances Esther Jack (modeled on Aline Bernstein). This famous love affair never came alive for me, it never did. But the chapter called "The Party at Jack's" is a masterfully satirical set piece that makes the city sections glow. The novel trails off as Webber sails for Europe, and a sojourn in Germany, having rejected Esther for some vague notion of the growth of his soul.

You Can't Go Home Again seems more of a piece than its predecessor, *Look Homeward, Angel*. Here Wolfe's lyrical prose and satirical eye seem more at home together than Webber and Esther (with whom he effects something of a reconciliation). In all the other novels the historical dimension becomes manifest in the memories of the Civil War past shared by the hometown characters. Here it is the boom mentality just prior to the Crash of '29 and the self-delusion leading to the rise of Nazism in Germany. This broadens the scope of what is, in essence, Wolfe's perennial fiction, the narrative of a young man setting out into the world to educate himself in its ways.

Webber's return to Germany during the Nazi period helps him to gain mastery of a way of seeing remarkably close to what John Fowles in *Daniel Martin* calls "wholesight." In Germany he puts his American past and the present danger in a similar perspective, and after

> such a night of seeing whole at last, day would come again, the cool glow of morning, the bronze gold of the kiefern trees, the still green pools of lucid water, the enchanted parks and gardens—but none of it was the same as it had been before.

Seeing things whole leads Webber to temper his original optimism about America with the historically inspired warning of the impending social danger of fascism. America will survive this, but in the final pages he announces his intimation of his own impending death.

> Something has spoken to me in the night, burning the tapers of the waning year; something has spoken in the night, and told me I shall die, I know not where. Saying:
>
> To lose the earth you know, for greater knowing; to lose the life you have, for greater life; to leave the friends you loved, for greater loving; to find a land more kind than home, more large than earth
>
> Whereon the pillars of this earth are founded, toward which the conscience of the world is tending—a wind is rising, and the rivers flow.

There's much here to move readers of a certain age, not eighteen but thirty-eight or older. *Look Homeward, Angel* is a young person's novel. *You Can't Go Home Again* speaks to all who find themselves, or remember finding themselves, passing like ships between the locks of some great canal from the blind optimism of young adulthood to the heroic pessimism of early middle age.

Asheville, North Carolina—In all this vast hummocky expanse of lawn that comprises the Riverside Cemetery, the only creatures stirring besides the birds and the squirrels are a photographer, two gravediggers far off down the gravel road—one sitting atop the high seat of a backhoe, the other directing him as he scoops out a grave deeper, deeper still—and me.

It is three o'clock on a warm afternoon, a kind of witching hour in Thomas Wolfe's fiction, and we're standing in front of his clearly marked grave.

At this time of day, Wolfe wrote in *The Web and the Rock*,

> we like the smell of old unopened rooms, old packing cases, tar, and the smell of grape wines on the cool side of the house. If we go out, we want to go out in green shade and gladed coolnesses, to lie down on our bellies beneath the maple trees and work our toes into the thick green grass.

But here we find none of the magic of three o'clock as Wolfe conjures it up out of the ordinary world of Asheville circa 1900. Here we stand in the graveyard of a quiet Southern mountain town feeling only an awareness of absence.

On the other side of Asheville, a town like many old places these days bisected by the cement-filled slash of an interstate highway, stands the "Old Kentucky Home," Mrs. Julia Wolfe's boardinghouse and the prototype of "Dixieland," the guest house in *Look Homeward, Angel* owned and operated by "Mrs. Eliza Gant," mother of the protagonist.

Guides who take us through the sprawling old white clapboard building point out the relics of "Tom's" life. They are paid for this by the State of North Carolina, which has maintained the house as a state and national landmark ever since Wolfe's surviving siblings became too enfeebled for the task.

"Here's a picture of Tom when he was three," a guide tells a tourist who is a graduate of the University of North Carolina at Chapel Hill. He signed up for the tour because he and "Tom" were fraternity brothers, he confides later. His statement baffles me for a moment, and then I realize that he means he and Wolfe belonged to the same Greek letter club. He and "Tom."

Tom! Tom! Tom!

The familiarity annoys me. Tom! I've just reread nearly three thousand pages of Wolfe and feel as though in doing so I've lost the sensitive, all-seeing, lyric-tongued alter ego that I had found when I first read him at sixteen.

"Here's where Tom and the family gathered around the piano on winter nights," our guide says, motioning for us to peer beyond the rope that prevents me from entering the front parlor just to the left of the hall. Leaning inside is like ducking under water—the air in the room, thick and antique, reeks of woolen carpet and antimacassar, the moisture of a thousand evenings of sweating boys standing around the music machine. Only the similarity between its odor and that of my own great-grandmother's house makes the room live a bit for me. Otherwise, despite its piano, easy chairs, tables, photographs, the cheap crystal lamp, the relies of turn-of-the-century parlor nights, it's empty.

Where are you, Wolfe? I ask in my mind. Not here, I have to reply to my own question.

I've visited other grave sites, and it was never like this.

In Old Bennington, Vermont, near the place that I called home for nearly a decade, Robert Frost lies buried behind the old First Church, the creamy marble slab that marks the space announcing: "I had a lovers quarrel with the world." Vermonters call him "Frost." I can't imagine anyone calling him "Robert," or telling me "Now here's the spot where Robert saw that boy who lived too far from town to play baseball swinging on those birches." The tone's all wrong. "Frost" suffices.

The kitchen where Mrs. Wolfe prepared all of the meals for the boarders, sometimes numbering in the dozens, offers no solace for my loneliness. It has all the warmth of an embalming room in a mortuary. The small bed-site off to one side where the mistress of this domain spent her nights so that bright and early she could begin to cook breakfast and set the black servants to boiling the sheets, that too remains palpably empty, despite the guide's assurance that all of the articles within view—a pair of spectacles on the night table alongside the guest register—are those that Mrs. Wolfe might well have kept at her bedside.

And next we see the dining room, where sparsely but carefully appointed places give the illusion of what passed for elegance among the widows and shop clerks, incapacitated bookkeepers and warehouse men who came to Asheville for their health—for the airs—sometimes to heal a lung, sometimes simply for the rest—the elegance of the captain's table on a coal barge or a river scow.

"Mrs. Wolfe cooked and cleaned for the guests all by herself," says our assiduous guide. "The children had to take care of themselves and each other."

Then we're led into a room that passes for a study, moldering editions of long-forgotten novels lining the shelves. In a corner stands a table holding W. O. Wolfe's stone-cutting tools. Light from the southern exposure illuminates the display with an intensity that nothing else on the ground floor deserves.

W. O., the novelist's father, did not fully approve of his wife's speculation in houses and land. When he settled in Asheville and married Julia, he bought the house on Woodfin Street where all of their children were born. Though Mrs. Wolfe soon moved herself, and those children who cared to stay with her, into the boardinghouse that she invested in across the road, the stonecutter did not leave the Woodfin residence except to take his meals with his family until he became so ill with cancer of the prostate that he could no longer care for himself.

Those tools on the side table glowing in the light mark his absence far more eloquently than the gravestone next to his son's in the Riverside Cemetery. They alert the passerby to the irony that the man who had refused to call the "Old Kentucky Home" his residence now lives here in the sign of his tools. The father is present, but where is the son?

On the second floor, where nearly two dozen rooms reveal themselves to the interested tourist, the stonecutter's last bedroom glows redolent with light that shows off the deathbed. Thomas Wolfe was at Harvard Drama School studying in George Pierce Baker's famous playwriting seminar when he heard the news that his father, after several miraculous remissions, was finally dying. He arrived in Asheville too late to see the man one more time. But the scene in *Of Time and the River* that he conjures up from eyewitness accounts of family members and his own febrile imagination stands as one of the most powerful and grotesque set pieces in American literature, with the old man bleeding his life away from all of his orifices while dreaming of reconciliation with his loved ones, nature, and the past.

There are a number of beds that speak of life on this second floor. The bed where Mrs. Wolfe gave birth to "Tom" was moved over from the other residence and installed here for public viewing. I press my hand on it and it sags nearly to the floor, like the belly of an old worn-out sow. On the upstairs sunporch, screened in for summer pleasures, there is the bed where Eugene Gant, the young protagonist in *Look Homeward, Angel*, supposedly consummated his affair with Laura James after crawling out in the middle of the night on the ledge opposite the window, leaping onto her ledge, and climbing in.

Wolfe, where are you?

Not here. The bed of adolescent joy holds the noon sunlight the way a basin holds water, but the actors remain absent.

There are more death beds here than life beds. Besides old man Wolfe's, there is the bed where Ben, one of Wolfe's older brothers, died of the flu in 1918.

O Lost, and by the wind grieved, ghost, come back again!

Ben's death gives birth to Wolfe's famous lyrical refrain in *Look Homeward, Angel*, in which he is a character with his own name. At the novel's end, Ben's ghost appears to charge his brother with poetic labor. Ben's spare, unpoetical bed stands in a room on the northeast side of the second floor no larger than a long, wide closet. No direct sunlight ignites it in our eyes.

Come back again?

The bed remains empty, the tiny room remains empty, the air gives back nothing but staleness and the sound of my own breathing.

Wolfe himself despised this house, preferring his father's residence across the road (where since 1956 a YMCA has stood on the site of his birthplace). He felt neglected here, houseless. The children had to move from bed to bed, room to room, depending upon the needs of the boarders.

In *Look Homeward, Angel*, he transcribed this aversion into Eugene Gant's

> silent horror of selling for money the bread of one's table, the shelter of one's walls, to the guest, the stranger, the unknown friend from out the world; to the sick, the weary, the lonely, the broken, the knave, the harlot, and the fool.

He despised even the odor of the place, which after his mother added on a new section reeked of "raw wood, cheap varnish, flimsy rough plastering." Ironic then that one room upstairs has been set aside to hold the remains of Wolfe's Brooklyn apartment—a desk atop which sits an old Remington typewriter, with photographs of Maxwell Perkins and of Aline Bernstein. As if Wolfe, who scribbled furiously into the nights of Brooklyn and then turned his mounds of handwritten pages to a harried typist, would have approved of that machine as a tombstone! Or of the photographs! Wolfe loved both of these people passionately—to such an extent that you can almost feel the room tremble with the quaking of his wild fury when he broke with each of them. Beneath a table lies an old battered leather suitcase still filled with Wolfe's Brooklyn belongings, the guide tells us. Never been opened. The moths tour this part of the house.

Some clothes hang for viewing, an enormous overcoat, a battered hat fit for a giant, relics that gather in the light and wait patiently for their owner to return. But to look at them closely gives you the idea that Wolfe shed them long, long ago, like a snake's skin or a cocoon. He'll never be back to claim them. He died just short of early middle age, and never wrote enough in his mature style to convince those who caretake his memory that he was ever anything else but a boy.

Almost within spitting distance from the porch of the Old Kentucky Home stands the Inn at the Thomas Wolfe Plaza, a many-storied motel that contains shops, restaurants. Look Innward, Angel! The Thomas Wolfe Memorial Plaza! For a town that Wolfe depicted in all its moral blindness and hillbilly rapaciousness in the "Boom Town" chapter of *You Can't Go Home Again*, the entrepreneurs of Asheville show a lot of steely nerve in naming this shopping-center complex after its ignored, and then reviled, and (once dead) most favored son. If only Aaron Burr had been born here, or Billy the Kid, or Dillinger, what a test of the mettle of Asheville boosterism that would have been! Do they serve "Look Homeward, Angel-food Cake" at local restaurants?

And would he who couldn't go home again, the Wolfe always questing for the fabled door that would open onto the life of fullness and pleasure, family, friends, lovers all intact and within the single circle of his mind and affection, would he be given a room at the Inn on the Thomas Wolfe Plaza? Would there be a bed large enough for Tom?

9

Stories of Deep Delight

Tell me a story.
In this century, and moment of mania.
Tell me a story.
Make it a story of great distances, and starlight.
The name of the story will be Time.
But you must not pronounce its name.
Tell me a story of deep delight.

Audubon: A Vision

At the age of seventy-six, Robert Penn Warren has a great deal to smile about. In his long and productive career as a poet, novelist, essayist, critic, and teacher, he has published ten novels, several volumes of short stories, more than a dozen books of verse, several collections of essays, and some of the most important humanistic pedagogical texts of the twentieth century. If he were a general, he'd have to strain to keep from tipping floorward—he'd have so many medals.

Despite all his books and honors, the Kentucky-born, Tennessee-educated master is still known best for his creation of Willie Stark, the governor of an unnamed Southern state in the Pulitzer Prize–winning novel *All the King's Men*. From the start, Warren's third novel, published in 1946, tolled a loud bell in modern American culture. Its broad allusions to the facts and legend of the life (and death) of one of the most intriguing politicians of the century, Huey Long of Louisiana, occasioned much of the early stir and helped turn the book into a best-seller. Willie Stark, like Huey Long, was a messiah in the eyes of the poor, from whom he came; an oppressor in the eyes of the rich, whose economic and political rule he overthrew; and a homegrown Mussolini in the eyes of the press and citizens interested in good government. And Stark, like Long, dies at the hand of an assassin, gunned down, as

Warren has described the actual politician's death, "in the brand-new skyscraper capital which he had built to his greater glory."

Warren has pointed out on a number of occasions that his acquaintance with Huey Long was slight. He saw him in person only twice: once when Long crashed a crowded banquet in honor of the founding of Louisiana State University and made an impromptu speech to the surprised diners, and again as he passed in a motorcade. But the life of Warren's novel and the life and times of Huey Long became from the start almost mythologically intertwined. Just as the events of Long's career gave power to the book, the novel has kept alive the memory of the internationally famous (and infamous) political leader in a period when our leaders tend to be flamboyant only in private.

In 1950 came Robert Rossen's film of the book, with the screenplay by the novelist himself (for which he later won a prize). The film starred Broderick Crawford as Willie Stark, Mercedes McCambridge as his fiery press secretary and mistress, John Ireland as Jack Burden, the journalist and would-be historian through whose eyes we view the action, and John Derek as Stark's handsome football-hurling, hard-driving, hard-drinking young Casanova of a son. The movie won a number of awards, including an Oscar for Crawford, and has become a classic of American cinema.

Since the mid-forties, the paperback edition of *All the King's Men* has gone through nearly fifty printings, selling millions of copies. In addition to its popular and monetary success, however, the novel stands out as perhaps the single most intriguing and discussed production in Warren's varied and successful career. In the eyes of a number of literary critics and those with an abiding interest in the political imagination of our culture, it remains his finest and most enduring creation. Although from time to time some critics may snipe at it—as did Roger Sale in an essay in the early sixties and Richard King in his book on Southern culture, *A Southern Renaissance, 1930–1955*—its place in the American literary canon seems unquestionable. As Robert Alter, a literary critic who also teaches at the University of California, wrote last year in the *New York Times Book Review*, the novel must be seen as the only important political novel of this century. Serious students of literature know that it is only the second major political novel to appear in our culture (after Henry Adams's nineteenth-century *Democracy*) that remains worth rereading.

From the opening passages, one knows in moments that the novel's language and sense of place as much as its depiction of the political life of a certain time and region make it a classic.

Mason City

To get there you follow Highway 58, going northeast out of the city, and it is a good highway and new. Or was new, that day we went up it. You look up the highway, and it is straight for miles, coming at you, with the black line down the center coming at and at you, black and slick and tarry shining against the white of the slab, and the heat dazzles up from the white slab so that only the black line is clear, coming at you with the whine of the tires. . . . Way off ahead of you, at the horizon where the cotton fields are blurred into the light, the slab will glitter and gleam like water, as though the road were flooded. You'll go whipping toward it, but it will always be ahead of you, that bright, flooded place, like a mirage. You'll go past the little white metal squares set on metal rods, with the skull and crossbones on them to mark the spot. For this is the country where the age of the internal combustion engine has come into its own. Where every boy is Barney Oldfield, and the girls wear organdy and batiste and eyelet embroidery and no panties on account of the climate and have smooth little faces to break your heart and when the wind of the car's speed lifts up their hair at the temples you see the sweet little beads of perspiration nestling there, and they sit low in the seat with their little spines crooked and their bent knees high toward the dashboard and not too close together for the cool, if you could call it that, from the hood ventilator.

Jack Burden, the novel's narrator, opens the story with a view of the territory of mirage, illusion, heroism, love, and great (though ultimately practical) virtue through which we will travel as he tells of the life and death of Willie Stark, whose rise and fall become so bound up with his own. Stark, a backwoods lawyer, rides to the governorship on the shoulders of the down-and-out rednecks for whom he seems to speak. With some irony, he gives a speech and calls his own rise "a funny story . . . about a hick . . . about a red-neck" like those in the crowd before him. This hick grew up, Stark goes on to say,

> like any other mother's son on the dirt roads and gully washes of a north-state farm. He knew all about being a hick. He knew what it was to get up before day and get cow dung between his toes and feed and slop and milk before breakfast so he could set off by sunup to walk six miles to a one-room, slab-sided school-house. . . . Oh, he knew what it was like to be a hick, summer and winter. . . . He didn't start out thinking about other hicks and how he was going to do wonderful things for them. He started out thinking about number one, but something came to him on the way. How he could not do something for himself and not for other folks or for himself without the help of other folks. It was going to be all together or none.

Warren himself on a number of occasions has spoken about the inspiriting germ of the novel as "Louisiana—that 'Banana Republic,' as I think Carleton Beals called it—at the time when Huey Long held it as his fief." Less well known is that *All the King's Men* was first created as a play, which Warren began in Italy in 1939 and later rewrote with the help of Francis Fergusson, a drama critic and director, in Bennington, Vermont, in the summer of 1942. It was first produced with the help of the critic Eric Bentley at the University of Minnesota—"a tight play about a dictator," as Warren has described it, about the Huey Long figure and

> the people around him. Now, the theory of that play was that the dictator, the man of power, is powerful only because he fulfills the blanknesses and needs of people around him. His power is an index to the weaknesses of others. In other words, his power lies in the defects of others rather than a thing exist-

ing in itself, and so he fulfills the needs of people around him. The idea that gradually developed in the course of writing the play was the contrast between the "hero" as a person and the "hero" as a reflex of history. . . . But this notion did not work in this little tight play . . . my dissatisfaction with it led a bit to the novel, to get some sense of the world around the man—the man as *seen* rather than the man as presented.

An unnamed reporter who happens to be present in the assassination scene of the play's first version becomes Jack Burden; a fugitive from the state's upper classes, the reporter and would-be historian who finds himself taking on power and new life in the presence of the dictatorial Stark. In Burden's life, in that of his childhood sweetheart, Anne Stanton, in the life of her physician brother, Adam, in the lives of Judge Stanton and the millions of individuals who make up the state's population, we see unfolding the redneck relationship between the personal miseries and the power of the hero who becomes the ruler of a Southern political empire.

By virtue of its narrative pace, its insight into character, and its broad and deeply serious depiction of the social fabric of that "Banana Republic" in the days of terrifying and wonderful events, *All the King's Men* endures as much more than a momentary swipe at understanding life in an important place at an important time. But above all, the masterly tension between Jack Burden's educated, necromantic rhetoric—a voice that in many ways approximates Warren's own—and Stark's plain—stark—and brutal rise to power gives the novel its claim on permanence. And while the local habitation is Louisiana and the name is Long, as the novel unfolds it speaks to political situations as old as Julius Caesar's and as timely as the rise of modern fascism. No better book about the ambivalence we feel toward public heroes and villains (and they for us) and the links between American crowds and individuals, between private neurosis and public history, has been produced in this century. It's a good bet that if Warren had not written it, none of his other estimable achievements would have won him the Presidential Medal of Freedom, the highest award made to a citizen of this country, which

Jimmy Carter bestowed upon him in a White House Rose Garden ceremony.

But when you catch Warren on a workday, as I did one July morning in Vermont, there's none of the pomp and circumstance of the Rose Garden about him. He's "Red" Warren, a man whose thick Middle Tennessee gargle rumbles over words like a coal truck over Appalachian highways. Time has gouged his face the way that fierce rains erode the western hills, and the once bright mop of hair—"as red as a termater," as he has a character in a poem describe it, hair that was once as thick as the pelt of a rhesus monkey, as he told an interviewer—has thinned out to mere wisps of its former self. One of his eyes seems slightly askew, the other watery. To see him dressed in a turtleneck sweater and old trousers, you might take him for a stockbroker or a big farmer who has retired to live on his earnings. The Mercedes parked beneath the screened-in porch hints, at least, of rewards for hard labor.

Warren grew up in Todd County, Kentucky. His adolescent dream was to attend Annapolis and become a naval officer, but the loss of an eye in a family mishap killed that hope. The man whom novelist William Styron has described as having the "seamed and craggy" face and the "salty presence" of an admiral swims every summer morning in the pond fed by the noisy stream behind the house (in the winter he runs instead). But it's drizzly today and clouds hug the mountains, so Warren skips his swim and talks about the rest of his regular schedule: work until one or two in the afternoon, then a break for a makeshift lunch with his wife, Eleanor Clark (who writes all morning in an old hunter's cabin across the road from the main house), and a nap following lunch. Nights in the Warren house, summer and winter, when they don't include guests for dinner, usually find the poet engaging in good old-fashioned reading out loud from the classics of Western culture, a practice he initiated when Clark's eyesight began to trouble her. (She has written about this problem brilliantly in her memoir *Eyes, Etc.*)

"The only poet my wife doesn't allow me to read to her aloud is Dante," Warren says as we begin talking on the porch. "She says my accent ruins it for her."

It does take a while to become accustomed to Warren's accent if you have a Yankee ear. You must listen hard and make an effort to catch hold, like reaching out for the brass ring on a merry-go-round. Although Warren hasn't lived in the South for more than forty years, the culture that has given us some of our most terrifying historical moments and our greatest writers lives in every vowel and elision that emerges from his throat. He is a thoughtful speaker, with an eloquence and intensity that grow out of intelligence as much as diction. He eschews grand terminology and highfalutin language, smacking home his points with the certainty and skill of a leadoff hitter rather than a man whose talents run either to the grand slam or the strikeout.

Warren is probably one of the most lauded writers in American history. The living room at the house in Fairfield, Connecticut, where he and his wife have lived since the early sixties and where they have raised their two children, Rosanna and Gabriel, has been described by a friend as "a trophy room" of literature. He is also one of the most interviewed writers.

Last year Random House published *Robert Penn Warren Talking*, a collection of eighteen interviews conducted over the past thirty years (by such people as Edwin Newman, Bill Moyers, Benjamin Demott, and Dick Cavett) and edited by two English teachers. On the porch this morning in Vermont, Warren strikes at a theme that becomes one of the main threads of social commentary running through that book of interviews—his "sadness about America" and the problems of preserving democracy in a culture that has become increasingly dependent upon technology.

"Students don't write well anymore," he says. "They don't know how to read the way they need to and a lot of them would rather watch television than pick up a novel—and that way lies madness. Maybe in the short run that keeps them off the streets and out of demonstrations, and it certainly sells television sets, but over a long period of time it chips away at the masonry that holds us all together as a culture. Or makes us a different kind of culture. Not that kind that I grew up in love with."

He talks a little about growing up in Guthrie, Kentucky, a town of twelve hundred that is tobacco-spitting distance from the Tennessee line, about forty miles north of Nashville. He reminisces about his friendship with the late Kent Greenfield, who lived across the street from the Warren family's small stucco house at Third and Locust and went on to pitch for the New York Giants. Greenfield was a hunter. Warren learned taxidermy. The two of them roamed the fields and woods outside Guthrie on many a pleasant foray. Warren's father, a small-town banker, was a secret poet, and both he and his wife, Mary Penn (whose ancestors had come over from Virginia the century before to settle in the rich tobacco and grain lands of the upper South), encouraged their children's education in literature.

But Warren's real tutorial began on a tobacco farm near Cerulean Springs, west of Guthrie, that was owned by his maternal grandfather, Gabriel Penn, who was nearly seventy at the time of Warren's birth in 1905. As Warren has described it in his meditation on the paradoxes of American history, *Jefferson Davis Gets His Citizenship Back*, he spent a great deal of his time as a boy on that farm,

> sitting tailor-fashion on the unkempt lawn, looking up at the old man, and then beyond him, at the whitewashed board fence, and then at the woods coming down almost to the fence. . . . I would be waiting for the old man to talk, or even sing, in his old, cracked voice, one of the few songs that might rise from his silence, sung only for himself. "We'll Gather in the Cane-brake and Hunt the Buffalo . . ." In spite of the obvious knowledge that I would grow up, I had the sweet-sad feeling that the world had already happened, that history had come to an end—though life did go on, and people lived, died, went broke.

Aside from the stories he told the boy about the Civil War—he had seen action at Shiloh—Gabriel Penn talked about Guthrie in the old days, when the tobacco wars raged between the farmers who wanted a good price for their prime leaf and the companies that conspired to keep the market price down. In addition to the tales he told from firsthand knowledge, Penn drew on his reading in European military history, Egyptian history, Romantic poetry, and other matters.

"He was an inveterate reader," Warren says, staring off into the morning mist. A logging truck whines past the driveway on its way up the dirt road toward the hamlet of West Wardsboro, and the poet listens intently, as though he might be waiting for the sound of a gray-coated cavalry unit tromping past his house.

"You've written," I said, "that you mistook that phrase about his reading when you first heard it as—"

"'*Confederate* reader'! That's right. Well, he was a Confederate reader, too, wasn't he? And I suppose I am, too." He clears his throat with a laugh and cocks his head toward the door that leads to the kitchen, where Eleanor Clark is still finishing her breakfast. "Now my wife and her family, they are all *Yankee* readers through and through."

Warren then plunges into a long narrative about the years when he began his formal education, first in the Guthrie high school and then at nearby Clarksville, just across the Tennessee border. He excelled in all his subjects as well as enjoying drawing lessons from a nun from a Nashville Catholic school who took him to the zoo and told him to sketch the animals—"while she fell asleep under a tree and snored like a horse," he adds with a chuckle.

He was fifteen when his dream of attending the Naval Academy collapsed. His older brother, Thomas, tossed a stone over a hedge and it put out Warren's right eye. The next year he entered Vanderbilt, signing up as an engineering major. Almost immediately upon taking his first English class, he changed his view of himself and changed his vocation.

His instructor in freshman English was John Crowe Ransom, "the first real live poet in pants and vest" that Warren had ever seen. Ransom soon persuaded him to give up thoughts of engineering for the serious study of literature. Warren joined the Blue Pencil, a writing club for freshmen and sophomores. By the second half of his freshman year, he was enrolled, at Ransom's suggestion, in an advanced writing course. (In another interview, Warren has described how he read Ransom's first book of poems "and discovered that he was making poetry out of a world I knew; it came home to me.")

Vanderbilt became, after Guthrie and the Penn farm, another home to him. Among the undergraduates a few years his senior, he made friends such as Allen Tate, and among the junior professors, Ransom and some of the others who gathered around the "strange Jew" named Sidney Mttron Hirsch for discussions of literature and philosophy in a group that came to be called the Fugitives, after the title of their poetry journal, *The Fugitive*.

Warren hesitates to impute the importance to this group that literary historians readily apply. It was, as one commentator has explained, "the most talented cohesive group of creative writers America produced since the Transcendentalists." Moreover, the group, if a bit philosophically retrograde, stands out as the only serious twentieth-century alliance of Americans that produced a manifesto rivaling in intellectual force and aesthetic value the documents of European surrealism. In the face of the growing industrialization of the South, these writers and critics, almost all of them associated with Vanderbilt, expressed their commitment to the traditional Southern agrarian way of life.

But for the young Warren, it was mostly a poetry club where "we read each other's poems and argued poetry . . . it was a good time to be there. Ransom was writing his best poems then, and Tate was just finding himself. I myself was 17 and I said, 'This is what I'm going to do.'" Warren helped organize the Verse Guild, a group within the undergraduate writing club devoted to poetry, and he published five of his poems in "Driftwood Flames," a small pamphlet the group produced in 1923, and more verse in *The Fugitive* in June of that year.

By the time he left Vanderbilt (graduating summa cum laude and with the Founder's Medal for scholarship) in the summer of 1925, Warren was well on his way toward a serious career in academia. He enrolled in the master's program in English at Berkeley and then went on to a doctoral program at Yale. Aside from his formal studies in poetry, he was working on a biography of the abolitionist John Brown, which he published—with the help of Allen Tate—while at Yale. *John Brown: The Making of a Martyr* appeared in 1929, while Warren, as a Rhodes scholar, was working on a B.Litt. at Oxford. It was, he recalls with hindsight, "a step toward fiction."

At Oxford, Warren was supposed to be working on his doctoral dissertation in poetry, but other writing assignments intervened. At the invitation of Paul Rosenfield, who was editing a volume of the *American Caravan* anthology along with Van Wyck Brooks and Lewis Mumford, Warren produced a novella, "Prime Leaf," based on stories he had heard about Todd County life during the tobacco wars. He also wrote an essay, "The Briar Patch," as his contribution to *I'll Take My Stand: The South and the Agrarian Tradition*. When it appeared in 1930 it was clear that the twelve contributors to the volume, all members of the Fugitives, saw poetry as the leading edge of an ideology that encouraged a return to a way of life already well lost in most other sections of the country.

Other interviewers, particularly his old friend Ralph Ellison—author of the definitive novel of the American black experience, *Invisible Man*—have asked Warren to talk about the view of race relations set forth in "The Briar Patch." Warren stands up and stalks about the porch, repeating, as he has said elsewhere, that he hasn't read the piece in fifty years now. He was, he has said, uncomfortable writing it: it remains a rationalization of and apology for the segregation of the races that at the time seemed to be inevitable not only in the South but in the rest of the country as well.

That embarrassing essay of his youth may be one of the few things Warren has not read and reread in the past half century. His capacity for literary study has been as enormous as his own production of poetry, fiction, and essays. And even if he had not written some of the most important and moving fiction and poetry in this century, he would have remained one of the most influential critics in our history. Later that morning, on a drive through the woods to the West Wardsboro Post Office, he talks about contemporaries he reads for pleasure—"not a great deal of fiction these days, though I admire Styron and Welty, Malamud, and young writers like Cormac McCarthy and John Yount, Michael Malone, a few others—but mostly I read poetry. I receive many, many volumes of poetry, and I try to dip into each book and read at least as far as I need to so I can get some sense of what the poet is doing." Among these, he mentions established authors such as James Merrill and John Ashbery and younger poets like Dave Smith and Robert Pinsky. The political and economic news of the past few years has made him feel that "certain sadness about America," but the writers he admires, he says, "are struggling against this."

All it takes for Warren to stiffen his American lip and say out loud that we do have some advantages here is to arrive at the post office and find a registered letter from the Bulgarian government (apparently not the first), asking him to appear at a ceremony in Eastern Europe. One of the most popular U.S. writers in the Soviet Union and its neighboring countries, Warren laments the way some writers have allowed themselves to be used by totalitarian nations in exchange for honors and medals. He takes his stand and draws the line against this.

But on the drive back into the woods, he just as quickly talks about his role in the committee of world-famous authors (including Malamud, Styron, and Michener) who are about to lodge a protest with the U.S. Justice Department on behalf of former CIA agent Frank Snepp, whom a recent court ruling separated from his earnings on a book about the CIA. And we're talking about sadness again, and censorship on both sides of the world. About the kind of "interpretation" of *All the King's Men* practiced in the USSR.

"It would be terribly hard," he says, "to have to live under that kind of government—a dictatorship that began with promises of good works for the people—it *is* terribly hard for a writer, a poet, anyone who needs freedom of the imagination. When I taught at LSU in the late thirties, I saw how people could get caught up in the ideas, the promises, of someone like Huey Long, who at the beginning of his career didn't sound so bad to some folks. Later in Italy I worked on a play that eventually became the novel of *All the King's Men*, that has Talus, a dictator who made me think of Mussolini. The first version of the play didn't pay much attention to the Jack Burden character—in fact, he was there only as a bystander, an onlooker at the end, at the murder. Later on, in other versions, he became just as important as the Talus–Willie Stark character."

We reach the turnoff for the logging road that leads to the Warren property and the car slows to a halt. I offer to get the mail, but the poet demurs, slides out of his seat, and lopes across the road in the drizzle to the rural delivery box at the corner. There's a determination and at the same time a certain jauntiness to his run that one would be hard put to find in one's friends over forty; at seventy-six Warren jogs for the mail like a man who loves letters and chilly summer rain.

We return to the house and head directly for the old wooden work shed at the side of the main building that has a screened-in room built directly over the stream that feeds his pond. Just beyond the entrance, the floor is awash with books, files, clippings, and old magazines; in the work area itself, discarded manuscript pages cover the floor, in some places ankle-deep.

As the drizzle outside turns to a steady downpour, we huddle around Warren's desk. He snatches up a black notebook stuffed with loose typescript and chants part of a poem in progress, a long narrative about the 1877 battle in Montana between the Nez Percé tribe led by Chief Joseph and the U.S. Cavalry under General O. O. Howard (Jefferson Davis's jailer at the end of the Civil War, about whom Warren had written in his recent meditation on Davis's life):

> If you were the eyes of the Eagle of
> eagles.
> And from the great height looked
> down on the bruised
> Thump-hump of the Bear Paw
> Mountains, then South
> You'd see a tangle of canyons and
> coulee
> Where water, long brack, had sliced
> at the high plain,
> And then the plains of great grass
> swales curried
> By wind-comb, or lying gray-green in
> its slickness
> Of windless sunlight, or worn down
> by
> The buffalo hoof or tooth-edge to
> earth's

Inner redness, and dust-devils rising
  in idle
Swirl, or the streaked poison of
Alkali flats, the whiteness marked
By the black standing stakes of
  poplar long dead.

"That's the scene, Montana," Warren says, pointing to the page of manuscript as though it were a map. It is a map of sorts, with its typed-over lines, crossed-out words, insertions, incisions, revisions, and notations in several kinds of ink and pencil, a map of Warren's method of composition.

As he explains, all his life, Warren has been "trying to be a writer." Each morning when he goes to his desk that's all he's been "trying" to do, and whether the road takes him one month to poetry and three years later to fiction doesn't matter, he explains. And all of the theory he knows and has promulgated as one of the founders of the "close reading" school of interpretation (in his textbooks with Brooks) has, he asserts, "no relation to composition except at the point of revision." He is interested primarily in the way that literature conveys a philo-sophical view of life, not in philosophical views *about* literature.

Striking a theme that runs throughout *Robert Penn Warren Talk-ing*, Warren says that poetry for him isn't working with a given but rather "toward the given, saying the unsayable, and steadily asking, 'What do I really feel about this?'" For him the process of writing is everything because it is "a process of trying to find out what the writer thinks. He is not working deductively from a highly articulated image, a careful scheme of values; he is trying to find the values, find the ideas, by a process of trial and error. . . . Life is a process of trial and error about our own values." And writing? A "continuing experiment with values."

Poetry and fiction are alike for Warren in that they are problems that the writer must solve. You find yourself writing, he says, a "story or poem that has some meaning that you haven't solved in it, that you haven't quite laid hands on. So your writing—it is a way of understanding it, what its meaning, the potential meaning, is. And the story that you understand perfectly, you don't write. You know what the meaning is; there's nothing there to nag your mind about it. A story that's for you is the one that you have to work to understand." So writing for Warren has always been an act of "exploration and interpretation . . . not just stenographic work."

He closes the notebook and clears his throat.

"Let me give you an example. The poem I wrote called *Audubon*. I'd been thinking about it for a long time, made a lot of false starts at it. And then one day I was helping my wife make the bed—that's right, I'm trying hard to change my old ways—when a line came into my mind. 'Was not the lost dauphin.' And right away I understood that method I had to use to approach the subject of Audubon, something that had eluded me for years. Angle shots! I'd come in on him as a subject by a series of angle shots, not just dead on." He slices his hand through the air. "I'd been exploring that problem in my mind for years, not thinking about it, but it was there, and then in that odd moment it just came upon me, the answer to my problem."

Recalling the Chief Joseph poem, I asked him, "What's the 'exploration' part for you in the long poem? What's the problem you're trying to solve in it? Do you sense any affinities between the embattled Nez Percé and the lost cause of the Old South?"

"Well, that might be there. But I can't say yet for sure—not until I finish it," Warren says, giving the notebook a good thump. "I am planning to go back to Montana to the site where Chief Joseph fought the final battle. He beat the U.S. Cavalry six times before they defeated him, and he only had a hundred and seventy-six warriors. But he had faith. He said, 'The Great Father tells a man how to defend himself.'" Warren pauses and listens to the rain. "'The Great Father tells a man how to defend himself.' Hell, the Great Father must have given him good instructions because right until the end he held off those soldiers, and then his people even had to carry their ponies into the mountains along with the sick women and children."

He picks up the notebook again, turns to the opening page, and begins to read. But Eleanor Clark's call from the main house informs us that lunch is ready. "It's slim pickins around here at lunchtime," Warren says, "because we both work right up to the wire." But Clark has put together a tasty and meaty soup.

She asks about the morning mail, and he informs her about the invitation from the Bulgarians. He talks a little about the "shadowy autobiographical" aspect of the new collection of poems but at the same time eschews any desire to have anyone write his biography.

"What's worth anything is all there in the books," he says.

"Tell that to the press," says Clark, passing around some cookies. "A writer is red meat to them."

"Does red hair count as red meat?" Warren asks, sipping tomato juice along with cookies.

We talk more about red men, about stories from the past that haunt their way into present creations, his new poem.

"I'm stuck on it, I know," he says. "But I hope that if I walk across that battleground I may stir myself into the ending. It just needs an ending. Maybe *that's* the ending! Me walking across the battlefield."

It's a compelling image: the septuagenarian Southern poet and novelist striding across the northern Montana battlefield where the heroic Nez Percé took their last stand against the encroaching cavalry, a man in quest of an ending for the latest story he wants to tell us about our country and ourselves.

10

Of Steinbeck and Salinas

There is that quality of light—as if some unknown hand had pried open the sky like a lid and revealed the brighter, almost translucent blue behind the óceanic tincture visible for miles before you actually see the sea—and the salt scent that flavors the air already pungent with the odors of fecund valley soil. Whether on first arriving here or on homecomings, after absences brief or long, the trip down the Pacific Coast road toward the Salinas Valley heightens the senses of both natives and strangers.

In this special locale, where natural science explains as much about the world as philosophy does (and where the two disciplines often become intertwined), one of our century's most popular and lauded—and controversial—writers, Nobel Prize winner John Steinbeck, was born, a little more than eighty years ago. Past dry, brown hills thick with live oaks, through field after field of lettuce and artichokes, I'm heading on a fine California autumn day toward Salinas, the town that gave Steinbeck a life and a subject, my own mind crammed full of the facts of his career and the stories and scenes and images from his substantial body of work.

A half century ago, Steinbeck published his first few books of fiction: *Cup of Gold*, based on the life of buccaneer Henry Morgan; *The*

Pastures of Heaven, a series of linked stories about life in a valley quite similar to his own native grounds; and *To a God Unknown*, a strange (because of its devotion to a vision we can only call pantheistic) and powerful early novel. As Jackson Benson, Steinbeck's official biographer, makes clear in the mammoth new volume *The True Adventures of John Steinbeck, Writer*, published this month by Viking Press, few American writers with as much pretension to greatness as Steinbeck received as much popular success and critical vilification.

Over the years, more than twenty million copies of his novels have sold in Bantam paperback editions alone, and millions more have been reprinted in the more recent Penguin paperback series, making Steinbeck perhaps the single most widely read North American writer in this century—more than Faulkner, more than Hemingway, the two novelists whom he always held above and ahead of himself, like true north. And of those readers who ingested the best of Steinbeck as students and remember, say, the experience of reading *The Grapes of Wrath* as an encounter as monumental as reading *Moby Dick*, even the most critical can go back on this occasion and read through the body of Steinbeck's work and find that if he is, at his worst (in some of the later books), exceedingly mawkish and sentimental and downright awful and deserving of the harshest criticism, he is, also, in the books from his middle period, in *Cannery Row* and *In Dubious Battle* and *The Grapes of Wrath* and *Of Mice and Men*, in the screenplay *Viva Zapata!* and in *East of Eden*, astonishingly good, even great, and worthy of our best time and attention.

Steinbeck's own story—the life that Jackson Benson so carefully chronicles and, with less success, evaluates—is itself sometimes astonishingly mawkish, sometimes sentimental, and upon occasion exceedingly good. Born in 1902, the young John Steinbeck, big-boned, homely, the son of second-generation German and Irish stock, stood out from the crowd of middle-class and farmers' children. Looking back on his childhood from the point of view of a young writer with all language and time at his beckoning, Steinbeck recalled how the land stood out for him: "I remember my childhood names for grasses and secret flowers," he begins in *East of Eden* in the plain, elegiac voice with which he tells much of that problematical but intriguing saga of the Valley's settlement.

Although he grew up in a pleasant, Victorian-style house in the middle of Salinas (a market center for the lush and productive Northern California valley), the young Steinbeck never found himself far from the fields and mountains that dreamy Westerners love to ramble in. He also never found himself far from his books, from the romances and pirate stories and Arthurian legends that he fed on during his early years, or from the great narratives of Western literature that he encountered in high school and in his truculent years at Stanford and afterward. Out of his fanciful thoughts about nature and literature came the first stories, clumsy fiction that he sent out under a pen name, without a return address, to the editors of magazines he admired. Later, after work in a local sugar refinery and in the fields, after sojourns in San Francisco, diffident years at Stanford (where chemistry and marine biology appealed to him as much as poetry), and a stint in New York City as a journalist and then a laborer, he composed intense works of fiction based on the lives of those among whom he had lived. Unlike Thomas Wolfe, whose sensibility otherwise resembles Steinbeck's, the native son of the Salinas Valley would go home after his travels, find there the subjects of his best passions as a writer, and remain a long while.

Tortilla Flat, his fourth book (published in 1935), extricated him from the obscurity that had enveloped him while he lived and wrote in a small house in Monterey which belonged to his parents. Local people began to take notice of the gangly, boisterous bohemian who caroused with Ed Ricketts, owner of the marine biological laboratory run on a shoestring in the center of the canning district. But it wasn't until the publication of his next novel, *In Dubious Battle*, in 1936, the lean, well-plotted story of a fruit pickers' strike in which two Communist labor leaders play the predominant parts, that the middle-class inhabitants of his native Salinas came to regard Steinbeck as a rabble-rouser. By the time *The Grapes of Wrath*, his longest and best-known creation, appeared in the spring of 1939, Steinbeck's first marriage was coming undone, his reputation as a writer as well as a "radical" was growing nationwide, and he had moved to Los Gatos, on the other side of the Santa Cruz mountains, hours from Monterey. Along with such financial success and notoriety, both locally and across the country, the question was this: Did he really want to go home again?

The answer came after various interludes in Los Angeles, Mexico, New York City, and the European front: yes. And out of his love for Monterey, his friendship with Ricketts, and his nostalgia for cama-raderie—for the warm fellowship of the Arthurian tales he so loved as a boy—came *Cannery Row*, published in 1945. Ten years after *Tortilla Flat*, a whimsical treatment of the Monterey underclass, this lovely novel evoked a world exponentially more serious and more engaging. But as in *The Grapes of Wrath*, in which a great theme elevated a tale of ordinary people, the vision behind the comedy of *Cannery Row* turned what might have been merely charming and forgettable into some-thing magical and memorable. The result was a supreme example of Steinbeck's ability to encapsulate the essence of the lyric experience.

Consider the image of the Great Tide Pool, where Doc—the Ed Ricketts figure in *Cannery Row*—collects his samples. Steinbeck pres-ents to us a "tranquil and lovely and murderous" microcosm, "fantas-tic with hurrying, fighting, feeding, breeding animals." The hermit crabs, the starfish, the limpets and lovely nudibranchs—dozens of creatures occupy briefly the bright water-world left by the receding tides. And as a rising wave breaks over the pool, "the smells of life and richness, of death and digestion, of decay and birth, burden the air."

Clearly, in this strikingly sensuous passage, Steinbeck's training in marine biology does more than merely enliven a novel about tramps and dreamers in an out-of-the-way pocket of the country. The novel-ist uses his knowledge of how the natural world works—or doesn't—to elevate his seemingly random sampling of our species to the level of cosmic metaphor, giving us a picture of a world with plenty of action but no apparent purpose other than appetite, and no radical motive other than biology. It is a vision of human life in relation to the rest of nature, and it suggests that the belief in purpose is a great romantic illusion and motive is nothing more than the vagaries of a nonteleo-logical universe. We've had a few American naturalistic novelists before—Stephen Crane, Frank Norris, Theodore Dreiser—but their worldviews were overwhelmingly tragic. Only Steinbeck, with his novel of a "lovely colored world [that] is glassed over," managed to turn an ordinarily bleak view of life into an existential comedy of magical and incongruous moments in which men and women transform basic hungers into the stuff of amusement and dream, and time turns into what he calls "hours of pearl."

Ironically, the tide went out for Steinbeck after the appearance of *Cannery Row*. The book was only a minor success in comparison with *The Grapes of Wrath*, and though aesthetically *Cannery Row* stands among his best works, it has been honored more for its entertaining effects than for its vision. For the next seventeen years, Steinbeck appeared to be squirming on the beach, both in his life and in his work. His reverse migration—a move to New York City just after the war, and his eventual middle-class homesteading on the eastern acres of Long Island—might have offered him a much-needed distance on his subject, but in effect it dramatized his retreat from the ironies of the changing California valleys and thus from the realities of American life.

No longer the sharp and careful observer who knew human beings to be a tough, defiant, and often comical species struggling against the shifting tides of their native habitats, Steinbeck turned into a windy and platitudinous spokesman for traditional values, an artisan of the superficial. Instead of deepening with time, his vision thinned to nearly nothing, and for a while he produced vacant allegories like *The Moon Is Down* and *The Pearl*; and sentimental fiction like *Sweet Thursday*. He let out one last great gasp of genius in the novel *East of Eden*, a mixture of elegy and melodrama, while his last novel, *The Winter of Our Discontent*, seemed to combine all the worst aspects of his efforts from 1945 onward. In his life he appeared to lapse into a round of trivial show-business acquaintances and political ties in which he kowtowed to a number of presidents, and his art declined so markedly that his Nobel Prize, in 1962, came as a tremendous surprise to almost everyone except Steinbeck himself, whose sense of irony appeared to have been left behind in California.

What happened to Steinbeck? How does one account for the way in which his power declined after the mid-forties? I'm traveling along California's Highway 1 with James Houston, a tall, lanky California

novelist and my guide on this trip, down the coast to Steinbeck country. Houston's own books, among them the novel *Continental Drift* and
the nonfiction *Californians*, share certain themes with the works of the
state's only Nobel Prize winner, and he is a knowledgeable guide to the
Salinas Valley and the salty environs of Cannery Row. I wonder aloud:
Was it Steinbeck's permanent move to New York that crippled him as
a writer, or did that signify some inner change?

Houston gives a hearty laugh, blinking into the autumn sun as he
steers toward the center of Salinas. Except for an occasional excursion,
Houston would sooner reside on the moon than depart from his native
soil. To a visitor from the East like me, New Jersey–born but cut loose
and rambling from home to home, region to region, such loyalty to a
local base seems so admirable, like fidelity in marriage, more than a
state of mind, almost a state of grace.

"That's one theory," Houston says. "But some people think Ed
Ricketts was the brains and inspiration behind his best work, and when
Ricketts died, in 1948, *that* was when Steinbeck's work went into
decline." He laughs again as we slow down for a parking space on West
San Luis Street, alongside the John Steinbeck Library, Salinas's public
tribute to its best-known—and only—native writer: "In California,
the surf's always up as far as his books are concerned."

We walk through the warm late-morning air past the life-size
statue of the novelist, which stands in the garden in front of the library
named after him. It makes Steinbeck appear more gnomelike than
normal, a reduced local representation of a man for a long time dis-
liked in this part of the world once he had become a success. Inside the
building is a room set aside for Steinbeck memorabilia, including a
copy of the 1919 El Gabilan–Salinas high school yearbook, opened to
his graduation photograph, and still photographs from the films made
from his novels and scripts. There is a copy of the Nobel Prize speech,
with a handwritten message to his fellow townspeople: "Not everyone
has the good fortune to be born in Salinas, but to those so favored, this
is inscribed."

In the basement of the busy library—are readers spurred on to
new and better books, as writers sometimes are, by the presence of a
local writer in their lives?—there's a vaultlike space where the young

Steinbeck's home library, the reading that moved him, is shelved, along with a few original manuscripts—*The Pearl*, his World War II notebooks, the typescript of the story "The Snake"—and the bulk of the collection's 300,000 photographs, newspaper clippings, and other mementos of the man, his town, and time, including an old Eddie Condon recording of a tune called "Tortilla B-flat," with Pee Wee Russell on the clarinet, George Wetling on drums, and Max Kaminsky on the cornet.

Library director John Gross is about to embark on a fund-raising expedition to bring in cash to build a John Steinbeck Center annex to the existing library. According to a recent story in the *San Jose Mercury News*, his plans call for a 7,500-square-foot structure that includes a large vault, study rooms, a 130-seat movie theater, and a souvenir shop. If he were alive to know about this, says Teresa Hickey, an archivist for the Bank of America, one of the major corporations that Gross hopes to approach for a large contribution, Steinbeck, the foe of large Valley landowners such as the bank, "would be rolling over in his grave." He was an extraordinarily shy man at times, as Jackson Benson points out, and would have been put off by crowds in any building, let alone one named after him. But three thousand people showed up for the Steinbeck Festival in Salinas last summer for more than ten days of lectures, movies, plays, panel discussions, and guided tours based on the work and life of the local writer. As literary industries go, this one seems only just to have gotten off the ground.

Nothing makes that more plain than a trip to the Steinbeck birthplace for a sit-down lunch prepared by the volunteer women of the Valley Guild. "Dining at the large, frame Victorian house where John Steinbeck was born will be a unique California experience," the Valley Guild's flyer announces. "The Steinbeck House is a gourmet luncheon-restaurant located at 132 Central Avenue, Salinas, California. Menus feature a delicious gourmet entree each day, Monday through Friday, utilizing fresh produce from the fields of the famous Salinas Valley. . . . 'The Best Cellar,' the basement shop . . . features Steinbeck's books, antiques, and gift items."

Houston and I follow the hostess to our table, admiring the Steinbeck family bric-a-brac on the walls and shelves as we pass through the outer rooms.

"Today we're serving *poulet au broccoli*," says our waitress, a middle-aged volunteer from the Valley Guild.

"*Poulet au broccoli?*" The living California novelist raises an eyebrow, in honor of the dead writer. "We should be eating beans and drinking campfire coffee brewed with eggshells. Or we should drink that dollar-a-gallon jug wine from Mrs. Torrelli's in Tortilla Flat."

"This is real life, not a Steinbeck novel," I remind him.

"It's real," Houston says. "They wouldn't have let the young Steinbeck in here."

"The young Steinbeck probably wouldn't have tried to get in. He once was coerced into attending a banquet in honor of Thomas Mann, and he lasted five minutes."

"The older Steinbeck would have come, though," Houston says. "He would have toured here with Charley, his poodle."

We eat our *poulet au broccoli*, wishing for campfire beans. After lunch we talk our way past the assistant manager and up the narrow staircase to the second floor, where the Steinbeck family slept. From the gabled window of young Steinbeck's bedroom you can look to the southwest, over the town, toward the lower end of the valley, the sunny Gabilans to the east, the dark and brooding Santa Lucias to the west. We picture the aspiring writer, dreamer, would-be Galahad of the modern age, all ears and elbows, leaning on the window ledge. Benson tells us that high-school chums chugged by in roadsters on the street below. They sometimes called out to him: "Hey, John! Hey, John! Johnny! Steinnie! Hey, John—you got any ideas yet, John?"

A half-hour ride westward through the fringe of the valley, over on Cannery Row, in Monterey, we can see that his success gave some wily entrepreneurs some (bad) ideas. There's little left of the magical community that Steinbeck made famous, not even the stink. That went when the sardines disappeared, a few decades ago. Only the quality of light reminds us of the spirit of the early books, and of the great-hearted, humane talent that was mostly lost when Steinbeck moved three thousand miles east of his Eden. Now the swarming fish have been replaced by schools of tourists, who roam the streets in search of some connection with the present, rather than the past, stopping to eat at the John Steinbeck Lobster House and buy knickknacks at the nearby souvenir shop that someone converted from the prototype of Lee Chong's grocery store in Cannery Row.

Several of the most important sites here remain unmarked, as well-hidden from the tourists as Steinbeck's best works seem to be from the minds of the critics who enforce our country's literary canons. There's Ricketts's old laboratory, a shabby, warehouselike structure right in the middle of the block. And there's the railroad crossing where Ricketts, driving to town to buy some food one twilight hour in the spring of 1948—"and he probably had had a few beers," Houston suggests—failed to hear the signal of the approaching evening freight.

And there are the tide pools south of town, still teeming with life.

II

The Return of James Agee

On the movie screen of the newly renovated Bijou Theatre in downtown Knoxville, Tennessee, one pleasant evening in October, a famous man shows us his famous teeth in a famous smile while, in careful Southern cadence, he praises a book he says he admires second only to the works of Henry David Thoreau.

"I give the book to friends and tell them not to worry about the style when they read it, just to relax with it, I tell them it's poetry," says Jimmy Carter. He is talking about *Let Us Now Praise Famous Men*, a nonfiction study of three Alabama tenant farmer families in the 1930s. The president: "I was never poor like that but I knew people who were, they lived just down the road from us."

Jimmy Carter, an unemployed candidate for the presidency when he gave this interview, smiles a bit harder into the camera as he jokes about the book's initial commercial failure and its present acclaim. He likes obscure candidates who come from behind, out of nowhere, to win the highest prizes.

The first of a number of people who appear on the screen—most of them Agee's family, colleagues, and friends—Carter is talking into a camera directed by Ross Spears, an East Tennessee filmmaker in his early thirties. We're watching the world premiere of a ninety-minute documentary, *Agee, a Sovereign Prince of the English Language*. Seventy years ago this month, Agee was born here in Knoxville.

The theater is crowded with celebrants, some in furs, long gowns, dinner jackets, and cravats; others in beads, beards, headbands, and jeans. There are loyal local fans of the writer, undergraduates, elder churchmen, the mayor and his wife, teachers from the English Department of the University of Tennessee, critics from New York and Nashville, actors, filmmakers, the director and crew from Knoxville, Los Angeles, and points east. How Jimmy Carter himself would love to be here amid a crowd of hundreds—all of whom agree about little other than his excellent taste in books.

It seems appropriate that the man from Plains, Georgia, should speak convincingly about Agee's writing, which is so full of passion and pity for the common clay farmers of the Deep South. Carter epitomizes what Agee calls, in one passage from *Let Us Now Praise Famous Men*, the humanity of the Southern "white man owner of the land."

After the plaudit from Carter, the film begins with a tableau depicting "Knoxville: Summer, 1915," the prose poem that precedes the first chapter of Agee's most popular work, the novel called *A Death in the Family*.

Spears first encountered Agee as a sixteen-year-old high-school student in Johnson City, Tennessee, when he had to read *A Death in the Family*. Throughout his undergraduate years at Duke, Spears was deeply influenced by the special balance in Agee's work between love of the printed word and love of the movies. When he enrolled in the California Institute of the Arts, he majored in filmmaking and wrote a script about Agee for his master's project. In so doing, Spears was grappling with an overwhelming task, since Agee was not only a superb artist of prose but also one of the finest film critics ever to see print.

After five years, one grant from the Tennessee Commission on the Arts, several private contributions, the formation of the James Agee Film Project, and the labor of a group of good actors and crew, the film glides upon the screen. It features interviews with each of Agee's three wives; with his friends Robert Fitzgerald, Walker Evans, John Huston, and Father James Harold Flye; and with several of the surviving family members of Famous Men who talk about what it was like to have Agee move in with them to do his research. It also contains footage of Agee himself performing a bit part in a Hollywood movie for which he did the screenplay. And it has, among other mementos, mostly visual, an aural souvenir, a tape of Agee improvising a letter to a friend.

Spears's film stands as the best biographical treatment of the legendary Agee now "in print." If this made the two Agee biographers in the audience nervous, they didn't show it. David McDowell, now in semiretirement after a long career in publishing, was the writer's lifelong friend and heads the Agee Literary Trust. His long-promised biography of Agee is suffering from an excess of material, and he has yet to find the best way to cut the manuscript down to size.

"I know too much about the subject," McDowell says during the reception on the stage of the Bijou after the film. He and Mia Agee, the writer's third and last wife, edited the manuscript of *A Death in the Family* and published it two years after Agee's death. "And my approach is too personal," McDowell adds. "I have to discover a way of leaving myself out."

McDowell, like Spears, is a Tennessee native. Erik Wensberg, in his late forties, is a dapper New Yorker, a former editor of the *Columbia Forum* and *Esquire* who, like most of Agee's readers, discovered the writer first and his home state later. In fact, just that afternoon, before he and Spears, along with a few maintenance men from the Bijou, washed down the movie screen in preparation for the evening's premiere, he had his first look at the hilly streets that make up "Rufus country," the Fort Sanders district of north-central Knoxville where Agee was born.

Wensberg's biography of Agee is a few years away from completion. Its progress has not been complicated by his friendship with his subject but by what Wensberg calls Agee's promiscuously friendly attitudes. This means that there's always one more old pal of Jim Agee's whom he must interview.

A number of people in the film, particularly Robert Fitzgerald (who has published a wonderful memoir of his friendship with Agee), attest to the power of Agee the man. But why does his work have the impact it has had, particularly since it was rather meager compared to the enormous production of most of the other writers who shared Agee's world? How does Wensberg explain that the man's work survived and acquired the kind of audience that it has?

"If Agee doesn't captivate you with one talent, he does it with another," Wensberg says. "He appeals to different audiences at the same time, to the young by the acuity of his sense impressions and to older people by the power of his moral realism."

The mayor of Knoxville nods his head. Patrons of the arts, students, editors, writers, moviegoers, priests, poets, projectionists, novelists, and politicians all seem to agree that tonight we're celebrating not only the seventieth anniversary of Agee's birth but also the flowering of the already healthy reputation of one of our nation's finest writers.

When you leave the Bijou Theatre and head north, past Market Square and the Louisville and Nashville Depot, across the viaduct that carries you over the railroad tracks, you reach Forest Avenue, the once trim and well-kept middle-class neighborhood that now has the faded look of an abandoned movie set. You find yourself in the Fort Sanders district, the scene of Rufus Follet's mournful days following the demise of his father, Jay, in *A Death in the Family*. Another few minutes' walk west, and you are standing on Highland Avenue in front of the James Agee Apartments. It is the only monument in the city to one of its most famous men, built on the site of Agee's birthplace, which was razed in 1963.

He was the son of Hugh James Agee (known to family and friends as James), a white-collar worker with a mountain heritage, and Laura Tyler, a middle-class, college-educated Episcopalian town girl. The writer was born on November 27, 1909, into a household of relative comfort, good feeling, culture, and health. But life didn't give him much time to enjoy these advantages he had over most of the children growing up in Appalachia and the rural South in those days. From the *Knoxville Journal and Tribune* for May 19, 1916, news of his father's death: FOUND DEAD ON CLINTON PIKE JAMES AGEE OF THIS CITY PINNED UNDER AUTOMOBILE WHEN CAR STRUCK EMBANKMENT AND OVERTURNED — WAS RETURNING FROM LAFOLETTE.

Not all of Agee's comforts had been material. His mother had tended his childish soul carefully, fertilizing it with the Doxology and watering it with her own affection. But it was his father to whom he cleaved, and his death when James was only six reverberated through Agee's life. The headline from the Knoxville newspaper signals the transformation of one morning in a life to a life of mourning, a shift from the possibility of comedy to the emotions of tragedy, to laments for the loss of one of the fundamental pediments of home.

In an interpolated chapter in *A Death in the Family* presented after we have learned that Jay Follet has died in an auto accident on the way home from his own father's sickbed, we witness Follet musing to himself on this same subject:

> "How far we all come," he thinks to himself. "How far we all come away from ourselves. So far, so much between, you can never go home again. You can go home, it's good to go home, but you never really get all the way home again in your life . . . and once in a while, once in a long time, you remembered, and knew how far you were away, and it hit you hard enough, that little while it lasted, to break your heart."

Losing home is an old story, the theme of Homer's *Odyssey* and the song Dedalus sings in Joyce's *Ulysses*. The late Hungarian scholar Georg Lukács once claimed it was endemic to modern Western man and dubbed the condition "transcendental homelessness." Agee felt the disease come upon him early in life. His father's death uprooted him and dispersed the family.

Agee's fate was to emigrate to New England, always looking back over his shoulder at what he had to leave behind. But before he headed north, Agee first turned south. His mother enrolled him in St. Andrew's Episcopal School in Sewanee, Tennessee, on the Cumberland Plateau about a hundred miles southwest of Knoxville. She moved there so that her son could live with her on weekends. Fortunately for Phillips Exeter Academy (and novelist John Knowles, author of *A Separate Peace*), Agee already had student life at St. Andrew's impressed so deeply on his feelings that the New Hampshire preparatory school, where his mother enrolled him after her marriage to a minister and a move to Maine, escaped his pen.

Agee's mixed feelings about the Ivy League emerged at Exeter, but so did his burgeoning talent for verse and fiction. At Harvard, in 1928, he found his place as an editor of the *Advocate* and among friends such as Robert Fitzgerald. Though he continued his ties with St. Andrew's through his correspondence with Father James Flye, who had befriended him there, he was moving swiftly toward a career as a New York man of letters.

In the summer of 1932, publisher Henry Luce gave him his start in the professional world of writing and editing. The *Advocate* parody of *Time* that Agee had produced as his final undergraduate project impressed Luce enough that he hired Agee to write for his new magazine, *Fortune*. The average serious writer trying to preserve his stylistic integrity while working for the Luce organization might seem today a bit like a man trying to stay sober at a New Year's Eve party.

But these were years when Agee's colleagues in the ranks of *Time*, *Life*, and *Fortune* writers included John Kenneth Galbraith, Archibald MacLeish, Dwight Macdonald, John Hersey, and Fitzgerald. Agee used assignments about the manufacturing industry, the Tennessee Valley Authority, and the American roadside to perfect his own writing strategy. In spare moments he completed *Permit Me Voyage*, the volume of verse that won him the Yale Younger Poets Series prize in 1934.

The restless writer took a leave of absence from November 1935 to May 1936. His first major assignment upon returning was a series of articles (to be accompanied by photographs by Walker Evans, on loan from the U.S. Farm Bureau) on the plight of Alabama tenant farmer families. After an eight-week sojourn in rural Alabama, Agee completed the articles, only to have Luce, after some agonizing, refuse the pages of the magazine to this latest work of his brilliant poet-journalist.

Over the course of the next few years, Agee worked intermittently for Luce while turning the articles into a book-length manuscript. He attempted to publish it with Harper and Row but withdrew it after the editors suggested what Robert Fitzgerald remembers as "a few domesticating changes." Meanwhile, Fitzgerald convinced the *Time* editorial board to sign Agee on as a book reviewer. Agee gladly accepted the position, working with Fitzgerald and another reviewer under the managing editorship of T. S. Matthews. At first a book reviewer and later a movie critic, he hissed and cheered the moving pictures of the early forties with fellow staff member and night owl Whittaker Chambers.

Houghton Mifflin published Agee's manuscript of *Let Us Now Praise Famous Men* in the autumn of 1941; Agee could now look back on nearly a decade of service for Luce's organization, a period during which he had published a volume of verse and had tested himself as a writer of prose, both "highbrow" and "middle-brow" (to use the terms devised by his friend Dwight Macdonald in a now-famous essay in the *Partisan Review*). The signed articles on film that he wrote for the *Nation* from 1942 to 1948 while he was also *Time*'s main film critic suggest that he moved with ease between both worlds—or perhaps that the two worlds were really one. Along with his freelance articles for *Life*, his *Nation* essays won him well-deserved attention among moviemakers as well as moviegoers.

By this time Agee had become a walking legend in the halls of *Time*. He was famous, within a certain circle of readers and friends, for his piercing critical intelligence that manifested itself in plain but beautifully persuasive language, for a wit that crackled fiercely in the midst of his lyric poetry, and for the kindness, generosity, and frankness he showed to friends. And for the ability, as he himself put it in a cabaret song about a prostitute (published after his death), to stay "Open All Night."

Agee graduated from movie watching to moviemaking in 1948. Three years into his third marriage, he left the East for Hollywood, giving up his job at *Time* to work full-time on film scripts for a production company owned by millionaire Huntington Hartford. His adaptation of Stephen Crane's short story "The Bride Comes to Yellow Sky" appeared in 1949; Agee himself showed up on screen for about three minutes, in the part of the town drunk.

Film work seemed to stimulate his fiction writing in a way that the job with Luce had not. In 1951 he published the short novel *The Morning Watch*, an initiation story based on his own experiences as a student and acolyte at St. Andrew's. He was drinking even more than his usual large amount by the time he began his collaboration with director John Huston, the man whom he called in a 1951 *Life* article "the undirectorable director."

Agee had written a favorable *Nation* review of Huston's film *The Treasure of the Sierra Madre*, and Huston had responded with a note of thanks, eventually inviting him to work on a script based on a C. S. Forester African adventure novel. The result was the Humphrey Bogart–Katharine Hepburn feature *The African Queen*.

Working with Huston all day (a day that began with several vigorous sets of tennis) and working on his own fiction at night became a great strain for the big-boned, lanky Tennessean. The man who had played the drunk in his own script of the Crane story had become, according to Huston's testimony, a bottle-a-night man.

Agee suffered his first heart attack on Huston's Hollywood tennis court. During the next few years he worked as hard as ever, though he tried, as much out of sympathy with those who cared about him as for his own sake, to cut down on his smoking and drinking. He wrote an Abraham Lincoln television series for *Omnibus*, a screenplay of Davis Grubb's novel *The Night of the Hunter*, published a few short stories, and worked steadily on a novel. On May 16, 1955, he died of a heart attack in the backseat of a New York City taxicab. He was forty-five years old.

Agee died a poet, journalist, critic, and screenwriter. He was reborn a novelist.

Mia Agee and David McDowell edited the book-length fiction manuscript that he left unpublished at his death and brought it out in 1957, published by McDowell-Obolensky, under the title *A Death in the Family*. In 1958 the novel won the Pulitzer Prize for fiction.

Twenty years later interest in Agee still grows. *A Death in the Family* has gone into fifteen printings in the paperback edition issued by Bantam Books in 1969, selling approximately 75,000 copies a year. Houghton Mifflin reissued a hardbound edition of *Let Us Now Praise Famous Men* in 1960 and has kept it in print ever since, having sold about 30,000 copies to date. The paperback, brought out by Ballantine Books in 1974, sells about 10,000 copies a year.

How do we account for the sustained success of Agee's books? Robert Fitzgerald, in a "point of order" at the end of the 1971 special issue of the *Harvard Advocate* dedicated to Agee, suggested that in the early sixties Agee's strength, and by implication his appeal to serious readers, lay in his "range of awareness, moral passion, and visualizing power." And that in the early seventies his prowess as a writer, his "discipline, delicacy, precision, and scruple" came first to mind. Erik Wensberg, when he talks of the power of Agee's "sense impressions" on the one hand and his "moral realism" on the other, might be seconding Fitzgerald's discriminations.

Other American writers live as much in their plots and their characters as in their language—and some in their language scarcely at all. For me, Agee above all others resides in his prose.

Knoxville: Summer, 1915

We are talking now of summer evenings in Knoxville, Tennessee, in the time that I lived there so successfully disguised to myself as a child. . . .

Supper was at six and was over by half past. There was still daylight, shining softly and with a tarnish, like the lining of a shell; and the carbon lamps lifted at the corners were on in the light, and the locusts were started, and the fire flies were out, and a few frogs were flopping in the dewy grass, by the time the fathers and the children came out. . . .

Now is the night one blue dew. . . .

On the rough wet grass of the back yard my father and mother have spread quilts. We all lie there. . . . All my people are larger bodies than mine, quiet, with voices gentle and meaningless like the voices of sleeping birds. . . . By some chance, here they are, all on this earth; and who shall ever tell the sorrow of being on this earth, lying, on quilts, on the grass, in a summer evening, among the sounds of night. . . .

This prose sequence, which serves as the "prelude" to *A Death in the Family*, has ever since its first publication led many a young reader to try to write poetry. The purity of its diction, the soul-satisfying rhythms of its lines, the way it charges nostalgia with energy and forms it into a breaking wave of emotion—Agee's five-page prelude stimulates in the reader an awareness of difficult things unspoken.

Consider young Rufus with his father, who is soon to die, walking from the movie theater in downtown Knoxville to their home in the Fort Sanders district:

> He knew these things very distinctly, but not, of course, in any such way as we have of suggesting them in words. There were no words, or even ideas or formed emotions, of the kind that have been suggested here, no more in the man than in the boy child. These realizations moved clearly through the senses, the memory, the feelings, the mere feeling of the place they paused at, about a quarter of a mile from home, on a rock under a stray tree that had grown in the city, their feet on undomesticated clay, facing north through the night over the Southern Railway tracks and over North Knoxville, towards the deeply folded small mountains and the Powell River Valley, and above them, the trembling lanterns of the universe, seeming so near, so intimate, that when air stirred the leaves and their hair, it seemed to be the breathing, the whispering of the stars.

What does Rufus know? His sense of estrangement and at the same time his need for proximity to his father, the awareness of solitude and the pull of family, his sense of childishness and maturity at once?

What do we know about what Rufus truly knows except for what we feel along the lines of this passage and others?

Like a good lyric poem, Agee's novel communicates its sense by feeling rather than by discursive means. Everything we've been taught about how narrative works suggests that Agee shouldn't be able to sustain successfully a novel based on this technique. A book that strings together a series of deeply evocative moments for several hundred pages should wear us down rather than buoy us up.

And yet we read Agee's book, we say it aloud, as though it were a rosary of middle-class emotions: Rufus's awakening into the world of death, the story of a boy's brief life with his father, and how he survives the period immediately following the man's unexpected death. It is a story with a clear, simple action that stays with us in a way that thousands of other more carefully and attractively plotted novels do not. Even in its unfinished state, Agee's emblem of his own childhood evokes fierce sentiments about our lives without ever crossing over into the sentimental.

A Death in the Family establishes a modern standard for emotional realism. For all of the familiarity of the material, there are few books quite like it—perhaps only Updike's *The Centaur*, among books with a similar theme, approaches the level of feeling that pervades Agee's uncompleted novel.

The only book-length nonfiction narrative work James Agee ever published was *Let Us Now Praise Famous Men*. It remains the only work he ever completed to some degree of satisfaction. A vast inland sea of words, it sustains the intensity Agee discovered in the five pages of "Knoxville: Summer, 1915" over the course of nearly five hundred.

Agee's meditation—or "structure of special exaltation," as he calls it—on the lives of three Alabama tenant farmer families and his own brief involvement in their lives may well be the one great book of its kind of the century. None of the so-called New Journalists have written anything to compare to it. We would have to look back to, say, *The Education of Henry Adams* for a nonfiction narrative of this stature. What else might we compare it to? John Reed's *Ten Days That Shook the World?* There's too much history, not enough reportage in that volume, and its power derives as much from the event as the style. Mailer's *Armies of the Night?* A gentleman in the rear of the hall makes this nomination.

However apt these comparisons, Agee's inventive book remains unbowed, and solitary.

But what is "a structure of special exaltation"?

It's part memoir, part serious journalistic study of Agee's association with down-and-out dirt farmers, part encyclopedia (with essays explaining the nature of their work, their habits, their housing, their educations or lack thereof, their sadness, their good cheer). It is part catalog (of the things in this world they call their own: their tools; animals, if any; knickknacks, gewgaws, relics; their bodies; faint hopes and strong hearts). It is part indictment of the social conditions these farmers endure. And part encyclical from a lay pope on the state of human labor and unhappiness.

Like photographer Walker Evans, who accompanied him, Agee wants to show the reader things just as they were when he witnessed them, from the suffering of his subjects to the quality of the light on the landscape in which they move.

"I will try to write," he tells us midway through the book, "of nothing whatever which did not in physical actuality or in the mind happen or appear; and my most serious effort will be, not to use these 'materials' for art, far less for journalism, but to give them as they were and as in my memory and regard they are."

There's a deep and abiding concern for realism, if not a theory of realism, here. The book slows down considerably when Agee argues it out with himself—art or not art, fiction or nonfiction—in constant struggle against categories and encapsulation, a dozen pages at a time.

Fortunately for him, and us, the crucial words in this argument are "my memory and regard." Agee's memory and regard stood him in good stead in the composition of the record of his stay in rural Alabama. His memory and regard, unique certainly among his contemporaries and perhaps among the entire crowd of twentieth-century prose writers, turn what started out to be a magazine article into an anomalous creation, as close to journalism as a butterfly is to a moth. It's a book in which the taste of homemade biscuits and the narrator's crucifixion by louse and bedbug seem to the reader as valuable as his careful explanation of how the cotton crop is planted, harvested, and ginned.

When it first appeared, no less a critic than Lionel Trilling declared the book a masterpiece. It is also one of the most difficult books to describe and define. It starts off slowly, ambles, shuffles, backtracks, mumbles under its breath, and then veers away from the subject before coming back to it.

Reading it sometimes is a bit like watching a film made with a hand-held camera. When Agee finally gets his subject in focus—the lives of these farmers, his own life, our own—I know nothing so beautiful. Here is our narrator, imagining the family on the other side of the wall from him preparing for sleep:

> George's red body, already a little squat with the burden of thirty years, knotted like oakwood, in its clean white cotton summer union suit that it sleeps in; and his wife's beside him, Annie Mae's, slender and sharpened through with bone, that ten years past must have had such beauty, and now is veined at the breast, and the skin of the breast translucent, delicately shriveled, and blue, and she and her sister Emma are in plain cotton shifts; and the body of Emma, her sister, strong, thick and wide, tall, the breasts set wide and high, shallow and round, not yet those of a full woman, the legs long thick and strong; and Louise's green lovely body, the dim breasts faintly blown between wide shoulders, the thighs long, clean and light in their line from hip to knee, the head back steep and silent to the floor, the chin highest, and the white shift up to her divided thighs; and the tough little body of junior, hardskinned and gritty, the feet crusted with sores; and the milky and strengthless little body of Burt whose veins are so bright in his temples; and the shriveled and hopeless, most pitiful body of Squinchy, which will not grow.

Night descends upon the holy family of earthbound tenants, and Agee is sitting on the porch of their cabin, feeling his way across the landscape for us so that we know what the world would be like without even this poorest of human congeries:

> All over Alabama, the lamps are out. Every leaf drenches the touch; the spider's net is heavy. The roads lie there, with nothing to use them. The fields lie there, with nothing at work in them, neither man nor beast. The plow handles are wet, and the rails and the frogplates and the weeds between the ties: and not even the hurryings and hoarse sorrows of a distant train, on other roads, is heard. The little towns, the county seats, house by house white-painted and elaborately sawn among their heavy and dark-lighted leaves, in the spaced protections

of their mineral light they stand so prim, so voided, so unde-
fended upon starlight, that it is inconceivable to despise or to
scorn a white man, an owner of land; even in Birmingham,
mile on mile, save for the sudden frightful streaming, almost
instantly diminished and silent, of a closed black car, and save
stone lonesome sinister heelbeats, that show never a face and
enter, soon, a frame door flush with the pavement, and ascend
the immediate lightless staircase, mile on mile, stone, stone,
smooth charted streams of stone, the streets under their lifted
lamps lie void before eternity.

Readers like me tend to dwell on passages in Agee's work that veer
toward the prose poem. There are many other varieties of narrative in
Famous Men, as other Agee readers will quickly point out.

For example, when Agee reports the words spoken by Mrs.
Woods, wife and mother of the third family in the white trinity of
Gudger, Ricketts, and Woods, the spare speech of this valiant, belea-
guered farm woman becomes as eloquent as the lyrical sequences:

"How did we get caught? Why is it things always seem to go
against us? Why is it there can't ever be any pleasure in living?
I'm so tired it don't seem like I ever could get rest enough. I'm
as tired when I get up in the morning as I am when I lay down
at night. Sometimes it seems like there wouldn't never be no
end to it, nor even a let-up. One year it'll look like things was
going to be pretty good; but you get a little bit of money saved,
something always happens."

Agee follows these direct quotations with a lyrical reprise based
upon them from the point of view of one of the daughters: " 'But *I* am
young . . . and I am too young to worry . . . for my mother is kind to
me; and we run in the bright air like animals, and our bare feet like
plants in the wholesome earth." He then restates Mrs. Woods's lament
in lines spaced apart like free verse. Next comes the text of the Sermon
on the Mount. This seems at once moving and ironic, but not half as
believable or starkly beautiful as Mrs. Woods's own speech.

A book of many colors and moods, Agee's monument in prose to the unknown soldiers of the Alabama cotton fields is also a spiritual tract. It calls attention to this aspect of itself by a quotation from the Gospels and by some section and chapter headings that are taken from the ritual of the Mass. Above all, Agee's insistence upon the nature of what he calls human divinity, a feeling for the link between the poorest human clod and the farthest star, is ubiquitous in these pages.

It is at the same time the American sequel to the working-day section of Marx's *Das Kapital*, a sophisticated self-styled country Communist's tone poem on the trials and rigors of the workers of this world. (One of the book's epigraphs is a famous quotation from the *Communist Manifesto*, which Agee explains, in a Hamlet-like aside, is quoted here "to mislead those who will be misled by them [the words]. They mean, not what the reader may care to think they mean, but what they say . . . neither these words nor the authors are the property of any political party, faith, or faction.")

No, as this book attests, Agee was nobody's property, although his faith appears to be a bit more orthodox than his politics. *Famous Men* may be read as a powerful critique of the inadequacies of Roosevelt's New Deal; as the testimony of a radical witness in the countryside; and perhaps even as a portent of, if not a precursor to, the spirit of the New Left organizers who went out to work with "the people" in the 1960s. Another sign of its enduring style is the way it may be read as one of the most powerful and subtly wrought documents on the subject of human rights that we will find in our language.

Agee today remains nobody's property, and everybody's. He is Knoxville's hero, but also New York's and Hollywood's. The curious element in his reputation is that though it increases annually, it has not really been aided or abetted by academia. W. H. Auden once wrote that "one foresees the sad day, indeed, when *Agee on Film* [two volumes of Agee's film criticism] will be the subject of a Ph.D. thesis." There have been a few such works, no doubt, but probably many more have been written on the subject of Auden. Agee may have lived too short a life and written too little and too variously to serve as the best subject for any but the most passionately devoted aficionado of his art. Of whom, according to the 1978 *Modern Language Association International Bibliography*, there were six writing in 1977 (as compared to five on John O'Hara, eleven on Joyce Carol Oates, and sixteen on Thomas Pynchon).

To be sure, Agee is taught here and there—in an American Studies class at Rutgers, in a sophomore course at the University of Tennessee. There is certainly no more tried-and-true Agee partisan in the university than Robert Coles, whose General Education course at Harvard, Social Science 33, requires the reading of *Famous Men, A Death in the Family*, and other Agee works as the main texts of "Moral and Social Inquiry." Coles has written at length about Agee's work and the effect it has had on his own work and life, most recently in a review of the Spears film in the *New Republic*.

The work rather than the legend of the tormented artist attracts psychiatrist Coles to Agee. He teaches him for his books. Or, as he put it in a recent telephone conversation, steeped in love and appreciation of the Knoxville writer's work—and edged with a bit of irony—"there are five hundred people we could find on the street right now who are as tormented and disturbed as Agee was. The great thing about this writer is that he turned his pain into books that ease or explain our own torment. Let's face it, an artistic gift is not to be confused with individual psychopathology. Nor does the latter 'explain' the former."

The reading list for Coles's Social Science 33 suggests the special appeal of Agee's work within academia, at the same time calling out to the social scientist, the admirer of fine prose, and the person of conscience. (This past spring Coles added the Spears film to his required list, showing it privately to his class in what amounted to its first—but what Spears hopes is not its last—Boston showing).

But Agee is as much at home where writers work as where teachers teach.

"I never knew Agee," novelist Walker Percy has written. "I wish I had. . . . I can only speak about his influence on me as a writer. I can best describe this influence as technical . . . in the way that he crafts an

English sentence, and uses poetic devices, metaphors, and sentence structure within a single paragraph."

Sentence for sentence, paragraph for paragraph, Agee remains one of the finest American prose writers of the century. In other words, as President Carter said, it's poetry.

12

Mario Vargas Llosa and Conversation in the Cathedral: *The Question of Naturalism*

Where have the critics gone wrong? The astonishing success during the past decade of Latin American novelists who employ the technique of "magical realism" seems to have blinded most readers to the persistence in the work of the Peruvian novelist Mario Vargas Llosa of a hardy strain of naturalism. But as any reader, new or initiated, of the stunningly broad, expansive context of Vargas Llosa knows or soon discovers, he is not merely roaming around in a traditional nineteenth-century novelistic world, immersed in the fiction of the most proficient Flaubertian or Balzacian in Lima. While apparently true to the naturalistic code that characters are basically determined by heredity and environment, Vargas Llosa questions the very idea of environment. His juxtaposition of jungle and city forges a new vision that leads us, at least as we read, to become aware of the inscrutable forces behind each of the figures in the various social groups in the novel.

In *The Green House*, Vargas Llosa added a new context to the geographical regions of city, desert, mountain, and jungle: this is the "region" of time past and the "region" of time present. This addition creates a three-dimensional narrative in which the traditional display of naturalistic principles cannot be separated from the modernist outlook. With regions of time overlaying regions of geography, the reader finds new and innovative time-spaces in which to ponder the activity of men and women under the internal pressures of psyche. Some of these land and time spaces unknown to traditional nineteenth-century fiction are city-present, city-past; desert-present, desert-past; jungle-present, jungle-past; and, to add to the deepening sense of uncertainty that abounds in the supposedly concrete environment of the natural-ist's world, city-past as narrative present, city-present as narrative past; desert-past as narrative present, desert-present as narrative past, jun-gle-past as narrative present. In the massive *Conversation in the Cathe-dral*, Vargas Llosa's contexts or zones of time and being appear in par-adoxical but equally effective form. Instead of associating time with various geographical locations, as in *The Green House*, here he con-structs temporal zones that imply specific kinds of topological pres-ences. In other words, in *The Green House* space seems to take priority over time whereas in *Conversation* time takes priority over space.

For those, like myself, who found much that was persuasive in Ronald Christ's important article on Vargas Llosa's "film sense" (which appeared in the Spring 1976 issue of *Review*), the time scheme within the fiction of *Conversation* must nevertheless be invoked as evi-dence against Christ's view that Vargas Llosa is wholly "filmic" in his use of rhetorical "montage" at the expense of linear progression.

Conversation opens in the narrative present ("Santiago looks at the Avenida Tacna without love"), in the middle of the life of Santiago Zavala, son of the late Peruvian industrialist Don Fermín Zavala. Lima is under the thrall of an epidemic of rabies. Zavala, a Communist dur-ing his university days, is writing editorials attacking the sloth of the city administration's handling of the stray dog problem for the muck-raking pages of *La Crónica*. The first chapter (of the first of the novel's four sections) carries the reader along for many pages in a single tense and plane (the present, in Lima). Zavala sets out in quest of his wife's dog, which has been dragooned by dogcatchers anxious to earn their commission (ironically, part of the city's response to Zavala's own edi-torials). He encounters Ambrosio, a black man, now a dogcatcher, who once drove his father's limousine, as well as the limousine of the noto-rious Cayo Bermúdez, minister of security under the regime of the dictator Odría (during Santiago's university days). Only then does the epic "conversation" commence in "La Catedral," the bar-restaurant-brothel where Santiago and Ambrosio retire for drinks and reminiscences.

Nearly twenty pages of linear narrative in the present tense prepare the way for the limited "montage" effects, those sequences in which the narrative shifts from present conversation (ostensibly moving forward in time present) to the scenes out of the past (various levels of the past, to be exact). This linear present-tense overture to the more complicated main body of the novel enunciates clearly Vargas Llosa's naturalistic assumptions. Following the epigram from Balzac ("le roman est l'histoire privée des nations"), Zavala's opening interrogation ("At what precise moment had Peru fucked itself up?") seems almost programmatically naturalistic both in diction and in ethos. The association between the epidemic of rabid dogs and the deterioration of the psychic lives of the city's inhabitants, the main motif of the opening sequence, further establishes the novel's roots in the naturalistic tradition. The everyday details of Zavala's progress, his encounter with one of his fellow reporters, his passage across town to discover that his own dog has been snatched, his arrival at the dog pound (where he witnesses the brutal murder of the stray dogs), all reinforce the naturalistic atmosphere. The scene is degraded, enervating, the spirit bowed. When Zavala and Ambrosio retire to La Catedral, the metaphor of the world as brothel (which Vargas Llosa plays on in *The Green House* by superimposing the image of the brothel called the Green House and the jungle in all its green and lush decay) emerges as the central image of the novel, an image clearly naturalistic in meaning and texture.

What, then, distinguishes Vargas Llosa's relentless attention to the smell and feel of the actual world from the nineteenth-century models of Balzac, Flaubert, and Zola? Or from the twentieth-century American novelists John Dos Passos and Dreiser, whose pages his seem to resemble? One immediate response must be that, as Ronald Christ has suggested, his meaning lies not so much in the nature of the materials as in the nature of the presentation of the materials. The habitual use of the "montage" effect, or, as I would prefer to regard it, the manipulation of the "environment" of time itself, clearly separates *Conversation in the Cathedral* from the methods of conventional naturalism (which presumes a steady, linear, temporal progression and a cause-and-effect relationship between past and present, action and actor).

Consider the opening of section 7, part 1, where Vargas Llosa juxtaposes the discussion between Bermúdez and an assistant against the flight of a desert buzzard and its subsequent demise at the hands of a hungry peasant.

> It was noontime, the sun fell straight down onto the sand, and a buzzard with bloody eyes and black plumage was flying over the motionless dunes, descending in tight circles, his wings folded back, his beak ready, a slight glimmering tremor on the desert.
>
> "Fifteen were on file," the Prefect said. "Nine Apristas, three Communists, three doubtful. The other eleven had no record. No, Don Cayo, they haven't been interrogated yet."
>
> An iguana? Two maddened little feet, a tiny, straight-lined dust storm, a thread of gunpowder lighting up, a rampant invisible arrow. Softly the bird of prey flapped his wings at ground level, caught it with his beak.

The effect is not that of conventional flashback. The reader seems to perceive the conversation about subversion at the university, which is the subject of the Prefect's remarks, and the flight and death of the bird of prey almost simultaneously. This lends the text a spatial quality. With respect to the novel's chronology, however, the scenes are widely separated in time. The former takes place early in the novel's time scheme (when Zavala is still at the university), and the latter occurs around the time of Bermúdez's downfall. Thus cause and effect cease to hold in this atmosphere in which time past and time near-distant stand in relationship to each other as hill to pond, dune to ocean shore—in "geographical" rather than causal positioning.

One time block reflects back or forward upon the other (in the manner, as Ronald Christ has accurately pointed out, of the "wandering rocks" section of *Ulysses*). For example, in the scene just before the one from which I have quoted, there is a three-time-tiered passage in which Santiago and Ambrosio in the present in La Catedral evoke by means of their discussion Zavala's infatuation with the proto-communist student Aida during his days at the University of San Marcos. At the same time, the reader stumbles on one of the mysterious patches of dialogue between Don Fermín and Ambrosio that threads its way through the novel. This micro-conversation refers to Ambrosio's murder of Bermúdez's mistress "La Musa" in order to end the possibility of her blackmailing Don Fermín, whose homosexuality remains as much a mystery to the uninitiated reader as the murder itself:

> "I don't know what to do, I feel confused, I have doubts," Aida finally said. "That's why I called you, I thought all of a sudden that you could help me."
>
> "And I began to talk about politics," Santiago says. "See what I mean?"
>
> "Of course," Don Fermín said. "Getting away from the house and Lima, disappearing. I'm not thinking about myself, you poor devil, I'm thinking about you."
>
> "But what do you mean when you say that," as if startled, he thinks, scared.
>
> "In the sense that love can make a person very much an individualist," Santiago said. "And then he gives it more importance than anything, the revolution included."
>
> "But you were the one who said that the two things weren't incompatible," hissing, he thinks, whispering. "Do you think they are now? How can you be sure you're never going to fall in love?"
>
> "I didn't believe anything, I didn't know anything," Santiago says. "Just wanting to leave, escape, disappear."
>
> "But where, sir?" Ambrosio said. "You don't believe me, you're kicking me out, sir."
>
> "Then it's not true that you have doubts, you're in love with him, too," Santiago said.

In Zavala's quest to discover at what point he, like Peru, has "fucked himself up," this juxtaposition of conversations about love—love between himself and Aida, between Aida and Jacobo (another member of their radical group at San Marcos, who is the cause of Aida's "confusion" and the referent of the pronoun "him" in the last statement), and love between Don Fermín and Ambrosio—dramatizes the fluctuating nature of meaning with respect to the relationship of past and present. For one moment it seems that Don Fermín is telling Santiago to leave town; in another it appears that he is advising Ambrosio (after the murder the black driver commits as an act of love for his employer) to disappear. The love that Santiago speaks about in relationship to his thwarted feelings for Aida (and her masked affection for the hypocritical Jacobo) also refers the reader to Don Fermín's feelings for Ambrosio and vice versa.

The effect clearly sets Vargas Llosa's pages apart from those of conventional naturalism, where any confusion of the intellect or the senses must belong to one or another of the characters but never to the reader or the "character" of the text itself. The reader senses here, as he does in *The Time of the Hero* and *The Green House*, a kind of psychic leak in which emotions abound that may or may not be attached to any single character, thus lending the text or scene an emotion as though it were a character itself. This dispersal of individual character for the sake of the success of the text is not a new invention. Joyce lends *Ulysses* a "character" above and beyond that of either Dedalus's or Bloom's. Call it tone, mood, or whatever, clearly the totality of the narrative's language takes on a life that the reader cannot easily forget. We can go back to Flaubert, mentor of both Joyce and Vargas Llosa, to find the first serious instances of the character of the text becoming a salient feature of the narrative. With this in mind, we can consider that psyche itself becomes a geographical or topological location—mind turns into landscape, a spatial phenomenon as well as a temporal one in which the reader may roam about and ponder the view.

Time becomes not so much a major constituent as the entire complex of time-plus-space and character-in-context; it functions as a musical key, or as color in a painting, a defining but not a definitive factor. This is hardly the sustaining metaphysics of a programmatic twentieth-century naturalist. Rather, it stands as a major revision of the naturalist belief in the substantiality of nothing but the physical and chemical world. Yet even the feeling imagination working through the links between present and past, and the relationship of one mind to another in the present, may be seen in a larger natural context, the context of society, a complex tapestry of geography, tribes, and time.

There is yet another problematical element that arises out of a reading of Vargas Llosa as a pure naturalist. As Luis Harss has pointed out, individuals tend to get lost in Vargas Llosa's vast landscapes. Add the vastness of the "time-scape," and one might wonder how, if at all, Vargas Llosa's characters manage to survive in our memories (where all books finally live or die). Here we must admit the presence of myth, and the notion that myth, usually considered antithetical to the naturalistic novelist's disposition, plays an important role in these dramas. For how else do we recall the fascinating criminal Fushía of *The Green House*, a figure as memorable as Balzac's Vautrin, if not by the paradoxical means by which the environment itself forges characters who represent it as a way of being? What Harss describes as the "tidal movement of shadowy figures up and down the river of life and death" rises up from the text as river fog emanates from the moving waters, suggesting to the reader that it is not for the facts but for the mystery rising from the facts that he reads.

The creation of myth and mystery might at first seem antithetical to the naturalist's purposes. Balzac's quest, and Flaubert's, we assume, was to enlighten us about the patterns made by human figures as they dance to the music of the Bourse. How does society in its plenitude function? How does it "work"? As Erich Auerbach suggested in *Mimesis*, Balzac's methods may be intelligently compared to those of nineteenth-century zoology. But is the generation of myth and mystery finally alien to the naturalistic writer? Not if the reader recalls Balzac's lifelong interest in the occult. Not if we consider Flaubert's pursuit— through the figure of Emma Bovary—for meaning beyond the actual things of this world. Not if we recall the attempt to lay bare the mysterious driving forces of life in the best work of Dreiser.

Vargas Llosa stands in the tradition of the great practitioners of the nineteenth-century novel, presenting the world as it appears to the senses while at the same time extending the form by using the feeling imagination with the same extraordinary results as the so-called magical realists. His effects thus upset the critical reader's customary notions of naturalism, realism, and fantasy. They bring to light once again—as does all important narrative fiction—the knowledge that beneath the smooth flowing surfaces of the text a vitality abounds that no method or rubric can either quantify or diminish.

13

Where Is She Going? Where Has She Been?: Elizabeth Tallent's "No One's a Mystery" and the Poetry of Female Initiation

When I think of great initiation stories, it's always Joyce's "Araby" that immediately comes to mind, and after that, "I Want to Know Why," Sherwood Anderson's powerful American tale with its distinctive race-track setting. These stories, with their near-miraculous fusion of the vernacular and sensitive and wondering portrayals of the crucial moment in the education of two quite distinctly different adolescent boys (one a turn-of-the-century Irish Catholic from Dublin, the other a country boy from the Middle West) set the highest aesthetic standard for the coming-of-age tale. Moreover, they reveal to us that all short fiction in essence cries out to be lyric poetry.

Short stories are as close as I get myself to writing lyric poems, and these two stories come as close as any in creating the effect of the lyric. It's nothing short of miraculous the way they reveal to a young man just how much of the chaos and near-insanity of his floundering childhood and youth present a certain pattern of understanding and loss. A story such as this thrills you with the intensity of its unfolding, gives you hope that in your own hopelessness you are not alone, and creates on your blood a particular emotional effect that we associate usually with only the finest short poems.

But after all of the polemics and lamenting and honest skull-scratching that we've all suffered through during the past twenty years with respect to the question of equality for women in the modern world, the question comes to mind: what's a *girl* to do? Where does a young woman go to find a portrayal of female initiation that is as beautifully made and emotionally unsettling as the Joyce and Anderson stories?

In fact, there's a story of Maine writer Sarah Orne Jewett's—"A White Heron"—that precedes both the Joyce and the Anderson, and arguably rivals both of these in its powerful final effects. And lately, among our contemporaries, women have produced initiation stories of similar quality right alongside the men. Aside from Richard Ford's "Communist," the finest coming-of-age stories of the past several decades have, in fact, been written by women. One of these is Joyce Carol Oates's "Where Are You Going? Where Have You Been?" and the other comes from Elizabeth Tallent. It's called "No One's a Mystery."

Oates's story has been widely anthologized. With its dark undertow of a narrative pulling its heroine closer and closer to a fate so awful that Oates only hints at it in the end, it captures the worst fears of contemporary girlhood, and leaves little to hope for except a strong voice to tell about the barren truths of modern life. Tallent's story has been anthologized only a few times—in the first volume of the *Sound of Writing* anthology of stories from the NPR short-story radio show of the same name, in one of Tallent's own collections, and in the first volume of James Thomas and Robert Shaphard's *Sudden Fiction*. Given its compact and forceful rendering of an eighteen-year-old Wyoming girl's coming of age—and the ironic counterpoint of the perspective of her middle-aged rancher lover—the story deserves a much wider audience. Given the relation of its brevity—it's only about a thousand words, or less than three pages, in length—to its impact, the story deserves wide recognition as a little masterwork of short fiction.

It's certainly short enough to quote in its entirety right here in this space:

No One's a Mystery

For my eighteenth birthday Jack gave me a five-year diary with a latch and a little key, light as a dime. I was sitting beside him scratching at the lock, which didn't seem to want to work, when he thought he saw his wife's Cadillac in the distance, coming toward us. He pushed me down onto the dirty floor of the pickup and kept one hand on my head while I inhaled the musk of his cigarettes in the dashboard ashtray and sang along with Rosanne Cash on the tape deck. We'd been drinking tequila and the bottle was between his legs, resting up against his crotch, where the seam of his Levi's was bleached linen-white, though the Levi's were nearly new. I don't know why his Levi's always bleached like that, along the seams and at the knees. In a curve of cloth his zipper glinted, gold.

"It's her," he said. "She keeps the lights on in the daytime. I can't think of a single habit in a woman that irritates me more than that." When he saw that I was going to stay still he took his hand from my head and ran it through his own dark hair.

"Why does she?" I said.

"She thinks it's safer. Why does she need to be safer? She's driving exactly fifty-five miles an hour. She believes in those signs: SPEED MONITORED BY AIRCRAFT. It doesn't matter that you can look up and see that the sky is empty."

"She'll see your lips move, Jack. She'll know you're talking to someone."

"She'll think I'm singing along with the radio."

He didn't lift his hand, just raised the fingers in salute while the pressure of his palm steadied the wheel, and I heard the Cadillac honk twice, musically; he was driving easily eighty miles an hour. I studied his boots. The elk heads stitched into the leather were bearded with frayed thread, the toes were scuffed, and there was a compact wedge of muddy manure between the heel and the sole—the same boots he'd been wearing for the two years I'd known him. On the tape deck Rosanne Cash sang, "Nobody's into me, no one's a mystery."

"Do you think she's getting famous because of who her daddy is or for herself?" Jack said.

"There are about a hundred pop tops on the floor, did you know that? Some little kid could cut a bare foot on one of these, Jack."

"No little kids get into this truck except for you."

"How come you let it get so dirty?"

" 'How come,'" he mocked. "You even sound like a kid. You can get back into the seat now, if you want. She's not going to look over her shoulder and see you."

"How do you know?"

"I just know," he said. "Like I know I'm going to get meat loaf for supper. It's in the air. Like I know what you'll be writing in that diary."

"What will I be writing?" I knelt on my side of the seat and craned around to look at the butterfly of dust printed on my jeans. Outside the window Wyoming was dazzling in the heat. The wheat was fawn and yellow and parted smoothly by the thin dirt road. I could smell the water in the irrigation ditches hidden in the wheat.

"Tonight you'll write, 'I love Jack. This is my birthday present from him. I can't imagine anybody loving anybody more than I love Jack.'"

"I can't."

"In a year you'll write, 'I wonder what I ever really saw in Jack. I wonder why I spent so many days just riding around in his pickup. It's true he taught me something about sex. It's true there wasn't ever much else to do in Cheyenne.'"

"I won't write that."

"In two years you'll write, 'I wonder what that old guy's name was, the one with the curly hair and the filthy dirty pickup truck and time on his hands.'"

"I won't write that."

"No?"

"Tonight I'll write, 'I love Jack. This is my birthday present from him. I can't imagine anybody loving anybody more than I love Jack.'"

"No, you can't," he said. "You can't imagine it."

"In a year I'll write, 'Jack should be home any minute now. The table's set—my grandmother's linen and her old silver and the yellow candles left over from the wedding—but I don't know if I can wait until after the trout à la Navarra to make love to him.'"

"It must have been a fast divorce."

"In two years I'll write, 'Jack should be home by now. Little Jack is hungry for his supper. He said his first word today besides "Mama" and "Papa." He said "kaka. . . ."'"

Jack laughed. "He was probably trying to finger-paint with kaka on the bathroom wall when you heard him say it."

"In three years I'll write, 'My nipples are a little sore from nursing Eliza Rosamund.'"

"Rosamund. Every little girl should have a middle name she hates."

"'Her breath smells like vanilla and her eyes are just Jack's color of blue.'"

"That's nice," Jack said.

"So which one do you like?"

"I like yours. But I believe mine."

"It doesn't matter. I believe mine."

"Not in your heart of hearts, you don't."

"You're wrong."

"I'm not wrong," he said. "And her breath would smell like your milk, and it's a kind of bittersweet smell, if you want to know the truth."

The poet John Ciardi, one of my undergraduate teachers, used to talk about the two parts of a poem—the wave and the counterwave. You reach a moment in the lyric when it has gone as far as it can go in one direction, and then, like a wave pulled back out to a certain distance from shore by the undertow, the poem breaks back on itself. Paul Fussell, another one of my old teachers, calls this movement "elegiac action." You can certainly see this—better yet, you can *feel* it—"elegiac action" at work in the Tallent story as the narrator attempts to come to terms with her first understanding of the love affair that has taken up several years of her teenage life. You feel it deeply after the last exchange between Jack and the narrator as a pulse of emotion and as a sting of awareness and regret.

That comes after one reading. If you bear down on the story and reread it closely, its spare, brief surface opens up like a desert flower in a sudden rainstorm. The first line announces the gift of the diary, with its duration of five years of space—an ironic beginning. It's not until she receives the blank book that the narrator talks—thinks? and possibly writes?—about anything at all related to her affair with the older man. The opening phrase indicates to us that for two years the girl, always nameless, has not thought or recorded anything about her illicit liaison. The presumption is that for the next five years at least she will be paying attention to her own behavior and emotions.

But not yet. For the brief duration of the story, which is told in "real time," that is, in the same amount of time that the characters live it, she will remain unaware, conveying to the reader her perceptions of the next few minutes with a sort of raw innocence much purer, for all of her sexual experience, than that of the boy in either the Joyce or the Anderson story. Tallent quickly conveys this mixture of innocence and experience in the first paragraph when Jack, her lover and the driver of the pickup truck in which they're riding, sights his wife's Cadillac coming down the highway in the opposite direction and pushes the narrator to the floor of the truck.

She hovers there, at eye level with the seam of the crotch of his Levi's and its zipper glinting "gold" in her view. She doesn't see the wife's car as it passes, merely hears the betrayed woman—also innocent in her own way, we have to suppose—honk twice. The narrator's eyes fall from the view of her lover's crotch to a lower level, where she notices his boots, with their "elk heads stitched into the leather" and the "compact wedge of muddy manure between the heel and the sole." This descent of vision, reminiscent of the fall of the narrator's eye in "Araby" when he sees standing at the porch railing the object of his infatuation, the girl he refers to only by the phrase "Mangan's sister," takes us from the sexual level to the primal realm of excrement. It's an animal world down here, with the elk heads and the cow manure the reigning materials.

189

It's also the realm of infancy. Jack emphasizes this aspect of her place in his life—his child lover—and her own state of being during the past two years—innocent participant in adult games—by responding to her complaint an instant later about the mess of pop-tops on the car floor. A child might cut herself on those, except that no child gets into the car except her, he reminds her.

Leaping forward, you can make the connection between his view of the narrator as a child and his remark about the infant that she imagines they would bear if they married, finger-painting on the bathroom wall with his own excrement. Ranging back again to the first few moments in the truck, we also notice the Rosanne Cash tape that's playing on the tape deck. This implicit musical background to the entire story, with that brief additional honking of the horn as counterpoint, and the voices of the man and the girl in the foreground—annunciates the father–daughter shadow that lurks behind this illicit love affair, as in country singer Johnny Cash and his daughter the singer Rosanne. But rather than emphasizing the incestuous side to their romance, the story dramatizes those qualities that we normally associate with the coming-of-age story: the exploration of values and the ceremonial passage from innocence to experience that we find in both the Joyce and the Anderson.

The pickup zooming along, with Jack behind the wheel and the kneeling girl on the passenger side, is a small interior location, but as the girl tells us, there is a wider world beyond the truck into which she implicitly puts the story of her two-year teenage love affair with the older Jack. This news comes to us in a striking visual effect, with some interesting wild-life diction. As she tries to imagine what future they might have together, she "cranes" around while kneeling now on the seat "to look at the butterfly of dust printed" on her jeans, and in doing so she glances outside.

"Outside the window Wyoming was dazzling in the heat," she declares. "The wheat was fawn and yellow and parted smoothly by the thin dirt road." More senses than sight come in to play. "I could smell the water in the irrigation ditches hidden in the wheat." These lines about landscape suggest more stillness than passage. But the fact is—or is it the irony?—the truck is moving the pair through time, and the girl has yet to begin to recognize the inexorable passage that will carry her through the next five years of discovery about herself and the world.

The concluding beat of the story comprises statement and response between the girl and Jack on the nature of that future. She states as fact her dreams of a perfect marriage. He counterposes his realistic view of any such situation that she might conjure and suggests that she has an underdeveloped imagination. Their exchange builds to the stinging pathos of his final comment, which leaves the reader in a certain mood of understanding.

Whether the girl feels what the reader feels we can't tell. So we have to look at the story as completely ironic. No final epiphanic insight presents itself to the main character, as in the Joyce and Anderson stories. It remains for the reader to enunciate this girl's feeling for her. But it is a big emotion that we're left with, this sense that the girl, as certain of herself and her vision as she seems to be, has a number of years of trials and tribulations lying ahead of her.

We can feel, too, for Jack, her lover-teacher, the father surrogate who initiates her into the world of loving and love. All her life lies ahead of her. His best years may have come to an end, even as he hints at the end of the affair, and, worse than that for him, the eventual eradication of even any specific memory of him in her life.

Two and a half printed pages. About four minutes of "real" time in which this story unfolds. But four minutes of "real time" at eighty miles an hour. For the narrator the predication of a lifetime to come, and for Jack a life just reaching its zenith and about to descend. That's quite a lot for one small story to impress upon us, but Elizabeth Tallent's brief lyric miracle quite easily bears all the weight.

A Wintry Saga

It's been a downward-turning spiral here in the United States with respect to reader interest in Russian fiction since the end of the Cold War. With the Berlin Wall having fallen long ago, and the last few self-proclaimed Western Marxists currently isolated in such unlikely places as the Syracuse University English Department, serious American readers seem to have given themselves leave to turn their attention away from the calamities and horrors of the Stalinist period and ponder other matters.

When Solzhenitzyn's work was all the rage, the result was all outrage about the Gulag. Then came the end of communism and the bearded Vermont resident turned on his hosts, blaming U.S. culture for a decline in Western morals and sounding like a Russian version of Jerry Falwell. When Solzhenitzyn departed for home, our ranking Russian writers in exile were reduced to two: Anatoli Rybakov (whose *Arbat* trilogy, suppressed for two decades under Soviet rule, appeared here in translation, though receiving much less attention than Solzhenitzyn's work)—and Vassily Aksyonov. Since the death of Rybakov, Aksyonov stands alone as the finest Russian novelist living in America.

Still, I worry that what may be the finest fiction yet on the subject of twentieth-century Russian life, Aksyonov's trilogy, *Generations of*

Winter, may not find the audience it so well deserves. A version of that old paradox that obtained during the Cold War seems to be holding true: in the old Soviet Union, writers weren't allowed to publish their best work and everyone wanted to read it, and in the United States, the best writers could publish everything and no one wanted to read it.

Aksyonov certainly saw his share of censorship. After much early popular acclaim as a novelist, he watched his star decline when he published prohibited manuscripts in his Moscow magazine, *Metropol*. The result was his self-exile in Paris in 1980 and his immigration a few years later to take a teaching post in California. Like many Russians, he had known worse times. His mother, Eugenia Ginsburg (*Into the Whirlwind*, etc.), a teacher and journalist, had been arrested during the political purges of the late 1930s when Aksyonov was four years old, and he did not see her again until twelve years later when he took up residence in Magadan, the Siberian town adjacent to the notorious prison camp where his mother was interned. (The second half of Aksyonov's novel *The Burn* tells a story quite similar to his own.)

America for Aksyonov was like Siberia turned inside out, another sort of exile. He felt welcomed in the best way that a writer can, as a number of his books began to appear in translation in the prestigious International Writers series published by Vintage. Then came a professorship at an Eastern university. But his fiction wasn't having anything close to the impact on the reading public that Solzhenitzyn's did.

To be fair, it wasn't just that the Cold War was on the wane. Aksyonov is quite a different sort of novelist than the other Russian writers who gained currency here since the end of World War II, from Pasternak on to Solzhenitzyn, Valeri Grossman, and Rybakov. He does not demonstrate anything resembling the symbolic realism of the former or the impassioned naturalism of the others. His strengths are enormous, but he draws them from some of the most obscure and avant-garde aesthetic movements of the century, taking as much from the well of constructivism and futurism as from the realistic or naturalistic tradition.

This makes for a style that is slightly more difficult than the American public usually embraces. But it's also a style that's quite memorable and distinctive, a way of telling the story that allows for the maximum amount of passion while keeping enough distance to prevent a lapse into sentimentalism and its counterpart in the plot, melodrama. This becomes immediately apparent in the opening pages of the first volume of *Generations of Winter*.

"Just think"—the book begins—"in 1925, the eighth year of the Revolution, a traffic jam in Moscow!" We're given a picture of the traffic jam itself, with trolleys and trucks and automobiles and horse-drawn carts all making a commotion in front of an open-air food mar-ket on Nikolskaya Street, "which runs from the Lubyanka prison through the heart of Kitai-gorod down to Red Square."

"Just think"—that opening phrase is echoed in a moment in the comments on the street scene by Professor Ustryalov, a contemporary social commentator dubbed a "class enemy" by the Bolsheviks for his less than sympathetic analyses of their progress. He's making his com-ments ("Just think, only four years ago there were famines and epi-demics here . . . and the only vehicles on Nikolskaya Street were the Black Marias of the Cheka") to a visiting American journalist, the somewhat supercilious Townsend Reston. Reston is on assignment from a Chicago newspaper to cover the Soviet story. It's Reston's dis-tanced perspective on the new society that informs this opening scene, along with the attitude of his guide. The journalist is bemused by the attitudes and thought of the Bolshevik leaders he has encountered and, moreover, he doesn't enjoy caviar—these " 'controllers of history' with their confounded fish eggs," he laments to himself.

At that moment, among the crowd on the street Reston happens to notice "two young Red officers . . . trim and ruddy complexioned, wearing tightly drawn belts . . . chatting with each other, taking no notice of anyone else." One of these soldiers is Nikita Gradov, son of Boris Gradov, a well-known surgeon of excellent reputation; he is brother to Nina, young revolutionary and poet, and to Kirill, Marxist and Party man. Gradov's mother, Mary, is, like Stalin, whose nasty fig-ure hovers above all the action in the novel, a Georgian. The family has been living a long time in their comfortable house in Silver Wood on the outskirts of Moscow.

They are a tremendously appealing group, this family of sur-geons, soldiers, artists, and political organizers. The Gradovs stand at the center of Aksyonov's story, which follows them from this opening moment in 1925, through the period of the Purges, World War II, and on into the middle of the Cold War. They seem perfectly representative, adding more breadth to the story of political, spiritual, and physical survival under Stalin than the solitary figures in Solzhenitzyn's fiction, but as a group compact enough to avoid the drain on the reader's attention that comes with the extremely large cast of characters we find, say, in Rybakov's *Arbat* trilogy.

The story unfolds in fairly straightforward fashion over the course of three decades, beginning in the optimistic years of the 1920s. Although the elder Gradov is compromised by Stalin and drawn into a plot to do away with one of the rising dictator's perceived rivals, the Gradov children, particularly Nina and Kirill, enthusiastically throw themselves into politics, the daughter as a member of the still-viable opposition, the son as a programmatic Bolshevik. While Nina writes poetry and Kirill gives polemical speeches, Nikita rises in the army and his wife, Veronika, becomes known as the most beautiful woman in Moscow.

Within a decade, all the optimism has been drained from these characters. Stalin's political purges take their toll, and even the dedicated officer Nikita finds himself in a forced-labor camp in Russia's Far East. Only the impending threat of a German military victory allows Stalin's practical side to triumph over his paranoia and allow for Gradov's rehabilitation. By the early fifties, Nikita's son Boris, a Stalinist commando and much-sought-after athlete, has made a place for himself in the Russia of the Cold War. The rest of the surviving family members suffer the heavy fist of Stalinist repression under the supervision of the cruel and perverted security chief Beria. Only Stalin's death makes for some release.

While exercising a perfect sense of perspective, Aksyonov also avoids sentimentalizing the family's story or romanticizing any of his characters, such as the dashing officer Nikita. The Russian writer possesses the genius to move fluently from person to person throughout the narrative, making sharp, clear portraits of each of these interesting and attractive figures. Nikita's troubled love for his wife, dented badly by their respective sentences to labor camps, Nina's poetry, scenes from the battlefield—all this will stay with you a long time after reading the novels. Creating an atmosphere first of optimism, then of fear, then of a rather undaunted realism in the face of Stalin's horrors, Aksyonov makes the reader feel all too powerfully what it was like to be alive in these times.

But as you probably can tell from the flavor of the first novel's opening scene, this trilogy is not simply a realistic novel. Stealing a move from our own John Dos Passos and the "newsreel" sequences of his epic trilogy *USA*, Aksyonov punctuates the end of his long realistic sequences with what he calls "intermissions." These he makes up out of headlines, articles from Moscow and abroad—from everywhere from *Pravda* to the *Washington Post*—so that we can trace the evolution of public opinion, pro and con, about the Soviet regime, seeing some of the absurdity and also some of the clear-eyed views of observers at home and around the world.

But there is another level in these "intermissions" that turns us further away from realism and faces us toward the fantastic. For example, early in the first volume, with a nod toward Tolstoy, Aksyonov devotes a sequence to the Gradov family dog, Prince Andrei, and offers us a glimpse into the family's life during good times from the dog's point of view. As Stalin consolidates his power and the Gradovs' fortunes darken, we hear about life from the perspective of an eighty-year-old oak tree that seems to have been informed with the spirit of military rebellion and then from the point of view of Lenin, whose soul has been reborn into the body of a squirrel.

The effect of these vignettes is quite startling, throwing the human drama into a bitterly comic and sometimes even something resembling a cosmic perspective. At the end of the second volume, for example, with the family having survived the torment of arrests, years in the Gulag, and deaths at the front, the Gradov patriarch, surgeon Boris, now seventy, walks along the shore of a lake at sunset and encounters a flock of geese. Perhaps, he thinks, for a moment merging his mind with the honking birds, some part of his own being was once a migratory creature. "Who can say," he asks himself, "by what transformation our souls pass beyond the boundaries of everyday triviality?"

As if Lenin reincarnated as a squirrel were not enough, midway through the third volume in the trilogy, while the young Boris, the surgeon's grandson, is making his wild way through the frenetic nightlife of Cold War Moscow and Beria is stalking Boris's beautiful young cousin in order to add her to his collection of conquests, Aksyonov turns the screw tighter. In one of his animal fable "intermissions" in which the novelist reports on what he calls an "astral reincarnation," he recounts the story of an elephant named Hannibal in whose large body has been reborn the eighteenth-century poet Radischev. In this fantasy come to life, Hannibal the elephant becomes a nocturnal companion of Stalin's at the beginning of the 1950s and before too long incurs the tyrant's steely wrath. This particular vignette not only establishes the mood for the period of post-purge-trial Stalinist intrigue, it sets the stage for a final astonishing metamorphosis at the trilogy's end involving no one less than Stalin himself.

In the heightened reality of Aksyonov's trilogy, the fantastic mingles with the everyday, and there is also another level of play that he engages in, now and then introducing his own voice into the narrative. Stepping back from the story, he may talk about the difference between the way he sees his own work and that of other writers, or how he views the role of fiction in everyday life. "The reader may say," he states at one point, "that there is no comparison between reality and novels, that in life events occur spontaneously, while in a novel they occur according to the whim of the author; this is both true and untrue." He then talks about the surprises he finds in his own work as he moves the story along.

In the third volume, in a masterstroke of modernist practice, Aksyonov deploys a version of his younger self as a character in the pathetic story of Beria's abduction of Boris's cousin, one of the Gradov granddaughters. The portrait of the dreamy young man from the provinces, not yet a writer, who hopes to take Moscow by storm is an endearing and painful piece of creative autobiography. Many years would have to go by before this shy and hopeful fellow would find his metier, perfect it, then suffer official harassment for it, lose his citizenship because of it, move to another country—and create this absorbing novel about the land and times he left behind. As the elder Gradov muses when gazing upon the migrating geese, "Who can say by what transformation our souls pass beyond the boundaries of everyday triviality?"

15

Bernard and Juliet:
Romance and Desire in Malamud's High Art

In art, as in life, romance sometimes strikes when you least expect it. In Bernard Malamud's short fiction, it's certainly an anomalous occurrence, a sometimes almost comical state in contrast to the pathos of many of his other motifs. Romance à la Malamud is expressed by a number of quite traditional turns—one of the most apparent being the notion, formed in the Middle Ages, that attraction moves from the image of the desired one straight into the eye of the beholder with a certainty that we usually associate with the laws of physics.

On the question of love, Malamud is nothing if not a traditionalist. Most of his young female characters serve as the objects of the male characters' affections and are represented without question as simple objects of sex and love. But there is, over the long course of Malamud's story-telling career, a serious and subtle transformation that occurs in the attitude of his men toward their women.

Take Rabbi Leo Finkle, for example, in "The Magic Barrel." Having invited a matchmaker into his life in order to make an orderly search for an appropriate wife, he finds himself staring at a photograph left accidentally by Salzman the marriage broker in an envelope of suitable prospects.

He gazed at it a moment and let out a low cry. . . . Her face deeply moved him. Why, he could not at first say. It gave him the impression of youth—spring flowers, yet age—a sense of having been used to the bone, wasted; this came from the eyes, which were hauntingly familiar, yet absolutely strange. He had a vivid impression that he had met her before, but try as he might he could not place her although he could almost recall her name, as if he had read it in her own hand-writing. No, this couldn't be; he would have remembered her. It was not, he affirmed, that she had an extraordinary beauty—no, though her face was attractive enough; it was that *something* about her moved him. . . . Her he desired. His head ached and eyes narrowed with the intensity of his gazing. . . . Only such a one could understand him and help him seek whatever he was seeking. She might, perhaps, love him.

Love at first sight. And it occurs by means of the eyes. Although we don't usually think about Malamud's fiction as a repository of stories about physical love, this moment of peculiarly Malamudian amour also stands solidly in that European tradition of how passionate desire is formed. Think of Dante telling of his first meeting with Beatrice in *La vita nuova*. One look fixes him forever as her devoted love slave. And how does she first greet him when he sees her again in the higher spheres? By a piercing look! But this early Renaissance version of passionate love has its origins in the pagan notion of eros as an oppressive condition in which the lover finds himself in the throes of emotions beyond his control.

Certainly for most of the second half of "The Magic Barrel" Leo Finkle would agree. Love takes him over, as a disease takes over the body and the mind. He rushes off in search of Salzman. When he does not find him at home in his drab apartment, he rushes back to his own place, caught in that music, as Yeats would say, that works its way on the young and the impressionable, the melody and chords of romantic love. When he finally meets his match, the sky lights up in a Chagallian display of romantic, sexual fireworks: "Violins and lit candles revolved in the sky. Leo ran forward with flowers outthrust."

If this diagnosis of Finkle's condition seems paradoxical—it's classic, it's also romantic—that's only because Malamud himself, like any good modernist writer, draws his water from both wells. Consider, for example, such a classic scene as the man smitten as he observes the beloved at her bath, as in the myth of Diana. Readers of *The Assistant* will recall a similar moment, when Frankie Alpine works his way up from the basement of Morris Bober's store in the shaft of the dumbwaiter so that he can observe Helen Bober in the bathroom. "But if you do it," Alpine tells himself, "you will suffer." After crossing himself, Frankie turns himself into a classic voyeur, grabbing the dumbwaiter ropes and pulling himself slowly up the shaft. "A light went on over his head," we're told. Then, leaning forward, "he could see through the uncurtained crossed sash window into the old-fashioned bathroom." Notice, among other things here, the double cross, as Frankie, for all of his naturalistic qualities as a low-life Peeping Tom, fulfills the requirements of the young man in love, laboring hard in order to reveal the depths and intensity of his passion. As Prospero says, "Light winning makes the prize seem light."

So let's watch Frankie Alpine as he spies on Helen Bober:

> Helen was there looking with sad eyes at herself in the mirror. He thought she would stand there forever, but at last she unzippered her housecoat, stepping out of it. . . .
>
> He felt a throb of pain at her nakedness, an overwhelming desire to love her. . . . Her body was young, soft, lovely, the breasts like small birds in flight, her ass like a flower. Yet it was a lonely body in spite of its lovely form, lonelier. Bodies are lonely, he thought, but in bed she wouldn't be. She seemed realer to him now than she had been, revealed without clothes, personal, possible. He felt greedy as he gazed, all eyes at a banquet, hungry so long as he must look. But in looking he was forcing her out of reach, making her into a thing only of his seeing, her eyes reflecting his sins, rotten past, spoiled ideals, his passion poisoned by his shame.

The situation here is rich with allusions and transformations, both classic and romantic: Frankie's ascent from basement to higher up in the building, suggesting his rise in the world from criminal to shop assistant (and his moral elevation from ignorant neighborhood thug to reader and thinker, though one wouldn't know it from his pathetic pose at the moment) and Helen's instant metamorphosis from neighborhood girl to object of mythological observation; and her body's transformation in pure metaphoric terms from human to animal and plant—her breasts to birds, her posterior to flower.

There's also that classic trope of love fixing itself by means of the eyes. And an angular, almost geometrical modernist positioning, with Helen staring at her own eyes in the mirror in a self-conscious pose that is actually truly innocent because she is unaware that precisely at that moment Frankie Alpine is stealing his look at her. The classic transformation undergoes as well a modernist twist, since her change from girl to bird and flower takes place in an instant beneath his intense gaze, while Frankie's change from gentile to Jew articulated in the book's final paragraph needs the glacial force of the entire novel to make happen.

A number of other significant protagonists in Malamud's work take walks on the wild side of love. S. Levin, in *A New Life*, for example, before entering into a more mature and devotional relationship with Pauline Gilley, falls quite easily into an affair with Nadalee, a student at the Oregon cow college where he has come to teach. The language in the scene of their tryst tells us something, as does the language in the voyeur scene in *The Assistant*, about how we are to read the overpowering emotions rampant in the scene.

Levin drives west to the motel belonging to Nadalee's absent aunt, "aimlessly on, in sadness contemplating all the failures of his life, the multifarious wrong ways he had gone, the waste of his going," but, in a moment reminiscent of Dedalus's apprehension of the sea in the opening scene of *Ulysses*, he soon sniffs "a sea smell. Whirling down the window, he smelled again and let out a cry. . . . The ocean! . . . He beheld in the distance a golden lace of moonlight on the dark bosom of the vast sea." Liquid becomes the central metaphor of this discovery. "He saw himself as stout Cortez—Balboa, that is—gazing down at the water in wild surmise, both eyes moist." When he reaches the motel, he finds Nadalee waiting for him wearing "a sheer nightie." He says to her, "I got lost." But "before he could say where or why, she had shucked off her garment and her gloriously young body shed light as he hungrily embraced it."

Interesting here that the language seems lively when it describes Levin's sight of the Pacific and falls a little flat when it takes us into the sexual scene in the motel room. Still, desire remains a triumph of the eye. As in, to go to another interesting piece of Malamudian work, the presumably hallucinatory pornographic vision of Yakov Bok's in *The Fixer*. When lying at night in his cell he imagines a visit from Marfa Golov, the widow who has accused him of murdering her child for ritual purposes. Here it's mostly all done with the eyes. Bok sees her enter his cell and becomes a passive spectator to her striptease as she silently removes her clothes—"the white hat with cherries, the red rose scarf, green skirt, flowery blouse, cotton petticoat, pointed button shoes, red garters, black stockings and soiled frilly drawers. Lying naked on the fixer's mattress, her legs spread, she promised many goyish delights if he would confess to the priest at the peep-hole."

Sexual desire comes naturally by means of the eye to ballplayer Roy Hobbs in *The Natural*. When we first see him on the train in the opening of Malamud's debut novel, he's stirred at once by a boarding passenger, "a girl in a dressy black dress. . . . Her face was striking"—neat pun here, given Roy's profession, and the fate he is about to meet—"and when she stepped up into the train her nyloned legs made Roy's pulses dance." Within a short while his desire leads to his wound as he makes his rendezvous in a Chicago hotel with this woman who is packing a gun loaded with silver bullets—in a scene where lust and water merge.

> Opening the door, he was astonished at the enormous room.
> Through the white-curtained window the sight of the endless
> dark lake sent a shiver down his spine. . . .
> Then he saw her standing shyly in the far corner of the
> room, naked under the gossamer thing she wore, held up on

her risen nipples and the puffed wedge of hair beneath her white belly.

When she fires the pistol at him at close range the bullet cuts "a silver line across the water."

Later in the book water and sex come together in a brief romantic encounter between Roy and Memo when they drive to Jones Beach. There's liquid in the sky as the night is "lit up by a full moon swimming in lemon juice, but at intervals eclipsed by rain clouds that gathered in dark blots and shuttered the yellow light off the fields and tree tops." They don't reach the shore, stopping instead alongside a small stream where a sign announces that the water is polluted. They talk a while, stare at the water, finally kiss.

> He trapped her lips, tasting of lemon drops, kissing hard. Happening to open his eyes, he saw her staring at him in the middle of the kiss. Shutting them, he dived deep down again. Then she caught his passion, opened her mouth for his tongue and went limp around the knees.

So there's as much sexual lip service as there are meetings of the eyes in this young writer's first novel, where the tone still allows for the suggestion of something more than lust—that is, for romance.

In the later novels—in, say, *The Tenants*, though the writer in middle age has much more on his mind than sex—sexual desire still plays an important part, but the senses shift away from the eye to the touch. Such matters Malamud describes rather explicitly. Even as Lesser begins an affair with the black woman Mary Kettlesworth he falls in love with black writer Willie Spearmint's young white girlfriend, Irene. We hear that, in bed together, "they kiss, grope, bite, tear at each other. He licks the floral scent of her flesh. She digs her nails into his shoulders. He is aroused by their passion." In a novel whose themes appear more interesting in the abstract than they do in the execution, the writer seems to behave in similar fashion, stirred by the prospect of writing about sex but not drawing us fully enough into the scene itself.

A late work, *Dubin's Lives* is clearly not a young man's book. The motifs deal deeply with the length of a life nearly fully lived, and the sexual drive portrayed in its pages is not the hot ejaculatory rushing of a neophyte but the melancholy thrustings of a man who seems himself on the downward slope of desire. Maturity may account for the fact that the descriptions of the couplings between Dubin, the fifty-eight-year-old biographer, and the ex-student Fanny are the most explicit in the Malamud canon even as the passages are punctuated by annotative sentences about the meaning of the mixture of lust and desire—as in this scene toward the end of the book when ripeness is all there is to their love affair:

> She glanced at him momentarily anxious as he took the water glass from her hand and held it as they kissed. Their first kiss, after a season of separation, loss, before renewing joy, hurt. Dubin set the glass down and began to unbraid Fanny's warm hair. She shook it out, heavy full. Her shoulders, breasts, youthful legs, were splendid. He loved her glowing flesh. Fanny removed her heart-shaped locket and his bracelet, placing them on the bookcase near the dripping red candle. She kept the ruby ring on. Forcefully she pulled his undershirt over his head; he drew down her black underpants. Fanny kissed his live cock. What they were doing they did as though the experience were new. It was a new experience. He was, in her arms, a youthful figure. On his knees he embraced her legs, kissed her between them. . . . Dubin slept with his arms around her; she with her hand cupping his balls.

At the end of the novel, Dubin returns to his wife, his vitality recharged by his exciting affair with Fanny. And he returns in a pose similar to the stylized posture of Leo Finkle in the little Chagallian cameo in the sky above the New York street where he meets his match in "The Magic Barrel." Leaving Fanny's bed and house, Dubin runs up a moonlit road "holding his half-stiffened phallus in his hand, for his wife with love." The comedy is ended with the hero outthrust.

The human comedy, anyway.

In Malamud's last completed novel, the allegorical postnuclear war fantasy *God's Grace*, the Malamudian sexual comedy continues by other means, parodying the European romance tradition even as it breaks from it with a jarring sexual disjuncture. Cohn, the scientist hero, finds himself stranded on a Pacific island with only chimpanzees and baboons and gorillas as his company. Good intellectual that he is, he teaches the animals to speak. And because he worries about the demise of the human species, he eventually thrusts himself into a sexual situation with a female chimpanzee whom he calls Mary Madelyn. Mary the sexy chimp goes into estrus, with, as Malamud describes it, "the jeweled pink flower of her swollen sexual skin visible from the rear," and gives off a "dense scent" that hits the wind like "a compound of night-blooming jasmine and raw eggs."

It's not only the chimps who desire her. Cohn decides, as Malamud puns it, to "monkey with evolution," dressing the female ape in virginal clothing and then, one night, lifting her white skirt from the rear, "and with shut eyes, telling himself to keep his thoughts level," dipping "his phallus into her hot flower." There is "an instant electric connection" and Cohn parts "with his seed as she possessed it."

The intercourse between Cohn and Mary Madelyn is the most outrageous sexual coupling in all of Malamud's work—and it ranks along with Faulkner's scene of a Snopes standing on a stool behind a beautiful cow as one of the most outrageous romantic pairings in all American literature. Yet it remains completely logical within the confines of the plot because of Cohn's hope to save some part of the human species. Bestiality thus becomes a necessity in this odd futurist fable.

"'I wov you,'" Mary Madelyn says to Calvin Cohn.

> He said he found her very engaging. She was even alluring these days, amiable brown eyes, silken black hair; her features approached human. Though Mary Madelyn could not be said to be classically beautiful—facts were facts—still beauty existed, derived to some degree from her intelligent, generous nature. She came to something. Having become aware of her quality, her spirit, Cohn thought, accounted for his growing feeling for

her. . . . Sensing receptivity, Mary Madelyn presented herself to him, crouching low.

So while there may not be any lit candles and violins revolving in the sky, as in a young man's passion, there is, from Cohn's side, the certain evidence of the cultivated affection of mature love. As Cohn puts it, just before committing his seed for the hope of the future,

> if two daughters, in a dark cave on separate nights, lay incestuously with their wine-sotted, love-groaning father, why not Cohn, a clearheaded, honest man, lying with biophilial affection and shut eyes, against the warm furry back of a loving lady chimpanzee who spoke English well and was mysteriously moved by *Romeo and Juliet*?

A good question.

16

Fitzgerald's Christmas Carol, or the Burden of "The Camel's Back"

Writing only seems difficult to other writers, Thomas Mann once remarked. In the case of F. Scott Fitzgerald, in some of his stories at least, the writer seems to have produced such wonderful fiction in such effortless fashion that even longtime practitioners of the art have to bow their heads in amazement at just how simple he makes it appear.

That's the effect that his story "The Camel's Back" had on a young student of literature at Rutgers—yours truly—and that's the effect this story has had on me after a recent rereading. Here is true genius, which makes such wonders come with such a little stirring of the pot.

The history of the story's composition pictures a junior whirlwind at work. Just after Christmas of 1919, Fitzgerald moved to New Orleans in order to avoid the worst of the Minnesota winter. By the third week in January he was installed in a room on Prytania Street, where at eight o'clock one morning he sat down and began to compose this story, which he completed, as he told Maxwell Perkins, by seven in the evening. He recopied the manuscript in the middle of the night and mailed it early the next day to his agent, Harold Ober, who sold it immediately to the *Saturday Evening Post*. It was published in the issue of April 24, 1920. The five hundred dollars that Fitzgerald was paid for the tale he used to buy a six-hundred-dollar platinum-

and-diamond wristwatch for Zelda. What writer wouldn't have marveled at his own ease of concentration and success at production? The story was then selected for that year's O. Henry Prize Stories series and appeared in *Tales of the Jazz Age* in 1922. It was republished in England in *Borrowed Time* and in *Six Tales of the Jazz Age and Other Stories*, which in its paperback edition is now in its fourteenth printing.

"The Camel's Back" is a holiday story, the tale of a successful young fellow from Toledo named Perry Parkhurst who, at Christmas 1919, sues unsuccessfully for the hand of Betty Medill and, when refused, goes off on a drunk. In his altered state, he shows up at a swanky costume party dressed as the front part of a camel—with a cabdriver in the rear—and by a series of seeming misadventures finds himself in a supposedly mock marriage ceremony with the same Betty Medill. Some critics, possibly as the result of class bias, have dismissed the story because of its material. K. G. W. Cross offers only a slighting reference to the tale as one that "reveals, if nothing else, the indulgence with which he regarded the pranks of the very rich." Where praise comes forth, it seems slightly misdirected, as when John A. Higgins labels the story "good farce, although it fails to reach the level of superior farce because it does not, as superior farces do, show the fundamental folly of human nature." Milton Hindus makes only a passing reference to the story as one of Fitzgerald's "humorous anecdotes" that "makes no pretense to 'deep' meanings or satiric overtones of an intellectual kind," though he adds—here's the praise—that the story "seems as assured of permanence as any of the more self-consciously 'serious' literary efforts of our time because it will cause hilarity in this or any century."

The label of farce comes up again in a brief reference to the story by Sergio Perosa. Henry Dan Piper refers to it only as "a smooth little comedy," while Robert Sklar echoes Cross's charge that the story is a mean-spirited slur against "social inferiors," by which he means the cabdriver who brings up the rear of the camel. Only Alice Hall Petry, the most recent of Fitzgerald's critics to write about the story, takes "The Camel's Back" seriously enough to spend at least several paragraphs looking at the relation between the form—farce or fantasy, she calls it—and the subject of personal and social disillusionment that she

sees as played out in Perry Parkhurst's dive into alcohol after his initial rejection by the object of his marital suit.

If any of these readings in passing holds any truth, it is Hindus's
assertion that the story seems assured of some kind of permanence. It
held up for me more than thirty years ago, and it remains, in my view,
a marvelous holiday fable—an anti–winter's tale, if you will. With its
plot out of the tradition of new comedy—that of the disguised lover
who turns his romantic suit around in the midst of dark confusion—it
sounds the tune of "all's well that ends well" with a particular comic
twist, since it is the cabdriver who brings up the rear of the camel.

So it's an old story that Fitzgerald puts up here in twentieth-century dress, a festival tale, a sequence of white romance, a story about
change and transformation from one stage of life to another. Speaking
of the champagne that he supplies to Parkhurst when Perry comes to
him after being rejected by Betty, ready to drink himself into another
state, an acquaintance of Parkhurst's, "a bad man named Bailey, who
had big teeth . . . and had never been in love," says, "This is the stuff
that proves the world is more than six thousand years old. It's so
ancient that the cork is petrified." Playing the role of wizard in a hotel
room, Bailey describes in this playful way the strong medicine that will
preside over the rest of Perry's evening—the spirit of the Dionysian
ripening of his love and life.

It is, however, the fusion of old plots and details of the day that
make the story the wonderful, if neglected, work that it is. The opening lines build this double vision directly into the discourse of the narrative:

The glazed eye of the tired reader resting for a second on the
above title will presume it to be merely metaphorical. Stories
about the cup and the lip and the bad penny and the new broom
rarely have anything to do with cups or lips or pennies or
brooms. This story is the exception. It has to do with a material, visible and large-as-life camel's back.

It is no accident that Fitzgerald uses the traditional address to the
reader in order to announce the ironic entrance of a "large-as-life"

camel's back rather than the one broken by the proverbial final straw. All of the acutely accurate social observation of the holiday social scene among the Toledo rich that follows—the story of Perry Parkhurst's almost misspent but ultimately gloriously successful evening at a circus party during the Christmas of 1919—makes for a large-as-life tale that is also a fable about the trials of romantic love, whose airy superstructure is supported by naturalistic stonework.

"Now during the Christmas holidays of 1919," our narrator informs us, "there took place in Toledo, counting only the people with the italicized *the*, forty-one dinner parties, sixteen dances, six luncheons, male and female, twelve teas, four stag dinners, two weddings, and thirteen bridge parties." This active festival calendar moves Perry Parkhurst to propose, unsuccessfully, to Betty Medill. This in turn initiates Perry's idea to attend a winter circus party dressed in the front part of the "large-as-life" camel suit, which garners him the prize for most original costume and leads to the mock wedding to the other costume winner, Betty Medill (who wins for her snake charmer's outfit), presided over by the obese black waiter named Jumbo, who turns out to be an ordained minister.

Aside from the deft sketching in of characters and the easy management of the mob scene at the circus party (as well as a scene at an earlier party that serves as a kind of curtain raiser to the story's main spectacle), the most striking achievement of "The Camel's Back" remains the fusion of twentieth-century detail and mythic implication. The story opens in the Toledo of the Social Register, but it soon transcends the quotidian round by means of the introduction of alcohol— the "stoneage champagne"—and enters the realm of inebriated or festival reality. From the inebriation scene in the hotel we follow Perry and a cabdriver to the "dim and ghostly" setting of the costume shop run by the European—for Fitzgerald this apparently suggests some sort of wizardlike, alien stature—Mrs. Nolak.

The costume shop holds numerous portents of change to come— "glass cases full of crowns and scepters, and jewels and enormous stomachers, and paints, and crape hair, and wigs of all colors." When the costume shop owner produces the two-piece camel suit and Perry tries to wear both sections of it himself, more auguries show forth. Because of the hind legs of the costume tied "as a girdle around his waist," Perry gives the appearance "of one of those mediæval pictures of a monk changed into a beast by the ministrations of Satan. At the very best the ensemble resembled a humpbacked cow sitting on her haunches among blankets." Mrs. Nolak urges Perry to make a decision about the costume because she wants to close the shop. The cabdriver wanders in out of the cold, and Perry gets the idea to hire the cabbie to wear the hind part of the camel. Off they go to the party, except that Perry has forgotten the location. He thinks to ask Mrs. Nolak, since she has stayed open late in order to service the guests for this masked affair, but when he looks out the car window at the shop, it has gone dark, and "Mrs. Nolak had already faded out, a little black smudge far down the snowy street."

So the transition from the mundane to the magical is nearly complete. Perry, changed by imbibing the ancient drink and, as he arrives at the first party, donning the camel costume, loses his identity to the beast who, "as he walked . . . alternately elongated and contracted like a gigantic concertina." With his appearance, his identity, and, indeed, his very movement transformed from the everyday into the magical—into music—Perry moves into the festival round, first at the Tate house, where he mistakenly crashes a debutante party and is seen as a misfit, as a beast, and then merely as a guest from out of town. He becomes the star attraction, the young lawyer transformed, as if by the puckish powers of some hidden god of festival, into a beast with two parts (and his actions on the dance floor are a parody of Freudian schematics—with the taxi driver showing at first a will of his own that seems out of synch with Perry's desires to move in another direction).

The big party itself is a wonderful assembly of heated misrule under the sign of perpetual change—a sign over the bar that bears the slogan NOW FOLLOW THIS!

A great tent fly had been put up inside the ballroom and round the walls had been built rows of booths representing the various attractions of a circus side show, but these were now vacated and over the floor swarmed a shouting, laughing medley of youth and color—clowns, bearded ladies, acrobats, bareback riders, ringmasters, tattooed men, and charioteers.

In the midst of this festival, Perry, looking out through his camel's head, spies Betty Medill, who has so recently spurned him, "talking to a comic policeman." Betty is dressed as a snake charmer, which gives the impression, as Fitzgerald tells it, that she is already halfway along toward transformation into another form herself, since "Her fair face was stained to a warm olive glow and on her arms and the half moon of her back writhed painted serpents with single eyes of venomous green. Her feet were in sandals and her skirt was slit to the knees, so that when she walked one caught a glimpse of other slim serpents painted just above her bare ankles. Wound about her neck was a glittering cobra."

In this state—which some of the older and more reserved women at the party recognize as "perfectly disgraceful"—Betty is more than halfway ready to find herself matched up once again with Perry, who earlier that day had pled his troth to her, complete with marriage license in hand, only to be turned away. But since one of the conventions of comedy, as Prospero announces in *The Tempest*, is that "light winning makes the prize seem light," Perry must still struggle a bit more before ending up with his intended. That struggle comes in the form of the mock wedding in which Perry and Betty, after both winning first place for their costumes, must take front and center.

"Form for the grand wedding march," the costumed ringmaster of the party declares, "the beautiful snake-charmer and the noble camel in front!" Unaware that beneath the camel costume is the same man whom she had rejected earlier in the day, Betty steps up, as does Perry, still bearing with him the very marriage license he had carried to Betty's house some hours before. Music sounds: "The voluptuous chords of the wedding march done in blasphemous syncopation . . . in a delirious blend from the trombones and saxophones." Perry fits right in. Remember that he's already moving like a living concertina. And Betty is halfway there—half serpent, half woman. When Jumbo the black waiter is called on to serve as minister for what everyone has taken to be a mock wedding ceremony, everything has moved into place for the final major movement of the story.

Jumbo—bearer of the name of another beast—produces a Bible and proceeds to officiate, asking the camel for his marriage license.

Perry fumbles in his pocket, finds a folded piece of paper (the marriage license), and pushes it out through the camel's mouth. When Jumbo asks for a ring, Perry cadges one from the cabdriver to his rear and, in an action even more bizarre than the way in which he produced the marriage license, pushes the rhinestone "through a tear in the camel's coat" in a mythic variation of vaginal birth and slips the ring on the snake charmer's finger, "muttering ancient and historic words after Jumbo."

At this point in the scene, everyone participating in it—except for Jumbo, who knows more than he is saying—believes the event to be merely an empty ritual, a ceremony that is mere decoration, a playful moment in the passage from the dark heart of winter to the possibility of heat and light in spring. With the discovery that the marriage license is authentic and that Jumbo actually possesses the power to perform a marriage ceremony, the illusion flips over into reality, and Betty passes immediately from fury to acceptance. Just as Perry, ready to admit that he has failed miserably in his pursuit of Betty even in the playful form of the ceremony-turned-real, exits from the party, Betty, all "snakes and silk and tawny hair," avows her love for him. Exit camel accompanied by true love. The transformation is complete. The two parts of the camel, recognizing that their complicity, crossing over social boundaries and a number of difficult obstacles, has won Perry his success in love, exchange "a particularly subtle, esoteric sort of wink that only true camels can understand." The glazed eye of the tired reader that Fitzgerald alluded to in the first line of the story has been transformed as well into the complicity between writer and reader that allows such a "midwinter night's dream," a heated revel at the darkest part of the year, to seem true enough to win our attention and deserve our praise.

Of course none of this would work if it weren't for the meticulous buildup of naturalistic detail and sharply observed social gesture. This is not just any Christmas—this is the Christmas of 1919, through which Fitzgerald had just passed before he left for New Orleans and sat down to write the story. And "The Camel's Back" is not just any sentimental Christmas story but, rather, a pagan fantasy, the suggestion of the possibility of a new and happy beginning in the middle of what Blake calls in his ode to St. Lucy "the year's deepe midnight" that seems deeply rooted in the peculiar holiday antics of the American Midwest upper class. Coming from a twenty-four-year-old writer with a brilliant sense of form, a fine eye for detail, and a great heart for comedy appropriate to the season, the story is a rather marvelous gift in itself.

17

A Note on Landscape in All the Pretty Horses

They reached the Devil's River by midmorning and watered the horses and stretched out in the shade of a stand of black-willow and looked at the map. It was an oilcompany roadmap that Rawlins had picked up at the cafe and he looked at it and he looked south toward the gap in the low hills. There were roads and rivers and towns on the American side of the map as far south as the Rio Grande and beyond that all was white.

Cormac McCarthy, *All the Pretty Horses*

The Appalachian South and the American Southwest have served as Cormac McCarthy's fictional territory for the past thirty years, but with the publication of *All the Pretty Horses* he and his characters have come to the border of Mexico and crossed over into previously uncharted land. Despite the proximity of our countries, surprisingly few American fiction writers of merit have taken their characters south of the Rio Grande. Katherine Anne Porter, Wright Morris, David Markson, Harriet Doerr: the list is so short that I don't feel half shy about adding my own name to it, having set a group of stories there in my collection *The Tennessee Waltz*. But of writers in English outside of the United States, two major figures have focused upon the Mexican landscape, D. H. Lawrence and Malcolm Lowry. Cormac McCarthy's Mexico in *All the Pretty Horses* is transformed in such a powerful visionary fashion that his work demands to be placed in the company of this masterly pair of novelists.

In his brief essay "Landscape and the Novel in Mexico," Octavio Paz writes of Lawrence, Lowry, and the Mexican novelist Juan Rulfo as three artists whose poetic visions "give the landscape its concrete form" rather than vice versa. The landscape in their work, Paz suggests, "does not function as the background or physical setting of the narrative. . . . It is something that is alive, something that takes a thousand different forms; it is a symbol and something more than a symbol: a voice entering into the dialogue, and in the end the principal character in the story."

Using Paz's assertions as a standard, a reader can travel through the northern Mexico of *All the Pretty Horses* and notice certain rhetorical patterns that perhaps ought to be regarded as more than mere rhetoric. The landscape, almost a "character" in itself, becomes a force to reckon with rather than a mere reflection of mood. We get a sense of this at the very outset of the novel, while still in the charted portion of the book's geography, West Texas in 1949, when the young protagonist, John Grady Cole, disturbed by disruptive events in his family, rides his horse out from his house to the west. "The wind was much abated," we hear, "and it was very cold and the sun sat blood red and elliptic under the reefs of bloodred cloud before him." John Grady then has a vision of old Kiowa tribes, "nation and ghost of nation passing in a soft chorale across that mineral waste to darkness bearing lost to all history and all remembrance like a grail the sum of their secular and transitory and violent lives."

Thus having a map to the territory before you means having a past, both personal and historical, whose visions and outer signs you may easily read in order to find orientation. But John Grady Cole lights out for the territory ahead, or, to be specific, to the south, to Mexico and its blank and uncharted regions, unhappy with the known past of family turmoil and American blood. He seeks freedom from the old well-marked Texas spaces in the possibilities of an undiscovered country. In this way his quest becomes associated with the land and its representation in rhetorical passages focusing on landscape. It seems apparent from the start, however, that character, motive, and what we normally consider in fiction to be background are deeply intertwined.

They rode out along the fenceline and across the open pastureland. The leather creaked in the morning cold. They pushed the horses into a lope. The lights fell away behind them. They rode out on the high prairie where they slowed the horses to a walk and the stars swarmed around them out of the blackness. They heard somewhere in that tenantless night a bell that tolled and ceased where no bell was and they rode out on the round dais of the earth which alone was dark and no light to it and which carried their figures and bore them up into the swarming stars so that they rode not under but among them and they rode at once jaunty and circumspect, like thieves newly loosed in that dark electric, like young thieves in a glowing orchard, loosely jacketed against the cold and ten thousand worlds for the choosing.

More than a mere newly minted version of the romantic treatment of nature in fiction, in which landscape reflects the emotion of the characters, McCarthy's land and sky scape form an exterior version of the main characters' inner universe. And vice versa. We understand this more clearly in another passage offering us a glimpse of the night sky rather early in John Grady's flight into Mexico.

He lay on his back in his blankets and looked out where the quartermoon lay cocked over the heel of the mountains. In that false blue dawn the Pleiades seemed to be rising up into the darkness above the world and dragging all the stars away, the great diamond of Orion and Cepella and the signature of Cassiopeia all rising up through the phosphorous dark like a seanet. He lay a long time listening to the others breathing in their sleep while he contemplated the wildness about him, the wildness within.

"The wildness about him, the wildness within." That phrase suggests a certain geographical representation of psyche and natural world, with John Grady considering himself as a being possessing an inner nature who is embedded in a natural world of similar feel and texture. Holding inner and outer world in balance is McCarthy's prose, as represented in that phrase by the balancing comma.

The passage in which that phrase appears comes on a night just after John Grady and his companions Lacey Rawlins and the outlawin-training Jimmy Blevins have crossed the border into Mexico. There are few striking references to the landscape until they ride further south on the following day. But by early evening of that day they look to the north and see a rising storm front.

All the sky to the north had darkened and the spare terrain they trod had turned a neuter gray as far as eye could see. They grouped in the road at the top of a rise and looked back. The storm front towered above them and the wind was cool on their sweating faces. They slumped bleary-eyed in their saddles and looked at one another. Shrouded in the black thunderheads the distant lightning glowed mutely like welding seen through foundry smoke. As if repairs were under way at some flawed place in the iron dark of the world.

As if shut off from an immediate return along the way they have come by this massive storm, the three adventurous boys proceed ever southward, encountering minor dangers until an escapade with a stolen horse leads Jimmy Blevins to launch a criminal foray in a small desert village, for which all the boys take the blame. To escape they ride south and west through hill country toward a region they have heard of from a group of peasants they met in the desert, a lush section of farms against the western mountains in the state of Coahuila. Climbing the hills the next day, they catch their first glimpse of this fabled terrain.

The grasslands lay in a deep violet haze and to the west thin flights of waterfowl were moving north before the sunset in the deep red galleries under the cloudbanks like schoolfish in a burning sea and on the foreland plain they saw vaqueros driving cattle before them through a gauze of golden dust.

The land before him holds much promise for John Grady Cole, for his imminent education as a breaker of horses and prodigal son, as a boy turned man by means of love and tested by imprisonment and the blade. Readers who push forward through this provocatively lush and biblical chiaroscuro mystery about one young Texan's growth of soul will find that the land is more than promising. The Mexico that rises up before us in the subsequent sections of the novel is, as Paz argues about the Mexico of Lawrence, Lowry, and Rulfo, not so much a visionary landscape as a landscape of vision. The land is the promise, the promise is the land; alive, a symbol, a voice, a character; the book itself.

18

Rereading Traven

Time, that ethereal substance in which writers immerse themselves all their lives, is usually not good to them in death. Only the truest artist can remain a writer for his or her own epoch and then enter that ephemeral realm we call the universal. Few of us reach that place, and when we actually witness the work of a writer we admire "crossing over," it's cause for celebration.

With the reissuing of *The Kidnapped Saint and Other Stories*, we can all now observe the spirit of B. Traven soaring toward its rightful niche in posterity. The reclusive writer, a resident of Mexico for most of his adult life, had made something of a reputation for himself in Europe between the wars with the publication of the novel *The Death Ship*, but it wasn't until John Huston's filming of Traven's novel *The Treasure of the Sierra Madre* that a large North American audience discovered a taste for Traven's variety of fabulous realism.

It didn't take long for the man himself to become as important to his audience as the work he wrought, in no small part because Traven resisted the public eye. Imagine a chef who makes fabulous banquets for thousands of people year after year but keeps himself in the shadows of the restaurant kitchen, a shy creator who cannot bring himself to personally accept the thanks and praise of the grateful diners who have enjoyed his repasts. The chef's anonymity would lead many of these people—who, being human, are gossipers and dreamers and speculators—to talk as much about the chef as about his creations.

Writers are bound to speculate about the lives of other writers. Novices rely on established writers' work and lives to guide them from the realm of the normal to that strange condition we call the writing life. Established writers, too, use other writers' lives as reference points as they traverse the same literary paths. But when readers tramp through the private regions of a writer's life, another motive is at work: hero worship tempered paradoxically by iconoclasm. Although modern readers may appear to revere their writers and endow them with superhuman status, in fact they often seek to be convinced that their writers are not gods. But whatever their motive, they allow the life of the writer to distract them from the work.

B. Traven seemed to understand this human tendency, and he kept himself as much as he could out of the public eye. What he couldn't have anticipated was just how much the public, thirsty for information about the writer's life, would turn its energy into speculation about his identity rather than focus on his work. No one else in North America, except perhaps the novelist Thomas Pynchon, has had so much attention brought to bear on the question of his identity. And even Pynchon comes in a poor second to Traven.

I have to confess that as a young student of literature some decades ago I found myself on the Traven trail, his novels in one hand, a map of Mexico in the other. Fortunately for me I came to my senses fairly early in my quest for the "real" B. T.—aided by a little friendly advice from his widow, the gracious and intelligent Rosa Elena Luján de Traven, that finally it was the work that mattered and not the man. I reluctantly put speculation aside, or at least relegated it to the far corner of my writing desk, and threw myself into the pleasures of Traven's work.

Time has been good to Traven's fiction. In the autumn of 1975, a few years after I had started reading him, the *New York Times Book Review* asked me to review the stories gathered under the title *The Kidnapped Saint*. Here is the text of my review:

Filthy, unshaven, the man shuffles painfully across the cactus-studded desert, urging on his heavily burdened burros while the mountains brood darkly in the background. A band of destitute robbers confronts him at a waterhole. Machetes flash. A stone thuds dully on skull-bone. A dream of wealth fades like a mirage from the screen before us.

Most North Americans discover B. Traven's narrative by watching Humphrey Bogart perform such scenes in John Huston's film version of *The Treasure of the Sierra Madre*. Traven himself, who died in Mexico City in 1969, had a great interest in moviemaking and wrote the screenplays for several Mexican productions of his work. (One story, and there are many such, has Traven skulking about the set of the Huston production in the guise of his own agent, "Hal Croves.") But more important, Traven's spare but resonant narration, which harks back to the old wisdom tales of Indian-American mythology, has much in common as well with that alienated (Brecht called it "distanced") mode of presentation that we have come to associate with technologically produced works of cinematic art.

The Kidnapped Saint will give readers new to the Traven canon ample opportunity to discover this distinctive style at its best. The eight stories in the collection will in fact be new to all but the most intrepid Traven followers (and some will be new even to them). The title tale, which appears apparently for the first time in English, introduces us to Cecilio Ortiz, an illiterate miner who misplaces his precious pocket watch and then holds the icon of Saint Anthony, patron saint of those who lose valuable possessions, for ransom in a deserted jungle well. How Ortiz recovers his watch but loses his faith becomes a delightful comedy with serious social undertones. It sets the mood for the rest of these passionate and extremely witty fables of Mexican Indian and mestizo life.

"Submission" (one of several pieces that appeared in a now-long-out-of-print Traven collection and published here in new translations) depicts the period of adjustment between two headstrong though aging newlyweds from the "romantic" state of Michoacán. "Frustration" is an intriguing story (with a surprisingly Cortázar-like flavor) of a Chicano woman's bizarre spinsterhood in a Texas border town. "The Diplomat" sharply satirizes the court of Porfirio Díaz, Mexico's last dictator (against whom the mahogany-cutters struggle in Traven's six-volume *Jungle* series).

Of the remaining stories, only "Reviving the Dead" covers familiar ground, spinning a variation on the scene in *The Treasure of the Sierra Madre* in which one of the North American prospectors revives an apparently dead Indian child. It recalls a similar moment in Traven's lesser-known but equally wonderful novel, *The Bridge in the Jungle*, in which the narrator, a down-and-out oil worker named Gales, tries without success to bring a drowned Indian boy back to life. "The Story of a Bomb" and "Accomplices" starkly contrast country justice and city justice. "Indian Dance in the Jungle," a first-person account of an ephemeral night of music and ritual among the tribes of rural Chiapas, stands as a moving lyric coda to the fiction portion of the volume.

In addition to these tales, with their remarkable fusion of intense empathy and the self-conscious distance that prevents us from turning Indian passion to gringo pastoral, the collection contains the first seven (and most successful) chapters of a novel, *The White Rose*, Traven's uneven satire on the American entrepreneurs who ravaged Mexico's petroleum reserves before President Cárdenas nationalized them at the outbreak of World War II. Mina C. and H. Arthur Klein, Traven aficionados since the days of pre-Hitler Germany, also present their translation of a previously unpublished political essay, "In the Freest State in the World." Here the young Traven, apparently writing as "Ret Marut," fiery anarchist editor of the revolutionary Munich journal *Der Ziegelbrenner*, gives a stirring account of what seems to be his own capture and near-execution by right-wing police after the collapse of the short-lived Bavarian Republic in 1918.

As his widow, Rosa Elena Luján, suggests in her affectionate introduction, Traven's penchant for such disguises has made great headaches for scholars. Given some of the problems surrounding the "Marut" document and the variations in many Traven editions, the headaches will probably continue for some time. But as any reader trained to keep his gaze from wandering from the screen should know quite well by now, it is the stories themselves, whether fables of the downfall of avaricious gringos or tributes to the native wisdom of peasants bereft of modern technology, that remain the sites where the true Traven treasure abides.

I not only have just reread this review but have also just reread the stories in this collection. And aside from evoking a certain nostalgia for the time when I first read the book and was still ready to plunge heedlessly into the jungle in search of artifacts of the man behind the Traven mask (and for an era when a hardcover collection cost only $7.95), the review remains a valid statement of my opinions about Traven's work. If anything, I enjoyed the stories today even more than I did in 1975, a reaction that has as much to do with the timeless art of B. Traven as it does with the apparent maturation of a devoted reader of good stories.

Try this experiment yourself. Read the stories now, and then read them again after we pass the line that divides this century from the next. I think that you'll find what I found—stories for all time.

part 3

writing

19

Confessions of an Ex-Minimalist

I was riding in a car through downtown Chicago on the way to give a reading at a university when the driver, my host and one of the country's most accomplished writers of short stories, looked away from the wheel for a moment and said—we had been talking about the current state of the American short story—"I used to be a minimalist, you know, but I've grown up."

I asked him what he meant by that, since after all he began writing—like myself—only in his late thirties and by now, in his mid-forties, he had been writing for half a dozen years in a manner that I took to be quite mature.

"I started out as a writing student at Iowa," he explained, "after I'd made a little career for myself in documentary filmmaking. And out there I bought the whole Barth–Barthelme language-is-everything-reality-is-nothing-but-language package all tied up in a ribbon. I was in my late thirties, but I felt like a talented little kid, thumbing my nose at the realists, kicking up my heels by writing—and publishing.

"I started to publish early in my writing career even though I started that career quite late—publishing stories about writing stories and stories about the impossibility of writing stories, and if there were people in my stories at all they were stripped-down figures, not stripped naked, I don't mean that, hell, because then at least you might have seen some fat on them, some muscle, but these were voices, just voices, really, sketchy stick figures like something right out of a cartoon . . . the important thing for me then was to make stories in which I could show off my skill at manipulation—of language, of psychology, of everything that I knew about fiction.

"There were a lot of terms critics used to describe the kinds of stories I did, and a lot of the work of other writers of my generation—metafiction, sur-fiction, to describe the writing about writing. And then somebody came up with 'minimalist' fiction, which was the subgroup of stories in which you found people in situations stripped down to the bare wood, sort of like old country furniture that you find in a barn up in Vermont and take home to the city to strip and repaint, or maybe the best analogy is to European designer's furniture . . . nothing much to this chair except the idea that it will hold you if you sit your ass down in it. Functional stories, these were. Sort of like fast food. Call them fast-fiction. You're in, you're out, and part of the nourishment comes from the ambience of going in and out so quickly . . ."

This man went on a while longer with his impromptu confession—which turned into a statement—you can hear it—about what truly matters when making a good story.

"It's the truth of what's actually there that I try to get at now," he said. "In the old days I was much more interested in the truth of how I was seeing things rather than the truth about what I was seeing. I mean, since the turn of the century we've all been impressionists of sorts, but the stories I was writing were impressions for the sake of impressions and I was deliberately blurring what I knew to be there, the part of reality that was outside myself, outside the instrument of my vision. . . . Now I've grown up. And I write the stories that I find in what I see, not the story about how I am seeing."

He kept on speaking and I kept on listening as the traffic went on and on. Downtown Chicago rolled slowly past us in all its mixed splendor of high-rise glass and steel and burned-out housing projects standing against the backdrop of a sky as blue as or bluer than the lake that borders on the east side of this tough city. And I was thinking hard about what he was saying, about how even as he spoke I could hear him describe minimalism and metafiction as one and the same kind of story and how the labels didn't quite matter as much as what he was saying about the discoveries he had made about his art and how he came to see technique as a force at the service of the story rather than the other way around.

To throw some light upon this question of technique in contemporary story writing, I want to take a little excursion back into the tradition. American writers have made a unique contribution to the evolution of the short story, but in order to highlight this contribution we need to look first to the European antecedents of the modern story.

Though telling tales is an ancient art, one that we find playing a central role in the major works of poetry from the *Odyssey* through *The Canterbury Tales*, the modern story as we know it—the brief realistic depiction of a singularly important event in the life of a single figure, the leading up to a turning point in the character's life and then leaving him—begins quite late—really not until the advent of Chekhov. It's true that many decades before Chekhov, Poe's detective fiction certainly established the narrative rhythm of the short story—the discovery of a mystery, the search for an answer, and the uncovering of an answer—and that De Maupassant practiced the art of the sophisticated tale. But it wasn't until Chekhov that we find that elemental narrative rhythm—in Aristotelian terms, the action, or, that end toward which the story is moving—embedded in fiction about everyday life (and usually the life of the middle class).

Take, for example, the action in the Russian writer's story called "Gusev," a lesser-known tale but an extraordinary one nonetheless. Gusev, a consumptive soldier returning to Odessa by ship from the Russian Far East, languishes in the heat belowdecks with several other sick compatriots. One of them, Pavel Ivanitch, son of a clergyman, berates him for his ill health and suggests that he won't last the trip.

Gusev dreams of frost and a winter at home with family while the ship moves slowly forward through a sea indifferent to the suffering of the passengers. Pavel Ivanitch himself soon expires, and Gusev is left to cough and hallucinate. He climbs on deck, he returns below, "tormented by a vague craving." And he then goes to sleep for two days "and at midnight on the third day," Chekhov tells us, "two sailors came down and carried him out" onto the deck.

The last two pages of the story break all the rules about point of view—and make for a remarkable conclusion. We see Gusev wrapped in a flag and buried at sea, and then watch his body sink below the waves, where it is met by a school of pilot fish and then a shark that undoes the grave wrapping with its teeth.

"Overhead," begins the final paragraph,

> the clouds are massed together on the side where the sun is setting; one cloud like a triumphal arch, another like a lion, a third like a pair of scissors. . . . From behind the clouds a broad, green shaft of light pierces through and stretches to the middle of the sky; a little later another, violet-colored, lies beside it; next to that, one of gold, then one rose-colored. . . . The sky turns a soft lilac. Looking at this gorgeous, enchanted sky, at first the ocean scowls, but soon it, too, takes tender, joyous, passionate colors for which it is hard to find a name in human speech.

This is naturalism at its perfection, this ironically beautiful backdrop to the demise of the consumptive soldier who never makes it home. But the odd point of view at the end here advances Chekhov's great gift for allowing each of his subjects, from bureaucrats to physicians to soldiers and peasants, to speak for themselves. Taken together, the intimacy and the God-like perspective push the story form, or, as William Trevor calls it, "the art of the glimpse," beyond convention. Who else before Chekhov could dare to give us the point of view of the ocean and make it work?

Writers who adhere to the naturalistic persuasion usually have a penchant for looking upon the human comedy with the cold eye of a scientist. When the modern story arises in Ireland, in the work of Joyce, we notice directly what we can't truly ascertain in Chekhov in translation—that is, the beautiful relation of the language of the story to its dramatic action, beauty that takes the edge off any coldness that might obtain. Consider this moment from "Araby" when the narrator, entranced with the Dublin neighborhood girl he calls only by the title of "Mangan's sister," steps out at night under a streetlamp:

When the short days of winter came dusk fell before we had well eaten our dinners. When we met in the street the houses had grown somber. The space of sky above us was the colour of ever-changing violet and towards it the lamps of the street lifted their feeble lanterns. The cold air stung us and we played till our bodies glowed. Our shouts echoed in the silent street. The career of our play brought us through the dark muddy lanes behind the houses where we ran the gantlet of the rough tribes from the cottages, to the back doors of the dark dripping gardens where odours arose from the ashpits, to the dark odorous stables where a coachman smoothed and combed the horse or shook music from the buckled harness. When we returned to the street light from the kitchen windows had filled the areas. If my uncle was seen turning the corner we hid in the shadow until we had seen him safely housed. Or if Mangan's sister came out on the doorstep to call her brother in to his tea we watched her from our shadow peer up and down the street. We waited to see whether she would remain or go in and, if she remained, we left our shadow and walked up to Mangan's steps resignedly. She was waiting for us, her figure defined by the light from the half-opened door. Her brother always teased her before he obeyed and I stood by the railings looking at her. Her dress swung as she moved her body and the soft rope of her hair tossed from side to side.

The glimpse here is nearly ecstatic and exists as much in the ear as sound byte as in the eye. It makes a marvel of compactness that encompasses the back alleys and streets of Dublin as well as the initiation rituals of tribes much rougher than the Dublin lower bourgeoisie. It fuses—or deliberately confuses, we should say—the glories and perils of erotic love and devotion to the Virgin, and the technique of the camera eye of modern cinema. We can find the principles of literary naturalism at work here too, in the way in which the boys feel the cold. There's also in the image of the piercing temperatures a theo-logical/erotic fusion that derives from such baroque figures as Bernini's Saint Theresa, penetrated by arrows for her devotion and, by the look of her, desiring penetration all the while. When the boys reach the stable, we hear the horse making music with the shaking of its buckled, belled harness, like the art that we miraculously create out of the very constraints of our language.

In the finest stories that we know in English—and a number can be found in Joyce's *Dubliners*—the language of the story becomes an elemental part of the action, as in the use of prepositions and infini-tives, for example, in that sentence beginning "The career of our play," each of these serving as a conduit or gateway toward yet another stage in the downward-turning path toward the wisdom of the nether-side of bourgeois Dublin life, in the back streets, backyards, garbage heaps, and dung piles. Joyce shows us the way to marry language and story, sound and meaning, music and the images generated by beautiful noise.

In our own country a decade or so later we see a similar blossom-ing of the story in the hands of Sherwood Anderson. *Winesburg, Ohio*, that masterly volume of linked stories, ranks with the greatest short fiction we know. And outside of that collection Anderson created sev-eral masterpieces of brevity—"Death in the Woods," "The Egg," and what may be the finest coming-of-age story thus far written by an American, "I Want To Know Why."

We got up at four in the morning, that first day in the east. On the evening before we had climbed off a freight train at the edge of town, and with the true instinct of Kentucky boys had found our way across town and to the race track and the stables at once. Then we knew we were all right. Hanley Turner right away found a nigger we knew. It was Bildad Johnson who in the winter works at Ed Becker's livery barn in our hometown, Beckerville. Bildad is a good cook as almost all our niggers are and of course he, like everyone in our part of Kentucky who is anyone at all, likes the horses. In the spring Bildad begins to scratch around. A nigger from our country can flatter and wheedle anyone into letting him do most anything he wants. Bildad wheedles the stable men and the trainers from the horse farms in our country around Lexington. The trainers come into town in the evening to stand around and talk and maybe get into a poker game. Bildad gets in with them. He is always doing little favors and telling about things to eat, chicken browned in a pan, and how is the best way to cook sweet potatoes and corn bread. It makes your mouth water to hear him.

Language and action are wedded in this opening paragraph of "I Want To Know Why," in a vital way. Because the language is so simple (in the blind, bigoted idiom of the young speaker, of course) and straightforward, the product of several hundred years of use of the American plain style, in which redundancy, decoration, rhetorical flourish for its own sake play no role, Anderson's achievements may at first seem transparent. What's there but the story? However, his influence on modern American short fiction is undeniable, particularly the effect of his work on the fiction of Hemingway and, in a more complicated way, Faulkner. We all know the stories about Ezra Pound's impact on the work of Yeats and T. S. Eliot. Anderson deserves no less celebration for his role in relation to our own modern masters. As for his own prose, it makes your mouth water to hear him.

Certainly it's clear who our masters of the short story are: Hemingway, Katherine Anne Porter, John Cheever, Flannery O'Connor, Bernard Malamud, and the recently departed Raymond Carver and Wright Morris and Gina Berriault. Among the living there are Eudora Welty, Grace Paley, John Updike, George Garrett, Joy Williams, Evan Connell, and James Salter, and in my own generation Richard Bausch, Richard Ford, Robert Stone, Annie Proulx, Mary Robison, Laura Furman, Charles Baxter, Amy Hempel. And a few other fine writers whose names are not so well known as yet but ought to be, among them David Michael Kaplan, Alice Elliott Dark, and Matt Klam.

Which brings us up to the near-present, and the current state of the American story. So say now for the sake of the argument that if we started out talking about the contemporary short story in a car moving through downtown Chicago, now we're sitting in a German restaurant in the basement of a little shopping mall in San Jose, California. We're eating pretty good wiener schnitzel when all of a sudden lights go up on a little bandstand and a quartet of young men starts to play. The saxophonist, a kid about twenty-one, sounds just like Charlie Parker! If the lights didn't reveal him to be a student from a local music institute, you would think that someone had put a Parker recording on the sound system. But in music schools these days young white kids can learn how to play exactly like Parker and Coltrane. The technique they acquire has produced a generation of instrumentalists unparalleled in American jazz. Technicians of the first order roam the land, so many of them that even funky German rathskellers in San Jose can hire pickup jazz bands who sound just great.

M.F.A. programs have done something similar for American fiction. Dozens and dozens, perhaps hundreds, of writers between the ages of thirty and forty now write every day in the United States, and scores of books have come out of their workrooms, some of them with a technical proficiency that would make some of the masters of the West give pause and wonder. We live in a Silver Age of American fiction. Never before have so many well-made and interesting books, novels, and stories, been written and published. There are writers of every stripe and tendency, creators of short fiction and long, and they can write sentences and paragraphs and stories with skill that would make Theodore Dreiser weep and James Jones scowl.

The paradox is that hardly any of them has written anything worth reading twice. Most of the writers at work today have either closed themselves off from the world outside their workrooms, most of which seem to be located on or near university campuses—a point that E. L. Doctorow has emphatically made—or they have not given themselves over to the true stories of their own lives and stay, rather, within the fashionable boundaries of the styles in which they have been tutored.

The underside of our Silver Age is mannerism. The alternative would be a cadre of clunky writers with great stories to tell. I'm not suggesting that I want that, a gang of Dreisers rushing to the table with our big main meal of the day and in their haste and lack of grace slopping food over the tray and onto their trousers and shoe tops. You can't train to become a Dreiser, anyway. Ignorance and pain and accident do that for you. But you can imitate a Nabokov or a Barth or Barthelme. You can acquire technique—catastrophe that hurts you into story-making comes free of charge and at odd intervals in your life. You have to have the former in order to be ready for the latter. Most writers of our Silver Age seem to be indoors playing board games while the storms rage when they should be outside under the spreading oak, waiting for the lightning.

I guess what I'm suggesting is that a true distinction may exist between the achievements of writers who have given over their craft to their obsessions and those who have made an obsession of their craft. The difference for me is that the former can produce work of rough beauty that has the possibility of staying around for subsequent generations to take up. The latter make for natty little raves in the Sunday book reviews, jobs at the assistant professor level, and mildew of the imagination.

But in America in these days we all lie down with beast, wherever the place, whatever the position. That's what we do in order to bring the stories back alive. And it is fair to say that some of our finest writers have moved in and out of the faculties of colleges and universities. Some have simply failed to reemerge intact, while others have used the institutions as patrons for their art. For many it's a living, as the church was in nineteenth-century England. For those for whom it's faith, trouble might arise. In any case, their presence in academia has produced subsequent generations of these extremely competent technicians.

Nowhere has this development become more apparent than in the work of our so-called minimalists, the best of whom seem to emulate the plain style of Anderson and celebrate the aesthetic of Gertrude Stein. Stein, our major twentieth-century theoretician of American literary language, thought of it as a plastic medium, a medium to be shaped, formed, and manipulated for its own sake. From her vision, and the stories of Anderson, followed the pared-down style of Ernest Hemingway. Certainly Stein and Anderson and Hemingway among them invented the possibility of the acrobatic language tales we call minimalist fiction. With some help from Virginia Woolf around the same time. Because if you read her early stories such as "Kew Gardens" with its marvelously idiosyncratic perspective—the flowers'-eye view of reality—and its pulsating language, you can see that the self-conscious short story that makes itself known as a creation of language is an international event, something for which modern Western writers seem to have developed an affinity.

Our need for a short take on life in a busy industrial world produced this modern literary form. I have a less clear notion of why the peculiarly self-conscious story we've been calling contemporary minimalist fiction came about. If you go by the confession of my friend in Chicago it may have something to do with the precocity of these new generations of university-trained fiction makers, who think of language as a tool and a game, rather than as the means to tell the best stories they know. In that respect, minimalism may be the aesthetic response to the new high-tech civilization we seem to be on the verge of entering.

But there's another aspect, one that in the twenty years that I've been writing fiction, has seemed quite apparent to me. The highly compact and densely made invention of language we call the short story stands quite close to lyric poetry. Faulkner once remarked that all novelists were failed poets. Frank O'Connor in his *Paris Review* interview admitted that for him also the story was the next best thing to poetry. "A novel," he said, "actually requires far more logic and far more knowledge of circumstances, whereas a short story can have the sort of detachment from circumstances that lyric poetry has."

All the language and activity in a story builds toward creating a certain mood—that's the way the lyric writer would have it. Poe certainly stands as the forerunner of this view, if you take "The Fall of the House of Usher" as an example. *Son coeur est un luth suspendu; / Sitôt qu'on le touche il resonné*, goes the De Berenger epigram. And the story resonates one note and one note only to create and then reinforce the mood of dread and terror that ultimately brings down the House of Usher.

So I suppose I'm saying that at its best the so-called minimalist story works in two ways, compressing modern life into a very brief narrative and at the same time expressing strong emotions, as in lyric verse. A fine example of this dual effect is a short short story by Amy

Hempel, one of the best practitioners of this variety of fiction. It's called "San Francisco."

Do you know what I think?

I think it was the tremors. That's what must have done it. The way the floor rolled like bongo boards under our feet? Remember it was you and Daddy and me having lunch? "I guess that's not an earthquake," you said. "I guess you're shaking the table?"

That's when it must have happened. A watch on a dresser, a small thing like that—it must have been shaken right off, onto the floor.

And how would Maidy know? Maidy at the doctor's office? All those years on a psychiatrist's couch and suddenly the couch is moving.

Good God, she is on that couch when the big one hits.

Maidy didn't tell you, but you know what the doctor said? When she sprang from the couch and said, "My God, was that an earthquake?"

The doctor said this: "Did it feel like an earthquake to you?"

I think we are agreed, you have to look on the light side.

So that's when I think it must have happened. Not that it matters to me. Maidy is the one who wants to know. She thinks she has it coming, being the older daughter. Although where was the older daughter when it happened? Which daughter was it that found you?

When Maidy started asking about your watch, I felt I had to say it. I said, "With the body barely cold?"

Maidy said the body is not the person, that the essence is the person, and that the essence leaves the body behind it, along with the body's possessions—for example, its watch?

"Time flies," I said. "Like an arrow."

"Fruit flies," I said, and Maidy said, "What?"

"Fruit flies," I said again. "Fruit flies like a banana."

That's how easy it is to play a joke on Maidy.

Remember how easy?

Now Maidy thinks I took your watch. She thinks because I got there first, my thought was to take it. Maidy keeps asking, "Who took Mama's watch?" She says, "Did you take Mama's watch?"

From the realistic California setting on through the rivalry between the two sisters, their tangled relationship with their mother, and their father, this family drama reduced to the size of a brief but pithy monologue addressed to the dead matriarch, with its telling pun on "watch," make Hempel's little swatch of life a moving piece of lyric narrative.

Another fine example of minimalist writing is Mary Robison's story "Yours," in which you can hear another sort of elliptical story unfolding. Like Hempel's it happens to be about a death watch, this one set in the season of Halloween.

Allison struggled away from her white Renault, limping with the weight of the last of the pumpkins. She found Clark in the twilight on the twig-and-leaf-littered porch behind the house.

He wore a wool shawl. He was moving up and back in a padded glider, pushed by the ball of his slippered foot.

Allison lowered a big pumpkin, let it rest on the wide floorboards.

Clark was much older—seventy-eight to Allison's thirty-five. They were married. They were both quite tall and looked something alike in their facial features. Allison wore a natural-hair wig. It was a thick blond hood around her face. She was dressed in bright-dyed denims today. She wore durable clothes, usually, for she volunteered afternoons at a children's day-care center.

She put one of the smaller pumpkins on Clark's long lap. "Now, nothing surreal," she told him. "Carve just a regular face. These are for kids."

In the foyer, on the Hepplewhite desk, Allison found the maid's chore list with its cross-offs, which included Clark's supper. Allison went quickly through the day's mail: a garish coupon packet, a bill from Jamestown Liquors, November's pay-TV programs guide, and the worst thing, the funniest, an already opened, extremely unkind letter from Clark's relations up North. "You're an old fool," Allison read, and, "You're being cruelly deceived." There was a gift check for Clark enclosed, but it was uncashable signed, as it was, "Jesus H. Christ."

Late, late into this night, Allison and Clark gutted and carved the pumpkins together, at an old table set on the back porch, over newspaper after soggy newspaper, with paring knives and with spoons and with a Swiss Army knife Clark used for exact shaping of tooth and eye and nostril. Clark had been a doctor, an internist, but also a Sunday watercolorist. His four pumpkins were expressive and artful. Their carved features were suited to the sizes and shapes of the pumpkins. Two looked ferocious and jagged. One registered surprise. The last was serene and beaming.

Allison's four faces were less deftly drawn, with slits and areas of distortion. She had cut triangles for noses and eyes. The mouths she had made were just wedges—two turned up and two turned down.

By one in the morning they were finished. Clark, who had bent his long torso forward to work, moved back over to the glider and looked out sleepily at nothing. All the lights were out across the ravine.

Clark stayed. For the season and time, the Virginia night was warm. Most leaves had been blown away already, and the trees stood unbothered. The moon was round above them.

Allison cleaned up the mess.

"Your jack-o'-lanterns are much, much better than mine," Clark said to her.

"Like hell," Allison said.

"Look at me," Clark said, and Allison did.

She was holding a squishy bundle of newspapers. The papers reeked sweetly with the smell of pumpkin guts.

"Yours are far better," he said.

"You're wrong. You'll see when they're lit," Allison said.

She went inside, came back with yellow vigil candles. It took her a while to get each candle settled, and then to line up the results in a row on the porch railing. She went along and lit each candle and fixed the pumpkin lids over the little flames.

"See?" she said.

They sat together a moment and looked at the orange faces.

"We're exhausted. It's good night time," Allison said. "Don't blow out the candles. I'll put in new ones tomorrow."

That night in their bedroom, a few weeks earlier in her life than had been predicted, Allison began to die. "Don't look at me if my wig comes off," she told Clark. "Please."

Her pulse cords were fluttering under his fingers. She raised her knees and kicked away the comforter. She said something to Clark about the garage being locked.

At the telephone, Clark had a clear view out back and down to the porch. He wanted to get drunk with his wife once more. He wanted to tell her, from the greater perspective he had, that to own only a little talent, like his, was an awful, plaguing thing; that being only a little special meant you expected too much, most of the time, and liked yourself too little. He wanted to assure her that she had missed nothing.

He was speaking into the phone now. He watched the jack-o'-lanterns. The jack-o'-lanterns watched him.

In the wake of "Yours," it seems appropriate to speak of another of the most important, but least noticed, aspects of the modern short story, and that is its affinities with contemporary abstract painting. Perhaps, because stories are made of language, that most transparent of mediums, we usually assume that the story conducts itself as something belonging to the everyday world.

But as is so often the case, the modern story writer, like Robison, not only recognizes the true nature of language as a plastic medium—one of the essential characteristics of modernist fiction—but shapes and forms the tale with as much impunity as a hard-edged painter. The view from Robison's front porch is as foreshortened and designed as that from, say, Richard Diebenkorn's, and it is only our naïveté with respect to the purposes of modern fiction that allows us to forget this. So with story as with painting, we have, depending on the authenticity and genius of the writer, the deliberate distortion of everyday reality, which is to say, the deliberate shaping of everyday reality in order to achieve a desired effect.

There is another major contradictory element in contemporary short fiction it seems important to notice—the unfolding of a complete action standing opposed, or so it seems, to the lyric impulse. The unfolding action of the classical story takes place over time. The resonating activity of the lyric story gives the illusion, as does a lyric poem, of taking place in a single moment. (You can hear both elements at work in "Yours," a model of minimalism, of course, with its repressed truth about Allison's illness—not repressed for the sake of the effect, but rather kept below the surface of the story in order to augment the realistic atmosphere.) In the best stories the two goals, the quest for truth and the quest for effect, coincide. In the most fashionable modern stories effect becomes paramount. In the most obvious and clumsy of realistic stories the actual events or, as it so often happens, the personal—that is, autobiographical—material of the story weighs it down and sinks it.

As you may have noticed, length is also a factor in modern stories. Along with the legacy of Hemingway that less is more comes the notion that compactness is all. Brevity is the strong suit of the minimalists because the very nature of suppression of detail makes it necessary to go very short. It's aesthetically convenient that most of the so-called minimalist stories are brief, but not everyone who writes short is a minimalist, as in the case of the fine lyric story work of Stuart Dybek or Jayne Anne Phillips.

But as my writer friend in Chicago suggested, minimalism may have had its day. Lately, there seems to be a turn away from the overtly smart, sassy, and visibly technologically adept story toward a more mature and humane variety of tale, a deepening, in fact, of the realistic tradition that began in modern short fiction with Chekhov, with the writer deploying only when necessary the techniques of modernist composition. These stories tend to run much longer than those of the minimalist variety, some of them pressing the limits where story ends and something like "little novel" begins, as in, say, "The Fireman's Wife," by Richard Bausch, in which a despairing young woman discovers the truth about herself in relation to her troubled husband. (The story's very virtue—its complete and broadly told unfolding of a sympathetic story about the end of a modern marriage—makes it impossible for me to include it here in its entirety.)

Writer Susan Shreve has called this kind of story a resurgence of "the literature of the heart," passionate—but never sentimental—fiction in which technique works at the service of the humane tale. This renewed realism, if that's how we might think of it, separates its practitioners from the few minimalists, forever young, who are still writing in their own lean way, and continues the work of some of the most accomplished writers of an older generation, that of Peter Taylor, for example, and Raymond Carver, both of whom modified the storytelling techniques of the Anderson/Hemingway approach to enhance their personal visions and create coherent public statements.

I fear that I've been deceptively comprehensive in this essay, possibly passing off on you as definitive literary history and criticism what are merely my own visceral attachments. This little anthology with commentary that I've just presented to you doesn't pretend to be complete, only frank and forthright in its showcase of my ideas about the relation of technique and meaning and what bearing this might have on contemporary short fiction. There are other strains in contemporary fiction that you may have wished me to have praised. Maybe another time. That's the paradox and glory of short fiction. Even if a story takes only five minutes to read, we're always a little older when we finish it than when we began. If only we could be a little wiser; sometimes we are.

20

On the Contemporary

What does it mean to be a *contemporary* writer?

The word seems simple enough at first. *Contemporary* is made by adding the prefix *con*, or "together," to *tempus*, the Latin for "time." And the first meaning given to us by the OED is that of belonging to the same time, age, or period. The second meaning is that of being equal in age. The third meaning listed tells us that *contemporary* refers to people or things occupying the same definite period, as in one who lives at the same time with another, or others. The fourth meaning is specifically literary, as in when a publication or journal refers to others published at the same time.

We all knew these meanings. I knew them, didn't I? But it never hurts to go to the source upon occasion and double-check our sense of what's real and what may be something we invented.

So according to this definition the contemporary writer is everyone alive who is a writer, and it will apply to all of us until we go gently into that good night, or go kicking and screaming, by accident, design, or disease, old age. After that unfortunate event, the contemporary writer loses his or her contemporary standing and becomes a twentieth-century writer or, now that we've all been lucky enough to cross that imaginary line on the calendar, a twenty-first-century writer, with deep roots in the twentieth century. Or, in more general terms, a modern writer. (Not automatically a *modernist* writer, since that's a term referring to style whereas *modern* is a term denoting a time period, in this case, fiction made by writers from the late nineteenth century through the present, our so-called modern times.)

And right now, in addition to being contemporary writers, most of us will be thought of as fin de siècle writers, or, if you haven't published your first work until now, you will be known as an early-twenty-first-century writer. Does that make you feel uncomfortable? It is at the very least strange, to think that after all of the work you do, or will do, some critic of the future, if there are any critics left in the future, is going to come along and fit you into one neat pigeonhole or another. Or, if you prefer to think of yourself as another sort of winged creature, watch you flutter by, then net you, and pin you to a board in order to notice your genus and designs.

The manner in which critics have done this in the past is not entirely systematic, though, and leaves some room for us to interpret. Think, for example, of the way we talk about Hawthorne and Melville. We don't usually say, for the former, "early-nineteenth-century writer" and for the latter "mid-nineteenth-century writer." We just say "nineteenth-century writer." But now Mark Twain, by force of style, is more than a late-nineteenth-century writer. We think of him as a modern writer, and in fact we can mark the beginning of the modern period of American prose fiction with the publication of *Huckleberry Finn*. Then there's Henry James. Turn of the century? A good way to think about him. Certainly not a man of the twentieth century.

Now consider Dreiser. *Sister Carrie* was published in 1900 and set a new standard for literary naturalism in America. But though the Civil War was to the youthful Dreiser what the Vietnam War is to most of you starting out as writers in the last decade of the twentieth century, he never considered it a formative experience. Whereas many of us, at least those of us who have published a few books by now, look back to our century's sixties with a seriousness and sometimes even a fondness that marks us as twentieth-century writers. If we apply the Dreiser standard, it's clear that any of you who bring out your first book in the year 2000 will not be looking back at the sixties in the same way.

Of course no one thinks of himself, or herself, in these terms, except playfully or stupidly egoistically. It's dangerous business. Blake writes, "If the sun and the moon should doubt / They'd immediately go out." That's what would happen to any young writer who sits down and begins typing with the rubric in mind, "I'm a late-twentieth-century writer" or, better yet, "I'm a twenty-first-century writer."

Just call yourself lucky to be a writer. I called myself lucky to be alive and typing, when I first began. Twentieth-century writer? If I had been asked to put a name to it, I would have said, maybe, "June 24, 1984, writer." And on June 25, I would have changed the day. But that's not bad, though with hindsight I don't know how I managed all the pain that came along with separation from my children except with that vodka and a determined blind eye. June 24? June 25? I was a writer that morning that I wrote, and when I stopped writing, I stopped being a writer. Until the next morning, I was only someone who had written.

I feel pretty much the same today. But that's with a lot of experience to assure me that though I stop typing at one in the afternoon I will be able to begin again at eight-thirty the next morning. Probably.

When we start out, most of us begin in obscurity. (Quick trip over to the OED again to find that *obscurity* comes from the Latin *obscurare*, or "to darken," and that *obscurity* means "a dark place" or "to be unknown, inconspicuous, or insignificant.") And it is a good way for a young writer to be, especially in our age of celebrity. To be unknown, inconspicuous, or insignificant is a wonderful counterpart to Joyce's triad of silence, exile, and cunning. We gather our material best if we don't stand out. And unless we make a living by putting ourselves into the work, as, say, Mailer did to great effect in *Armies of the Night*, it's best to remain obscure, or at least off to the side of the scene rather than in it. Writers are like tape recorders. If seen, they cause people to behave other than normally.

When I first started out, I was not a late-twentieth-century writer but a bearded man in his late thirties, two marriages and a failed academic career behind him, three children living apart from him, and a troubled solitude that he carried with him like the shell the snail lives in and if wise never ventures out from. I had no resources but my wild hopes and few mentors outside of the great dead (not the Grateful Dead but the greats who are our literary ancestors, those who are there to teach us just about everything that we need to know).

I wasn't young, but I wasn't old either, so I suppose I saw myself as having an affinity with the paradigm of the older person who after years of working at some job or profession or other begins to write at the approach to forty. I call this the Sherwood Anderson–Henry Miller paradigm. The other is Rimbaud, or Alain-Fournier, the writer who burns with a cold, gemlike flame, as Walter Pater put it, but burns out quickly. Or Keats—who, like Mozart, had done his best work and had died before, as my first wife once reminded me, he had reached the middle part of his life.

There are dangers in both scenarios, but as Henry James explained, it is much better to become a writer in middle age rather than in youth because at least then after you're dropped by a fickle public you have a life to go back to.

So though while you are alive you will always remain a contemporary writer, there are a number of distinctly different phases of being contemporary. There is the beginning phase, the obscurity phase, if you will, and then the period of modest success, followed after a while by the period of obscurity regained. This happens to the best of us as well as the worst, and it's rare for writers to move beyond that third phase, in which they have fallen back into obscurity, though you do see it from time to time and sometimes in big ways. As in William Faulkner's resurrection in the mid-1940s, when Malcolm Cowley brought out the *Portable Faulkner*. For several years before that, everything Faulkner had published was out of print.

Then there is the case of the recently deceased Wright Morris, a generously talented writer whose entire body of work remained in print for the last decade of his life and who was one of the most gifted unread writers of our time. The books were all available but no one came to the party. (There are reasons for this, of course, since Morris was regarded by critics as a regionalist, and ignored because of it, in the same way that Faulkner was, until, in the case of Faulkner, Cowley came along and convinced the reading public that regionalism was a good thing, not bad. Poor Wright Morris—gone now, without ever finding his Malcolm Cowley in his own lifetime.)

Look at another writer of more than ordinary talent, the late James Baldwin. When he died, he left much of his work in print, and now he has just been republished in the distinguished Library of America series. A steady increase of his reputation, with only a few dips and falls during his middle years.

Saul Bellow, now in his mid-eighties, is the dean of American writers. By the publication of his third novel, *The Adventures of Augie March*, which came out in 1953, he was recognized for the strong swell of his sentences, nearly overwhelming in their strength of thought and the texture of their surfaces. His reputation has scarcely wavered.

Eudora Welty is the deaconess. Just as her language wedded the feel of Southernness to strong classic American syntax, her plots revealed that a keen-eyed stylist can use classical material to great everyday advantage. She has been silent now for years, alas. I wonder how her work and Bellow's will fare in the next half century.

Among other important contemporaries, we have to conjure with the work of John Updike, whose career, like Bellow's, has been one of consistent ascendance, to a place that seems like a plateau, until his next high leap. (Some recent bitter attacks on Updike seem like the work of sparrows trying to batter an eagle.)

Look at the work of Don DeLillo and we see another pattern. It wasn't until the publication of his fourth or fifth novel, *White Noise*, that he began to acquire a readership and a reputation. DeLillo happens to be of the pro-obscurity school of thought, having ventured out into media-land only once or twice during the recent publication of his magnum opus, *Underworld*, a book that is, as is often the case when a writer finally breaks through into the big sales brackets in American publishing, not his best work. In the career of John Irving, you can see a similar pattern, with *The World According to Garp* giving him that big boost into the pantheon of contemporary writing demigods.

Look to Joan Didion and you see another variation in the pattern. Early obscurity, middling success, and then celebrity, with the work declining steadily ever since the beginning of her middle period. Or Ursula LeGuin, toiling for years in the often disparaged genre of science fiction before suddenly turning out to be quite interesting to mainstream readers. Or Kurt Vonnegut, who, like LeGuin, never tried to hide his affinity with science fiction, because science fiction is the one form of American literature that allows for the dramatic expression of ideas.

It's Oscar Wilde, I believe, who said that success isn't enough but that you must see your friends fail. But in contemporary American letters in the past fifty years we have seen awful situations where some of the best writers at work were the least known and least appreciated.

I'm thinking of Evan Connell and James Salter and Paul Bowles. Now in their seventies or, in Bowles's case, in the Great Beyond, they hear applause and receive some recognition. But as my dear late friend Bernard Malamud lamented after receiving at the age of seventy-one the Award of Merit from the Governor General of Sicily, "Where was the Governor General of Sicily when I needed him?"

But after all this the sad fact remains that reputation quickly fades with the demise of a writer. When "contemporary" slides into the past tense, as in "he was our contemporary," a different set of critical judgments seems to apply. To be an entertaining presence is no longer enough to allow people to claim importance. The question of how a writer fits into the present turns into the question of how the writer's work fits into the time period in which he lived. And beyond that, into the century, and beyond that, into the culture. Some writers survive a bit longer than others because of some aspect of their work that coheres with a major style, as with, say, a Romantic poet like Leigh Hunt. But after a while even Hunt became a museum piece, while his friend Keats still soars. Obversely, greatness can withstand even great attack, as in the work of Fenimore Cooper, after assault and battery by Mark Twain. Or Joyce after being mugged by Virginia Woolf.

In Malamud's case, less than twenty years after his death, he still sits among the anointed dead. Most serious readers will be acquainted with some work by Malamud, and so are a number of students of American literature and the short story. The work of dear departed Wallace Stegner seems, at least at this date, to have a good chance of surviving (almost all of Stegner's work remains in print, but then so does Wright Morris's, and the difference in readership is, I'm afraid, quite noticeable). Your work can't survive, obviously, unless it is in print, but after that you do need readers. I don't have the figures on Morris's sales from the University of Nebraska Press, but I never meet anyone who has read him, while Stegner fans are legion. But, oh, this long step from the contemporary to the modern! The late John Gardner's reputation seems to have almost completely disappeared except as the author of his book on craft. Who could have foreseen this? But then, most contemporary work falls by the wayside soon after the author dies. Read George Garrett's poem "Anthologies" and see how many names you recognize before the list in the last stanza.

> Not only the pleasures of dust,
> of dry, stained pages and the out-of-date
> card that proves nobody has even checked
> this one out in a decade and not more
> than half a dozen times in my whole lifetime.
>   GENE DERWOOD . . . LLOYD FRANKENBERG . . .
>   ALFRED HAYES . . . COMAN LEAVENWORTH . . . JOHN
>   THOMPSON, JR. . . . .
>
> But also all of these names and so many
> more, not really forgotten, but not to be found,
> either, anywhere else but here in the stacks
> on shelves where Robinson's darkest inches
> preserve the anonymous dignity of the unfamous.
>   MARYA ZATURENSKA . . . CALE YOUNG RICE . . .
>   H. PHELPS PUTNAM . . . WILLIAM ELLERY LEONARD . . .
>   ALFRED KREYMBORG . . .
>
> And one great secret is simply this—how, taken
> together, cheek-by-jowl, these people, these poets,
> are often so much alike in form and substance
> and more democratic in excellence and virtue
> than anyone might have otherwise imagined.
>   MADELINE GLEASON . . . ROBERT HORAN . . .
>   MYRON O'HIGGINS . . . BYRON VAZAKAS . . .

Years ago in the Village at the San Remo
I bought poems from Maxwell Bodenheim
at fifty cents a pop. Once at the Museum
of Modern Art I watched W. H. Auden unsuccessfully
try to check a bottle of champagne like a coat.
    HELEN ADAM . . . EBBE BORREGARD . . .
    ADAM DRINAN . . . MURRAY NOSS . . . ELDER OLSON . . .

But what of all the unfamous others, ourselves
I mean, still alive and on fire and in love
with the taste of words and the making of poems?
Who will come here afterwards to blow the dust away
and disturb the peace and oblivion we have earned?
    FRED CHAPPELL . . . KELLY CHERRY . . . R. H. W.
    DILLARD . . . BRENDAN GALVIN . . . GEORGE GARRETT . . .
    DAVID SLAVITT . . . HENRY TAYLOR . . .

Garrett sometimes jokes that he wants to be buried in the Tomb of the Unknown Writer. For most of us, he seems to be suggesting in this poem, libraries will serve as tombs.

But why conjure up all this darkness?

When we peer beyond the edge of the word *contemporary*, the prospect seems frightening enough. And though *contemporary* sounds like one of the flimsiest words in the language when it comes up against the knowledge of what probably follows, it is, if you look at it in another way, one of the strongest words in the language. Remember what Emerson said about Aristotle and Plato in his essay "The American Scholar"? They too were once only young men in libraries.

Sophocles' plays were once contemporary theater. Virgil's poetry was contemporary verse. Except that they weren't regarded by their contemporaries as such. Without any work to compare it to, how do we rank such poetry and plays? The answer is that we don't. It just is. Or just was. A part of the world, a part of nature, a part of culture, with little distinction among these categories that we take to be timeless. Which they were not.

Think about this: *Sister Carrie* was once a contemporary novel. So was *Moby Dick*, the book that ruined Melville's career as a contemporary writer. *My Antonia. A Farewell to Arms. The Great Gatsby. As I Lay Dying.* Classics aren't born. They are made by generations of readers. All of these novels had mixed reviews. And many highly praised contemporary novels fade quickly away, like last season's fashions in clothes and music.

Now take one more trip to the dictionary with me.

Classic. A classic writer is a writer of the first rank. A classic work is outstanding work of the first order. Classic works are those works that endure over time, over generations, over centuries. And certainly of all the discriminations we apply when we read contemporary fiction this is the highest. After reading for enjoyment, and reading to notice the technical aspects of the fiction, and reading to see if the book will last beyond one reading, and reading to see if the book ought, in your opinion, to find its way into the hands of other serious readers, you begin to apply the highest standards. Might it endure into the next generation? And so pass from contemporary into the realm of the classic?

In English usage the adjective *contemporary* as applied to writers— that is, writers who were alive together in the same age—did not come into play until the late seventeenth century. And I wonder if that doesn't have something to do with the West's changing view of life in relation to eternity. To be a contemporary means to live in the same time as other writers, but in order to have this sense of ourselves living in a specific time with other writers we first have to have a special sense of temporal awareness.

Which question now leads me to deliver a one-minute history of time.

The Greeks looked back, not forward. Time for them was cyclical, and the passage of an individual life from birth to death was seen against the larger scenario of the passage of the seasons. They had no sense of a life after death, except that disembodied souls would end up in the place they called Hades.

The Greeks didn't see each other as contemporaries. They looked to the past, where they saw a long line of ancestors fading away into the realm of the heroic, where heroes and gods intermingled. Time for them was duration, a continuum that held no pattern outside the cycles of lives and the seasons, and because they had no sense of time as an accelerating process that led away from the past, they felt a deep kinship with the past and those mortals and gods who inhabited that temporal location.

Then came the rise of the Hebrews, with their peculiar notion of their tribe as having been chosen by Yahweh as the moral trendsetter of the Western world—followed by the spin-off of Christianity, in which singularity was expanded to include the possibility of a blessed afterlife. It was only then that the Western world began to look to a future with any sense of potential. And even after the continent-wide hegemony of Christianity ended in a rash of wars and theological bickerings, the idea of human progress within time remained behind as the legacy of the Christian notion of human perfectability in an afterlife.

Looking to the future as much as the past eventually led to our modern notion of progress, in which we turn our backs on the past in order to create a better future, all too often with bodies lining the road we travel oh so quickly toward our ever-receding goal.

And now I believe my one minute is up and I have arrived in the present of what when I began this little argument about time we looked on as the future we desired to reach. And it isn't all that great, is it? Better times lie ahead of us, yes?

Onward, ever onward!

Except that writers don't usually work this way. We create books with one eye on today's reader and one eye on the past. Which is a better way to proceed than keeping one eye on the present and one on the future, since the future doesn't exist and so is nothing much to look at.

This perhaps makes science fiction writers the only real avant-garde, since it is quite an experimental act to look upon nothing and describe what you see. The rest of us look to what has come before us, as a way of measuring what we are doing now.

In the last analysis our material as writers begins with time and extends to human psychology and the human environment (what we used to call landscape). In fact, without us there would be no time. As Auden writes in his elegy for Yeats, "Time loves language / And forgives everyone by whom it lives." Notice that Auden doesn't say everyone who lives *by* it. But everyone by whom *it* lives. Time loves language, because time *is* language. Without language, there would be nothing but duration, nothing but the duration that our bodies pass through as if it were air or water or light.

Painters work with space, in space. They teach us to love the world as it is. Writers make narratives that develop over time and teach us to hold the world precious because it is constantly spiraling away from us into the past.

So in the largest sense, to be a contemporary means to be with time, for a duration, and then to lose it. Which makes all human beings contemporaries, whatever time period they may inhabit—past, present, or future—because we all belong to time.

Unless, in the future, if I can try science fiction for a moment, someone in a laboratory comes up with a way to make us immortal.

Until then all we can do is work with our language and the time it takes to tell it in, with one eye on the present and the other on the past. And hope that our stories are good enough to become part of the seriously regarded and admired past of the writers of the latter half of the twenty-first century. We, who, as Garrett puts it, are still alive and on fire and in love with the taste of words.

21

Of the Making of Books

When I was an awkward dark-haired boy haunting the main reading room of my local New Jersey public library, I was disconcerted to discover that my efforts at reading sometimes outstripped the efforts of my favorite writers to produce new books—though of course back then I couldn't imagine an actual person making a book. I thought not at all about there being an actual writer behind every book I read. For me, the writer had already achieved the perfection that Joyce's Dedalus talks about to his friends in the schoolyard at Clongowes Wood School—like God, detached from his work, standing behind it, paring his fingernails. My complete lack of understanding of how books and stories got made was as innocent as my lack of understanding of, say, photosynthesis. I read books. I breathed air. These things occurred because I was alive.

I simply didn't associate the creation of books with human beings. They seemed to me to spring up on the library shelves like grass—or as in our vacant lots in New Jersey, mostly weeds. Which gave me the understanding that they would never run out. To think that we have an endless amount of time—or not to think about time at all in relation to such things—and that we can read and read forever, and that the books will keep on coming, now that is innocence.

And then one day we discover that there is a relation between makers and things made. I'm not sure how this happens. Maybe we see something break down—the family car, the kitchen sink—and observe as Father or Mother repairs it. Or we cut ourselves and watch the blood clot into a scab and the wound eventually heal. With respect to art, I'm not sure if our own drawings as children are something we link in our minds to great paintings. I do recall writing science fiction stories in eighth grade, inspired, I suppose, by the stories I was reading. But it still had not yet dawned on me that what I was writing had anything to do with authorship.

It wasn't until high-school days—maybe I should spell that *daze*?—that I made the connection. And it certainly wasn't in any highfalutin' manner. My first books were comic books. *Archie, Dagwood and Blondie, The Hulk, EC Comics*. But after the age of around ten I did raise the level of my reading by picking up *Classics Illustrated*. You know, everything from the *Iliad* and the *Odyssey*—I don't recall whether or not there was a comic version of the *Aeneid*, but I somehow doubt it— on through Jules Verne and H. G. Wells and everything in between. So this was education, Jersey style. To paraphrase Keats, I was first looking into the *Classics Illustrated* version of Chapman's *Homer*. I also discovered *Mad* magazine, the satirical comic book for the kind of boys who these days are mostly subdued by Ritalin.

Let me describe some of the earliest adventures in my literary education. I grew up in Perth Amboy, New Jersey, just across a narrow strip of water called the Arthur Kill from the lower tip of Staten Island, New York City's fifth borough. As soon as we were old enough to figure out that we could break free of our parents' watchful oversight, some of us young louts would use money from our part-time jobs handing out circulars for the local movie theater to pay for a cheap trip to Manhattan. It cost a nickel for the ferry ride from the watery east end of our main street over to Tottenville on Staten Island and then about a dollar to ride the shuttle train to the other end of the island where the Battery Park ferry waited to carry us across New York Harbor to the lower tip of Manhattan Island.

We boys would make a day trip into Manhattan to explore the great city, sometimes going to the Bowery to marvel at the alcoholics lounging in doorways or passed out on the pavement. Or to museums. To movies. And sometimes to make small pilgrimages. Such as a trip I made one summer morning to the offices of *Mad* magazine, where I knocked on the door and was admitted into the small two-room office and found editor and main illustrator Al Feldstein standing at his desk eating tuna from a can. I was shocked. A real person stood behind the magazine that I treated like Holy Scripture. (Shows you what my idea of the Holy was like back then!)

We had a conversation. He asked me who I was. I told him. He kept on eating his tuna. After a while, with a free copy of the latest issue in hand, I left for home.

My first encounter with an artist/author.

Around this same time I had graduated from reading sea adventure stories to science fiction. And in a science fiction magazine, I saw an advertisement for a convention in New York City listing the names of some of the writers whose work I was devouring. So I slapped my nickel down for the ferry ride across the Arthur Kill, stared out across the calm water at the green shore ahead, boarded that train for the other side of Staten Island, caught the ferry that churned across the harbor to Battery Park, and then rode the screeching subway train uptown. There in a rented hall that smelled of stale beer, sweat, and cooked sausage—the residue, no doubt, of some wedding held there on the weekend before— fans gathered to listen to talks by their favorite science fiction writers and to meet them and get autographs on their books.

In this crowd there were a lot of curious teenage boys (curious in several senses of the word) like myself. And mobs of men of all ages who never grew in their souls beyond their teenage years. Which is how we might imagine the readership of Stephen King (of which I am a statistic). Boys who haven't really grown up or boys who never will. In this hall I first caught sight of Isaac Asimov, one of the giants of the genre, his large head on short body moving in and out of various groups of men who seemed to know things that he wanted to hear. And John Campbell Jr., editor of *Astounding Stories*, one of the maga- zines I read regularly, and H. L. Gold, writer, and editor of *Galaxy Sci- ence Fiction*, the *New Yorker* of the genre as compared to *Astounding*'s *Atlantic Monthly*.

I overcame some initial shyness, asked for autographs, and returned home to New Jersey, my mind raised to a higher level. I had made the connection between the books and their creators. (And I still associate the thrill of that discovery with science fiction. On First Looking into Bradbury's *Martian Chronicles*, you might call it. Years and years later, when I was invited to share a podium with Ray Bradbury himself, I never did get over my awe of meeting this genial white-haired gent in Bermuda shorts who passed me little airline splits of vodka to pour into the melted Jell-O drinks we were served at the dry campus where we both were speaking. After I was introduced in the lobby of a Mexico City hotel to Gabriel García Márquez, I raced up to my room and jumped on the bed and did a little victory dance!)

Such are the thrills of meeting the masters of your adolescence and even those of your adulthood.

So there I was, in the next phase, having put innocence behind me and graduated into that condition where I recognized that writers possessed corporeal bodies. Though I still had no idea about how books got made. I tried to write stories and then a longer work—well, it wasn't work, it was some post-adolescent form of play compounded by a deeply romantic notion of how I thought I was supposed to live. There were a thousand reasons why what I wrote was awful. I lacked a number of important qualities necessary to the creation of good fiction, qualities that, if you think of it, are also germane to the life of the writer as well as his work: persistence, skill, and vision. Also honesty, a deep sense of humility, empathy, and a desire to be true to one's ideals.

Years went by, precious years; my family life ebbed and flowed, flowered, then turned to desert. For more than a decade I believed that I was bound for work other than that for which I had originally hoped, and my writing self stayed with me as a dessicated stillborn twin, something I dragged along with me but never talked about much, if at all. I remained a reader. Now and then I met a writer. But in my heart, I had given up that desire. You're an adult now, I told myself. Get an adult profession.

But there is a heart that beats deeper and more truly than the physical heart, and it was the rhythm of that grander organ to which I was dancing. It just took me a while to figure that out. The making of books lay ahead of me. But if my unwise self lived in suspense about my future, the side of me that kept on dreaming, if unconsciously, never had any doubt. It's that madness, that perilous hope, that faith, that demonic desire, that intense belief in the symmetry of things that keeps you moving toward your goal even before you know what the goal happens to be. I had given up. But my aspirations had not given out.

All this while, of course, I was reading books important to the formation of my sense of language, technique, and vision. That was part of the deeper truth that still lay beneath the surface of my life. As Borges has written, in a short poem, "I'm more proud of the books I have read than I am of the books I have written." I was reading, reading, reading, which meant that (even though I didn't know it) I was preparing to write. Meanwhile, my life seemed to move on the wheels of personal disasters. Marriages, divorces—and I went to graduate school, acquired a Ph.D. in comparative literature, took a teaching post at a small, prestigious New England college—and after eight years was fired. For a while it seemed to me as though I was just as bad at the making of life as I was at the making of books.

Not that there is any necessary correlation between the two. Shakespeare often gives his best poetry to bad men and bastards. Theodore Dreiser was a big galumphing jerk, and ugly, to boot. Robert Penn Warren in his poem "Homage to Theodore Dreiser" calls him "Potato Face" and records the difference—today's jargon would have this called the "disconnect"—between the flawed man and his great books. No one today wears disdain or bullying as a badge of pride. But there are writers we all know who behave badly and write like angels. (And, of course, many, many good people who wouldn't be able to write well, no matter how much they aspired to it, not even in order to save their own children from a burning house.) It takes a long time and great patience, awareness, energy, selflessness, insight, and passion to remain true to making a good life or good work. Why should we be surprised when those of us who are trying to do both sometimes falter? Or take a bad fall.

One must choose between the art and the life, Yeats tells us. Bernard Malamud used Yeats's statement as the epigraph for his linked stories about an itinerant American artist in Italy named Fidelman. And he includes a statement from Fidelman beneath the Yeats inscription: *Both*.

So part of the making of books is recognizing how different it is, and how difficult it is, in relation to the making of life. And even then, oh, yes, even then, when you reach a point where at least the former seems possible, the difficulties continue. This comes when you begin to live consciously in both realms, making a life of making books.

I've mentioned Theodore Dreiser, one of our great ones, however clumsy his style might seem by the sentence, paragraph, or page. As Robert Penn Warren makes us notice, in an essay that takes the same title as his poem on Dreiser, we have to read this novelist by the scene. And when we take him in that dosage the clumsiness turns by means of the miracle of the imagination into grace. A powerful dose of grace, prefaced by ignorance and suffering. Dreiser knew how to make books. You looked around at the interesting, self-destructive lives of your family members, or you read the horror stories in the newspapers. And then you sat down and you typed. (He'd learned this simple method from his own newspaper days, when he worked as a reporter for a couple of Midwestern papers.) And then you turned your manuscript over to your typist and told her to take out what she didn't like. And then you turned the manuscript in to a publisher, and he (and sometimes, as in the case of *Sister Carrie*, his wife) cut things out. When Dreiser completed the 750,000-word manuscript of his greatest novel, *An American Tragedy*, he delivered it to B. W. Huebsch, his publisher at the time, and a few days later Huebsch called to tell him that he thought it was a great book. But he did want a 50,000-word cut toward the beginning of the story. Certainly, Dreiser told him. What's 50,000 words between friends?

This is, of course, the next stage of the making of books. Composition leads to editing and revision. (It's a rare writer—and maybe rare in the sense of underdone or bloody as well as unusual—who doesn't need some editing. In our own time, we hear that Joseph Heller didn't like to be edited. Saul Bellow doesn't.) Some of our best, some of our greatest, have not only submitted their work to their editors and waited for advice, they have written about it in interesting ways, of how they made their books, by themselves and then with the assistance of their editors.

The editing of Thomas Wolfe's *Look Homeward, Angel* turned Scribner's Max Perkins into a publishing legend. Wolfe understood from the start that he needed editing. In his reply to Perkins after having been informed that Scribner's was accepting his manuscript, he wrote, "I want the direct criticism and advice of an older and more critical person. . . . I wonder if at Scribner's I can find someone who is interested enough to talk over the whole huge monster with me, part by part."

Yes, and it was quite a monster of a draft of a novel, with its expansive Whitman-like riffs on the details of the sensual world and its expansive Whitman-like rhapsodic passages on the joys and pains of being alive. Abundance, for Wolfe, is everything. As in this description of the feeding habits of the Gants, the family into which the protagonist, young Eugene, is born:

> They fed stupendously. Eugene began to observe the food and the seasons. In the autumn, they barrelled huge frosty apples in the cellar. . . . Smoked bacons hung in the pantry, the great bins were full of flour, the dark recessed shelves groaned with preserved cherries, peaches, plums, quinces, apples, pears. All that he touched waxed in rich pungent life: his Spring gardens, wrought in the black wet earth below the fruit trees, flourished in huge crinkled lettuces that wrenched cleanly from the loamy soil with small black clots stuck to their crisp stocks; fat red radishes; heavy tomatoes. The rich plums lay bursted on the grass; his huge cherry trees oozed with heavy gum jewels; his apple trees bent with thick green clusters.

Look out, Angel! Because, as Wolfe tells us, "Eugene was loose now in the limitless meadows of sensation." Between his living and his reading, he feels enough to fill large numbers of pages with his gargantuan recollections of what he has felt and perceived:

> He remembered yet the East India Tea House at the Fair, the sandal-wood, the turbans, and the robes, the cool interior and

the smell of India tea; and he had felt now the nostalgic thrill of dew-wet mornings in Spring, the cherry scent, the cool clarion earth, the wet loaminess of the garden, the pungent breakfast smells and the floating snow of blossoms. He knew the inchoate sharp excitement of hot dandelions in young Spring grass at noon; the smell of cellars, cobwebs, and built-on secret earth . . .

To read Wolfe is almost to become him. His rolling prolix paragraphs, reaching, grasping, the adolescent sensibility unleashed in a world of objects.

Ray Bradbury once wrote a story about choosing Thomas Wolfe—I think we retrieve him with a time machine—to be the first writer to be sent to outer space. Who else to record all that he sees and feels and smells and tastes and touches!

In the autumn of 1928 the manuscript—which at this stage was titled "O Lost"—swollen with these rhapsodic passages arrived at Max Perkins's office, pounds and pounds of manuscript, stacked and tied in bundles like old newspapers ready for the trash, 1,114 pages of onion-skin, 330,000 words, standing about five inches high.

Now, Wolfe had read everything. As he tells us of Eugene, so it was with his own education, beginning with the Bible and poetry. But now it was time for Wolfe, having read and written his massive draft, to go on to the next stage of making a book, which is the editing stage. And so, as Scott Berg describes it in his biography of Max Perkins, the gifted editor began the nearly overwhelming task of reading and rereading Wolfe's manuscript in preparation for his first meeting with Wolfe. Perkins was a great editor, not because he made his writers great but because he was up to the task of helping them to recognize their own gifts and genius. For example, "they began to talk about a scene early in the manuscript between the hero's father—the stone-cutter W. O. Gant—and the madam of the local brothel, in which she was purchasing a tombstone for one of her girls. In his eagerness, Wolfe blurted, 'I know you can't print that! I'll take that out at once, Mr. Perkins.' . . . 'Take it out?' Perkins exclaimed. 'It's one of the greatest short stories I have ever read!'"

So the legendary editing process proceeds, with Perkins going on to make some general suggestions "for keeping his hero in sharp focus" and Wolfe apparently ready and eager to take suggestions. As he wrote a friend back in his hometown of Asheville, "the publishers told me to get busy with my little hatchet and carve off some 100,000 words."

What's 50,000 or 100,000 words between friends? Apparently a great deal more to Wolfe than to Dreiser. Wolfe wrote in his journal that he was determined "First to cut out of every page every word that is not essential to the meaning of the writing. If I can find even 10 words in every page this wd.=10,000 or more in entire mss." In January of 1929 he began, and when he had finished, the book was only eight pages shorter. In *The Story of a Novel*, Wolfe's account of the genesis of what would become his next book, *Of Time and the River*, he admitted that "cutting had always been the most difficult and distasteful part of writing to me." And in a letter to a friend, he remarked, "I suffer agony over some of the cutting, but I realize it's got to be done. When something really good goes it's an awful wrench, but as you probably know, something really can be good and yet have no place in the scheme of a book."

Perkins would make suggestions, and Wolfe would cut. But he would also make some additions. So that often he would cut a prescribed 10,000 and add another 15,000. By his own estimate, he wrote another half million words of new material, though only a small part of this was used. As Berg recounts it, the wrestling back and forth often went like this: The hero's father dies and Perkins suggests that Wolfe do a 5,000-word funeral scene. Wolfe comes in the next day with thousands of words about the life of the doctor who attends the dying man. Perkins rejects this and the next day Wolfe returns with a long passage about Eugene's sister, her thoughts while out shopping and then later before she falls asleep that night. Perkins objects. Wolfe agrees. And the next day returns with thousands of more words about the older Gant's illness, all of it having nothing to do with the actual funeral scene.

This sort of back and forth goes on for many months. It's not until they begin work on *Of Time and the River* that Wolfe admits some of the necessities of his relationship with his editor, if not the editorial process. In the opening lines of *The Story of a Novel* he says:

An editor who is also a good friend of mine, told me about a year ago that he was sorry he had not kept a diary about the work that both of us were doing, the whole stroke, catch, flow, stop, and ending, the ten thousand fittings, changings, triumphs, and surrenders that went into the making of a book. This editor remarked that some of it was fantastic, much incredible, all astonishing.

What seems so astonishing to me is the way in which the editorial process remains on such display in the case of Wolfe and Perkins. For a new writer, their relationship is quite useful and exemplary. The romantic ego opposed to the steady-minded shaper of things. The reckless profligate talent for life in excess standing opposite the man who tries to discern the pattern into which much of the material will fit. The Wolfe–Perkins duo demonstrates for me just how much many of us need editors and editing.

Unfortunately for Wolfe, he was a bit too candid about his work with Perkins so that critic Bernard De Voto, writing some seven years later, attacked him as a terribly flawed writer precisely because of his seeming dependence on editorial guidance. "For five years," De Voto writes,

the artist pours out words . . . with little or no idea what their purpose is, which book they belong in, or what the relation of part to part is, what is organic and what is irrelevant, or what emphasis or coloration in the completed work of art is being served by the job at hand. . . . But works of art cannot be assembled like a carburetor—they must be grown like a plant. . . . The artist writes a hundred thousand words about a train; Mr. Perkins decides that the train is worth only five thousand words. . . . Until Mr. Wolfe develops more craftsmanship, he will not be the important novelist he is now widely accepted as being.

When we look at the writer–editor relationship between Fitzgerald and Perkins, we see something a lot less open to a De Voto–like attack. Fitzgerald in fact wrote to Perkins after reading *Of Time and the River* (a book he did not greatly care for). In this letter we can see just how much more innate than Wolfe's is his own sense of how to make fiction and that he recognizes his own particular profligacy, which was an excess of intake rather than Wolfe's excess of overflow. Fitzgerald writes that "the very excellent organization of a long book or the finest perceptions and judgement in time of revision do not go well with liquor." At least for a novel, for which "you need the mental speed that enables you to keep the whole pattern in your head and ruthlessly sacrifice the sideshows as Ernest did in *A Farewell to Arms*. If a mind is slowed up ever so little it lives in the individual part of a book rather than in a book as a whole."

In October of 1924, Fitzgerald had sent Perkins a manuscript titled "Trimalchio in West Egg," a novel that the author thought was "the best American novel ever written." Perkins, by his attention to it, seemed to suggest that he might well think just as highly about it. "I think the novel is a wonder," he wrote to Fitzgerald in a letter that every American writer dreams of receiving. "The amount of meaning you get into a sentence, the dimensions and intensity of the impression you make a paragraph carry, are most extraordinary. The manuscript is full of phrases which make a scene blaze with life." He then cites numerous instances of what he admires and goes on to say that "these are such things as make a man famous. And all these things, the whole pathetic episode, you have given a place in time and space, for with the help of T. J. Ekleberg [*sic*] and by an occasional glance at the sky, or the sea, or the city, you have imparted a sort of sense of eternity."

Perkins did have some suggestions for revision, but they were narrow comments, almost all of them having to do with, as Scott Berg points out, the character of Gatsby. And much more typical of the editorial process than the Sturm und Drang of his editing of Wolfe. "Couldn't *he*," Perkins writes to Fitzgerald, "be physically described as distinctly as the others, and couldn't you add one or two characteristics like the use of that phrase 'old sport,' not verbal but physical ones, perhaps . . . and I do not think your scheme would be impaired if you made him so." Fitzgerald was grateful for the suggestions. "With the aid you have given me," he wrote to Perkins, "I can make 'Gatsby' perfect."

Hemingway, whose work Fitzgerald had urged Perkins to publish, required less editing. When the manuscript of "In Our Time" first reached his desk in October 1924, Perkins worried only that it was so short that Scribner's could not publish it. He wrote to Fitzgerald, on whose recommendation he read the work, that the book "accumulated a fearful effect through a series of brief episodes, presented with economy, strength, and vitality. A remarkable, tight, complete expression of the scene." To Hemingway himself, he apologized for not making an offer on the book. "This is a pity, because your method is obviously one which enables you to express what you have to say in a very small compass."

Hemingway had his troubles, but most of these had to do with his life rather than his art. He seemed to have a natural gift, what he called the writer's necessary "sense of proportion," or, as he later put it more succinctly in an interview in the *Paris Review*, "a built-in automatic shock-proof shit-detector." He didn't believe that Wolfe had one. He wondered, as he mused to himself in the pages of *Death in the Afternoon*, "if it would make a writer of him, give him the necessary shock to cut the over-flow of words and give him a sense of proportion, if they sent Tom Wolfe to Siberia or to the Dry Tortugas. Maybe it would and maybe it wouldn't." Perkins said of this same book of Hemingway's that after finishing the manuscript he went to bed happy. "It gives the impression," he wrote, "of having grown rather than of having been planned.—And that is the characteristic of a great book."

Perkins's specific comments about Hemingway's work remain almost uniformly minor. He worries about the reception of the obscene words, and they go back and forth about this. He wants to change an epigraph. Hemingway lops off the first fifteen pages of the manuscript of *The Sun Also Rises* (not mentioning that this came at Fitzgerald's suggestion), and Perkins tries to convince him to keep the pages in. When he does have a serious criticism, as with the manuscript of *To Have and Have Not*, he refrains from raising it. As Berg writes, Perkins knew that Hemingway wanted "unquestionable support rather than constructive criticism, and that was what he gave him." In the editing of *For Whom the Bell Tolls* we can see evidence of these elements. Perkins raised small questions about style here and there, wondered about the reception of some material that might poke the public in the nose (Robert Jordan masturbating before a battle), and helped Hemingway to decide how to end the novel. Each of Perkins's three great writers had problems, but Hemingway's problems were of the variety that interfered least with his judgments about his work. And for a good number of years, he had a clear sense of how to edit his own work.

We can see a similar mature gift for self-editing in the editorial relationship between John Steinbeck and his editor, Pascal Covici, when we look at the evolution of the manuscript that became Steinbeck's novel *East of Eden*. From early winter of 1951 through mid-autumn of that same year, Steinbeck wrote a daily letter to Covici about the day's writing. Published in 1969, a year after the writer's death, under the title *Journal of a Novel*, these letters open a window onto the process of this writer's schemes for composition. Or, I should say, they open the window halfway. Without reading the novel in close relation to the letters, it is difficult to see those precise moments at which Steinbeck's references unfold into actual scenes. But he does, sometimes just in passing, often with some depth, refer to technique. His technique in the book, he says, "is an apparent lack of technique and I assure you," he says to Covici, that it is not easy to employ the various techniques he presumes to call upon as he is writing his draft.

Almost immediately Steinbeck stakes out the realistic ground. "My wish," he writes,

> is that when my reader has finished with this book, he will have a sense of belonging in it. He will actually be a native of that Valley. . . . This is an old-fashioned novel, Pat. It will achieve any effect it has by accumulation rather than by quick and flashing periods. And don't forget that it is going on for hundreds of pages. I only hope it is not dull. . . . This book is going

to take its own pace. . . . I'm going to use every bit of technique I have learned consciously and I am also going to let it go unconsciously—you will see if there is anything to see.

As guides to vision, Steinbeck announces that he will deploy every trick that he has learned in the forty years he has been writing fiction. He goes on to say that "since this book is about everything, it should use every form, every method, every technique." On creating characters, for example, he notes that it "is the custom nowadays in writing to tell nothing about a character but to let him emerge gradually through the story and the dialogue. This is what you might even call the modern fashionable method. But I don't have to do this. Using my method which is neither new nor old-fashioned, I can tell everything I can about a character but not only that. I can analyse and even say what I think about the character. Then if that person also comes through in the action and dialogue, one is pretty far ahead."

The deployment of symbols, the creating of a book's tone, the construction of plot, the awareness of narrative rhythm, the role of revision, and the function of chapters all enter into the letters as Steinbeck thinks out loud about his book's progress. Sometimes he seems to be talking to himself as he approaches a particularly difficult sequence. Sometimes he seems to be spinning his wheels, making a day's entry for the sake of making an entry. He reveals very little about his private life despite the personal tone of these journal entries, and he does not greatly illuminate either the process of composition or the editing process. But as a picture of a writer at the height of his powers, a mature writer who can take suggestion as well as give it to himself, a writer talking his way through nearly a year's worth of difficult labor, the journal is priceless.

I want to focus on a few more writers here in relation to the making of books, from the early draft on through the final editing process that goes on between writer and publisher. These writers are less well known than those I have already talked about here. One of them is Malcolm Lowry, whose 1947 novel *Under the Volcano* is one of the masterpieces of twentieth-century English prose. The novel is set on the Day of the Dead, All Souls' Day, in November of 1939. It takes place in and around Lowry's version of the town of Cuernavaca, just south of Mexico City, and it tells the story of the last day in the life of one particularly tormented soul, an alcoholic British consul named Geoffrey Firmin whose abandoned wife, Yvonne, and half brother, Hugh, have converged on him in order to try and save him from what seems from the very first an inevitable rendezvous with death.

Despite his weakness for alcohol—or perhaps because of it?—Geoffrey Firmin is a remarkably compelling character, since he trades willpower for sharp insight into the world around him. His long-suffering addiction is something that he wears with the dignity of a crown of thorns. Vast layers of incomparably beautiful prose slash across the pages of this book with all of the brilliance and sizzle of sheet lightning, and conjured up along with Firmin's exemplary soul in decline is a countryside—Mexican—and a country—Mexico—and a historical moment—the cusp of World War II—all of which makes the novel a nexus of exotic motifs and extraordinary breadth.

The genesis of the book is a short story with the same title that Lowry wrote in 1936. As he explains in his letters to various friends and potential publishers, he turned the story into a novel and then revised draft after draft, often making a new version of the book each time it came back from an unsympathetic publisher, of which there were many between the years 1939 and 1946. In a long letter similar in argument and intent to Dante's famous letter to Can Grande, Lowry writes from Cuernavaca to British publisher Jonathan Cape, dated January 2, 1946, making a powerful argument for his book by essentially explicating it for the sympathetic Cape. (The publisher's in-house reader, novelist William Plomer, had reported that the novel lacked action, strong characters, and was difficult to stick with at the beginning.)

"If the book were already in print," Lowry starts off by saying,

and its pages [were] not wearing the dumb pleading disperate and desperate look of the unpublished manuscript, I feel a reader's interest would tend to be very much more engaged at the outset just as, were the book already, say, an established classic, a reader's feelings would be most different; albeit he might say God this is tough going, he would plod gamely on through the dark morass—indeed he might feel ashamed not to—because of the reports which had already reached his ears of the rewarding vistas further on.

Lowry then talks about the composition of the novel, which, as he tells Cape, was first written in 1936, and rewritten in 1937, 1940, 1941, 1943, and 1944. (He doesn't mention that each revision came after a rejection by a different publisher.) First suggesting that his book is a poet's novel that requires a different set of principles for seeing into it, he then launches into a hyperbolic description of the novel "as a kind of symphony, or in another way as a kind of opera—or even a horse opera. It is hot music, a poem, a song, a tragedy, a comedy, a farce, and so forth. It is superficial, profound, entertaining and boring, according to taste. It is a prophecy, a political warning, a cryptogram, a preposterous movie, and a writing on the wall. It can even be regarded as a sort of machine: it works, too, believe me." And he then goes on for a number of pages, in what may be the sharpest and clearest and most convincing explication of any novelist about his own fiction, to explain precisely how it does work, concluding, as Joyce might have said about *Ulysses*, that the novel was "so designed, counterdesigned and interwelded" that it can be read an "indefinite number of times and still not have yielded all its meanings or its drama or its poetry."

Lowry, as you can see from this letter, represents yet another and possibly even more mature sort of writer—quite ironic, this word *maturity* when applied to Lowry the man, but utterly appropriate with regard to Lowry the artist—the writer who has made internal the best possible editorial perspective on his own work. From the profligate Wolfe to the necessities of Fitzgerald and Hemingway, the neatness of Steinbeck, we have come to the portrait of the writer as his own best editor. " 'O Time, Strength, Cash, and Patience!'" Melville's Ishmael cries out. And we can see that Lowry, despite his weaknesses, possessed all of these, at least when he was working on *Under the Volcano*. He had a living, the physical fortitude of his youth as a merchant seaman, and the perseverance to revise and revise and revise the manuscript of this great book. And then, alas, time ran out on him.

269

One more writer. Someone I know well enough to talk about the intricacies of his own editorial relations with editors and with himself. A writer on whose personal life I have an intimate perspective. Whose past I also know with a depth and particularity that I possess about no one else on this earth. Whose dreams, fantasies, hallucinations, grand leaps, and missteps I have witnessed over a long, long time. And yet someone who ultimately remains a mystery to me; no matter how close I get to him, he's always an arm's length or a hand's length away, constantly eluding my final understanding.

The writer is, of course, me.

About the making of my own books I could tell you a great deal, in fact, a great deal more than I should or will. Because one of the things I know about myself is that I understand that I musn't do this, out of humility's sake and for fear of angering the gods.

But I can say that I recognized early in my writing life that I needed the help of editors, particularly with long manuscripts, and that I have learned that the best editor is someone who tries to put him or herself inside your own skin and help you to figure a manuscript from the inside out. One editor with one word got me to make a final draft of a book that I had been rewriting over and over, with no end in sight. Another editor encouraged me to keep working in the same way as a coach might keep a player going on the field or court—with constant enthusiasm and expressions of faith always accompanied by, but never tempered by, suggestions for changes and transformations. The best editor out there is someone who is part mother, part father, part brother, part mentor, part disciple, part lover, part friend. I know that I will always need the assistance of a good editor, at least for small problems, not large, I hope. And I hope that that person will have something of Max Perkins's sense of taste and verisimilitude, and something resembling his sympathy for the difficulties of the writer at work.

Of all the advice that I've garnered from editors and from what I've read and heard of advice from editors to others, nothing seems more useful than what Steinbeck's Chinese American house servant, Lee Sing, says to his employer, Samuel Hamilton, in the ranch house in the Salinas Valley that Steinbeck so lovingly creates for us in *East of*

Eden. They're talking about the necessity of naming two newborn boys, and that discussion leads to a discussion of the Bible and some old Chinese poetry that Lee Sing is translating into English. While engaged in this enterprise, Lee Sing says, "I found some of the old things as fresh and clear as this morning. And I wondered why. And, of course, people are interested only in themselves. If a story is not about the hearer he will not listen. And I here make a rule—a great and lasting story is about everyone or it will not last. The strange and foreign is not interesting—only the deeply personal and familiar."

That's great advice for the making of books, past, present, and future.

22

Voices: A Conversation

Before I did this interview with Alan Cheuse, most of our conversations had taken place in his office at George Mason University, where I was a student in the writing program. I would enter the office and find Alan half-buried under books—books shelved from floor to ceiling, two and three rows deep, around the four walls of the office; books piled on the desk; books resting on the chair where I was supposed to sit; books stacked knee-high and thigh-high on every spare inch of floor space; books in the U.S. Mail tub that was perpetually overflowing with newly arrived review copies. Sifting through the contents of the mail tub was a Sisyphean chore. Alan's hands stayed busy sorting the entire time we talked.

In that bookscape, there were limits to where a conversation could go. Mostly we spoke about my work, Alan giving criticism on a story or chapter, suggesting things to read. Sometimes we spoke about literature in general, writers and the writing life. Alan is a private person and that office was no place to try and draw him out. Whenever I asked him about himself, he would take cover within his fortress of books.

Writer Andrew Wingfield conducted this interview, which appeared in the Autumn 1999 issue of *Pleiades*.

And so when I asked to interview him I was prepared to demur if he suggested meeting in his office. Happily, he did not. We agreed to have lunch in Washington, D.C., where he lives with his wife, Kristin. On a sunny June day we met for sandwiches in the shade of a leafy trellis behind a café near Alan and Kristin's home. The interview began when we finished lunch. A tape recorder sat on the table between us, along with cups of coffee and bottles of juice. There were no books in sight.

The interview's title refers not only to the wonderful variety of voices that speak in Alan's fiction but also to the variety of voices in which Alan speaks outside his fiction. As the book commentator for *All Things Considered*, he speaks with authority and insight about contemporary fiction. As a writing teacher, he speaks with equal acuity about the felicities (or infelicities) of a line of student prose and about, say, the structure of book 2 of the *Odyssey*. His essays—literary, political, personal—engage him in a wide range of civilized conversations. During our conversation that day, I hoped to invoke as many of these voices as I could.

ANDREW WINGFIELD:

One of the most impressive things about your fiction is the variety and authenticity of the voices one hears in it. How did you discover your talent for narrating "in character"?

ALAN CHEUSE:

I guess by getting thrown out of a lot of lower-grade classes for doing voices. A number of writers I know are the kinds of people who in the last decade would have been put immediately on Ritalin in the public schools. Hyperactive, as they're called, kids with a tremendous amount of verbal energy and highly active imaginations. So I think it starts very early. You become entranced with the way comedians do voices, the way actors do voices. One of my great childhood heroes was Paul Winchell. He had his own show in the early days of TV. His thing was ventriloquy, and he had this dummy called Jerry Mahoney. Also Señor Wences, another of my favorites, who just died at the age of 104. He cast voices.

I'm not saying writing is ventriloquy, because it's not. That seems to be the form, but what happens is the voice begins to talk on its own. It's kind of like a horror novel about a ventriloquist who becomes the captive of his own voices. You know, who's the real dummy in this picture? It's not the characters, it's you. You're just trying to keep up with them. As fast as they talk, you take it down. Voices are the characters. We first know our characters through the way they speak. At least for me, it's more the way they speak than the way they look. I hear their voices in my head and construct characters on the way they sound. Which makes sense if we work with language, not with light primarily. It doesn't seem out of the ordinary that we begin with sound rather than things unveiled by light.

WINGFIELD:

Are you sitting at your writing table when you hear these voices?

CHEUSE:

That's the last place you want to have something like that happen to you. No, you're in the shower, or you're eating lunch, or you're driving your car, or in the subway, or on the treadmill, or walking down the street, or playing with your kids, or kissing your wife, and suddenly you hear a voice in your head. I think when you're sitting at the typewriter, that's where you want to become the unsurprised conduit of surprising voices. You want to use the voices that you've heard. I sound like Shirley MacLaine, channeling. But the channelers are just very bad fiction writers. Their mistake is not to recognize what they do as fiction. If you don't recognize what you do as fiction, you get in big trouble.

WINGFIELD:

The Light Possessed is filled with a chorus of wonderful voices. As you were conceiving that novel, did you know that the voices of some characters would come more easily to you than those of others?

CHEUSE:

No, I don't work that way. My favorite creation story is not the biblical one where one thing gets made on one day, and the next day another thing gets made. Mine is the *Popol-Vuh*, the genesis story of the Central

American Mayans. The gods want to populate the earth after they've created it. They populate it with stick figures, but they're burned in the fire; paper figures, but they're burned in the fire; figures made out of mud, but they're washed away in a flood. Then they try jaguars, but they're too ferocious. Then they try monkeys, but the monkeys shit all over everything. Finally they come up with human beings. That's the way I tend to work. I create and then destroy, create and then destroy, create and then maybe not destroy the latest version. Sounds like Shiva. Maybe that's a myth we ought to look to for inspiration. Creator and destroyer, creator and destroyer—OK, if we get creation at the end.

WINGFIELD:

Minnie Bloch, the narrator of *The Grandmothers' Club*, is one of your most memorable voices. The author's note to that novel links her to the Jewish women whose talk and stories you listened to as a child. How have those women influenced you as a storyteller?

CHEUSE:

How much did they influence me? Very much, they influenced me, very much. It's the noise of their speech, the rhythms of those particular speech patterns. When I was first growing up, that was part of nature to me. I thought that's the way people spoke. The sounds of a particular immigrant group are the first sounds that some of us hear and they seem part of nature, so they stay with us in a very profound way, even though we ultimately recognize them as one person's way of speaking. They have an effect on us. Paule Marshall, a Caribbean-born writer, talks about having that same experience, sitting around the kitchen in Brooklyn talking to all these immigrant women, and she sees her goal as to reproduce those voices on the page. But to me the voices are a vehicle that I use for telling a story. It's not just the music itself, but the melody that I'm interested in, if you can draw that distinction.

WINGFIELD:

With Minnie, you also mention in that author's note a larger-than-life quality, a certain fecundity—producing stories and producing food.

CHEUSE:

I always liked the nanny-housekeeper in the household of the young Marcel, in Proust. She produces food, but it's more than just nourishment for the body. These women transcend the realistic and they move to a higher plane, and if you're lucky you can create that effect. In Minnie's case, she knows a lot more than she would know if I portrayed her simply in a naturalistic way. But the way I saw it, and the way I see it now, there's more to life than just the flesh, just the literal. As good as some naturalistic novels are, they deal only with the literal. Everything that I've been trained to do as a reader spills over into what I'm trying to do as a writer, and so I see them as something more than literal, something more than figures of the naturalistic realm.

WINGFIELD:

Do you think those women from your childhood have anything to do with your interest in creative women like Georgia O'Keeffe and the other women artists you read about in preparation for *The Light Possessed?*

CHEUSE:

I've always had an interest in women, creative or not. *[Laughter]* Goethe says in *Faust*, "The Eternal Feminine leads us ever onward." It's a quest for an understanding of the other. It's an old dance that's happened ever since the music started playing. Women see men as the other, men see women as the other, and we try to make an amalgam out of the two different ways of being in the world, and make up a greater reality as a result. If I'm drawn to some of these female characters, it's because I want to know more of the truth than I see at the moment. I think they offer ways of showing me things that I don't know. In a larger sense, that's what we do with any character.

WINGFIELD:

The Homeric epics have been very important to your literary education and your work.

CHEUSE:

Yes, growing up in New Jersey, one feels a close bond with the Homeric epics. *[Laughter]*

WINGFIELD:

It's a natural fit?

CHEUSE:

Sure, just think of all the great sea voyagers who started out from Bradley Beach. *[More laughter]* I knew nothing about Homer except what I read in a *Classics Illustrated* comic book until I got to graduate school, where I accidentally found myself in a tutorial, one on one, with a classicist named Cristophe Clairmont, who asked me what I'd read. When he discovered I'd read nothing, he put me on a very harsh regimen for a couple of years. So it wasn't until my mid-twenties that I really discovered that huge Homeric universe, and understood that it was mine and had been waiting for me all those years. Everything that I'd done before then seemed to fall into place.

WINGFIELD:

Why do you suppose Homer has had this effect on you? Why Homer and not Shakespeare, for example?

CHEUSE:

Shakespeare, certainly, for the language. But if one can say Homer is more universal than Shakespeare, I think it's true in that the anthropology and the mythology of family, as well as the road story and relations between the sexes, the relations among people of various levels at court, the visions of war and the visions of peace seem to me the most complete understanding of human life that we have, or at least the largest templates we have to compare our own lives to. What Homer offers us is an understanding of the relationship between physical action and symbolic action that no one else can show us. The way he takes the literal and turns it into the symbolic and transcends that to the cosmic is an astounding revelation when you see it for the first time.

WINGFIELD:

It's one thing to recognize it, and one thing to desire to have something like that going on in one's own work. It's another thing to actually achieve it. Is that in your mind when you're writing?

CHEUSE:

No, it's more like in my blood, in my brain, the interstices of my brain. You absorb these things. Look at dance, for example. The great dance pieces allow us to move with the dancers in our minds. Although physically we can never leap like Nijinsky, never move like Baryshnikov, we give our imaginations over to them as they move onstage, and we move with them. I think if you're reading as a young writer, whether you know you're going to be a writer or not, you learn to make those same moves in your mind. You show yourself that it's possible to do the kinds of things that the greatest artists have done. The Homers, the Rhapsodes, whatever you want to call them, that tribal group or familial group that passed the poems down from generation to generation over five to eight thousand years, they were the greatest artists ever known in the Western world.

WINGFIELD:

What about other literary influences?

CHEUSE:

Certainly Shakespeare for language, as I said earlier. Joyce, Faulkner, Hemingway, and Virginia Woolf. I think they're the main people. Not so much that I want to write like them, but they showed me what one could do with language and story. They're like the greatest coaches you could possibly have. Great athletes in their own right, and then they become coaches, and they show you how to do it. You go back to them and learn by watching old films of them doing their thing.

WINGFIELD:

All of them were writing around the same time.

CHEUSE:

Well, they gave birth to modernism. You wouldn't want to be influenced by a nineteenth-century writer, would you? You want to be influenced by the best writers around who immediately precede you. If you're influenced by people who are alive while you're trying to work, that's crazy, because you'll never break through to your own voice. You want to find the greatest immediate precedents you can find.

WINGFIELD:

What about teachers?

CHEUSE:

I had some great literature teachers. Francis Fergusson was my teacher as an undergraduate and in graduate school. He's probably had the greatest influence on me. Robert Pinsky and I were in Fergusson's undergraduate course in comparative literature at Rutgers in 1960. To this day, Pinsky and I still talk about how much Francis Fergusson taught us and how we still use the principles he taught us in that course. And this is forty years later. He based his understanding of how the work of art evolves in time, and how it's performed, on his reading of Aristotle's *Poetics*. Aristotle is the oldest teacher, and people like me and Pinsky get him through a great teacher like Fergusson.

At that time Rutgers was a hotbed of seriousness. Great teachers congregated there. My teachers at Rutgers had a tremendous influence on my reading, the way that I read. And that had a great influence on the way that I write. I think it's a perfectly normal thing. Show me a writer whose writing has an influence on the way he or she reads, and I'll show you someone whose vision is a small one, although it may be acute and accurate for what it reveals. I think the other way around is best.

As for writing teachers, I took one writing course my junior year with John Ciardi, and it was utterly useless. John was an interesting poet who couldn't teach fiction writing to change his boots, and I learned nothing from that workshop. For me, the real workshops were the ones that I took with Joyce and Flaubert and Hemingway and Faulkner and Virginia Woolf. At a certain point you start reading the masters and they teach you what they know by the way in which they make their work. So I've had workshops with the greatest.

WINGFIELD:

What is the difference between learning from what you read and attending an actual workshop?

CHEUSE:

In a workshop you learn how to become your own best editor. Everybody eventually learns something of that, if they work at it long enough. What we can try to do is accelerate that process a bit. That's what you get. Otherwise there's no real difference. Peter Matthiessen, a wonderful writer, never took a writing workshop, as far as I know, and he published three or four early novels that are not all that good. He worked with Joe Fox, a great editor at Random House, and eventually he learned to write really good fiction. So that's the equivalent of the M.F.A. process. It's a starting place, a springboard.

WINGFIELD:

Have any editors been influential with your work?

CHEUSE:

Yes, I had a fantastic editor named James Thomas, who's a story writer himself. He edited my second and third and fourth books, and he was wonderful. My first publisher was also my editor, Phil Zuckerman, at Applewood Books. He was terrific. They somehow figure out what it is you care to do before you turn to do it, and try to lead you a little further along in that direction than you might allow yourself to go without them. They train you to make your best moves, and to be a little more certain of making those moves that turn out to be your best.

WINGFIELD:

Your new collection of stories, *Lost and Old Rivers*, includes a horseback ride across mountains of Los Angeles landfill; a tunnel walk beneath Washington, D.C.; visits to a New Mexico bird sanctuary and Niagara Falls; a tour of various bodies of water significant to your life. Specific places—either natural or constructed—seem central to almost all your fiction. Do certain places suggest stories to you, or vice versa?

CHEUSE:

I have to say the former is probably true. Places do evoke stories for me. Or they solidify certain states of being that I might have in mind which need a place.

WINGFIELD:

Most place-sensitive writers keep returning to one or two favorite places. Your imagination is open to a wide range of localities. Mexico, New Jersey, New Mexico, Russia, Tennessee, Texas, Los Angeles, Santa Cruz, Vermont: these are some of the places your work returns to. Is there some common thread that ties them all together for you?

CHEUSE:

There's a writer I know from Tennessee named Robert Drake. Drake has spent his career writing tales and anecdotes, sketches and scenes, all of them set in this tiny Tennessee town about eighty miles north of Memphis, most of them set in the houses of his aunts and uncles and cousins and grandparents. I don't think Drake's ever written a story that wasn't set in this place. Drake once said to me, "You're a very cosmopolitan writer." At first I thought, That's some kind of insult, isn't it? That's what Stalin used to call Jewish writers in Russia that he didn't like, that he was about to execute. They were "cosmopolitan." So I thought to myself, I'm some kind of wandering Jew, I can't find one single place to write about.

But then, it's not so much being born Jewish as being born in New Jersey. I mean, just how long, lord, how long could you stay in New Jersey and write about New Jersey only? I got out. Lately I've been writing these essays for the *San Diego Reader* about border issues— Tijuana/San Diego stories. It's helped me to understand that New Jersey is a border state. Something about growing up in New Jersey, at least the part I grew up in, you know as soon as you're tall enough to drop a token in the subway that you're really part of New York. So you have this dual loyalty. You begin to see that you've got to forge out in other directions. And so you become a traveler. You want to see beautiful places, you want to breathe air that doesn't turn your lungs dark with soot, so you escape from New Jersey. You want to go back to your homeland, but if New Jersey is your homeland you want to find it somewhere else, and so you go looking.

WINGFIELD:

Lost and Old Rivers concludes with a beautiful long piece called "On the Millstone River: A Story from Memory." Can you explain the subtitle?

CHEUSE:

When I called it a story from memory I was trying to suggest that the material was autobiographical, but I wasn't trying to write history, and I wasn't trying to write autobiography. I was really just intensifying the normal process of the fiction writer, which is to take material out of one's own life or the lives of others and shape it and form it into a story. In this instance I was using material that was all true and shaping it and forming it in the way that one shapes and forms the material for fiction, rather than for nonfiction or memoir.

What that means is I didn't so much take liberties with the actual scenes or with the characters of the people I was dealing with, but I did feel free to move around in time and shape the arrangement of the scenes in a way that I wouldn't have done if I was trying to do straight memoir. I was trying specifically to deal with the way in which recollection plays a role in making the truth known to oneself when one thinks back on the past. I think that the same power we use to shape our understanding of time is the power we use to turn the unmediated stuff of life into fiction. So "story from memory" is more complicated than it first appears. You might say it's as much a story *about* memory as a story *from* memory.

WINGFIELD:

The critic John Aldridge has praised your fiction for its energetic evocation of specific historical epochs. According to him, this engagement of history makes you quite unique among your generation of American writers. Why is history important to your work?

CHEUSE:

It's other lives lived in other times, which is something we need to know about if we want to see our own lives in context.

WINGFIELD:

Can fiction teach us things about history that other sources of historical information can't?

CHEUSE:

The first historians didn't really recognize a line between history and fiction, between mythology and what we would call factual history. Herodotus and Thucydides, for example. The good fiction writers of today do the same thing. We work in the model of the greatest historians. We do that much more squarely than most contemporary historians do.

WINGFIELD:

You've written two books that can be described as biographical novels. In that work, how do you negotiate between the facts of your model's life and the demands of your fictional art?

CHEUSE:

I'll try to answer that with a story. I had finished a Ph.D. dissertation and I was teaching at Bennington. I was looking around for another project. John Reed had always fascinated me as an American figure, a sort of bold, naive adventurer. I had read *Ten Days That Shook the World* when I was in high school, and I'd read it again in college and I thought, Oh, I'll write about John Reed. Then I started doing a little research, and I discovered that a historian named Robert Rosenstone was coming out with a book on Reed. This little light went on in my head. A serious, trained historian is writing a book on Reed. You cannot do this, you are not a serious, trained historian. And then a little voice said, "Do it as a novel, Alan, do it as a novel." And so I obeyed.

When I mentioned to Nicholas Delbanco, a novelist friend, that I was doing it as a novel, he said, "Oh, you're really fortunate because I have to make up all the details in my fiction, and here you'll have all the details of this life laid out before you. You won't have to do all that hard work of the imagination." And I thought, very naively, he's right, I'm a very lucky guy. Inventing a life out of whole cloth is very difficult, as any novelist can tell you, but finding the pattern in bales and bales of cotton is also very difficult.

WINGFIELD:
You must have had a good experience, because you've done it since.

CHEUSE:
Are you talking about *The Light Possessed?*

WINGFIELD:
Yes.

CHEUSE:
That's a slightly different kind of book. The Reed novel—*The Bohemians*—is clearly bio-historical fiction. I didn't deviate from the facts of Reed's life, or Louise Bryant's, as I knew them. I could fill in gaps based on what they would probably do in certain situations, which is the method of Thucydides—knowing the traits of the historical figures you want to focus on, you can write their speeches. You know what they think, you know what they believe, you know what they would say under certain circumstances they might have faced when you weren't there. That was my principle in the Reed book, so I see it as straightforward historical fiction with some imaginative liberties.

The Light Possessed is different, since the main character is largely based on the life of Georgia O'Keeffe, but not entirely. I had read long and deep in the biographical material about a dozen American women painters, and some European women painters as well. Mostly twentieth-century painters. I made an amalgam in that character rather than a direct presentation of O'Keeffe alone.

WINGFIELD:

You have published novels, stories, a memoir, hundreds of book reviews, literary and personal essays, investigative articles, travel pieces, all kinds of other journalistic work. Is is it by design that you write so many different kinds of things well?

CHEUSE:

Yes, for at my back I always hear MasterCard's winged chariot hurrying near. It's a way to pay the bills. I guess there's a law that says people who can afford not to don't write as much of the peripheral material. If you don't have much money, you write a lot of occasional pieces in order to earn more money.

WINGFIELD:

Does that mean you see the fiction and the other writing as opposed and vying for your attention? Or are they complementary?

CHEUSE:

It's complementary. You use different muscles for different kinds of activities. I don't see it as a conflict. It's just a matter of how much time you have. I don't play cards as much as other writers may play cards. It just seems to work out all right for me.

WINGFIELD:

I know you're a very disciplined fiction writer. How do you manage to build writing time into your already full days and weeks?

CHEUSE:

I've been writing fiction for only about twenty years now. I started late. That's why my heroes are Henry Miller and Harriet Doerr and Sherwood Anderson, the people who started writing late. I had almost forty years of time to fool around in, so from the time I started writing I realized I didn't want to mess with the time that I had left. I just do it every day. Every morning I get up and I write some pages. It's just a habit. It's what you do if you want to work in this business. Most writers I know have pretty much the same pattern, give or take a week or a month here and there. Most of us work in the mornings and get tired by the afternoon and do something else. In the evenings I watch movies, if I can. They clear my head of prose like the sorbet between courses. That's why I have very little respect for movies—I do it as a trivial pastime. I love them, but I don't take them seriously. It's like taking dessert more seriously than the main course. If that's happening, you know you have a severe metabolic imbalance.

WINGFIELD:

In addition to being an American writer, you are an important American reader. How long have you been reviewing fiction?

CHEUSE:

I got my start writing reviews for the Kirkus service in 1962. We were living in the Village and my first wife saw an advertisement in the *Voice*. It said, "Writers Wanted." She said, "You call yourself a writer, why don't you answer this advertisement?" And I did. I was given a test assignment. They gave me a novel to review. Read the book and bring the review in the next day. So I started doing one review a day, and I did that every day for the next two years. They paid seven dollars a review, plus what you could get for the book at the Strand used bookstore over on Broadway and Twelfth Street. Some days you could make as much as twelve dollars. Winter was best, because you'd walk down this long hallway that led to this garden apartment where Kirkus had its headquarters. This hallway was lined with shelves that were filled with coffee-table books. So when you left in winter, you slipped as many of these coffee-table books as you could carry under your coat. Kind of like Harpo Marx in *A Night at the Opera*, getting food for the opera crew. When you left, you might have books that would bring you as much as four, five dollars apiece at the Strand. Some days you could even make fifteen or sixteen dollars—in winter. Winter was best.

That's where I cut my reviewing teeth, at Kirkus. I learned how to write fast. I learned how to read quickly, but not so overly speedy that I missed the book. I don't believe in anything called speed reading. (You know that Woody Allen joke? I took a course in speed reading and I've just finished *War and Peace*. It pertains to Russia.) Later I wrote for the *Nation* and for a couple of radical papers that no longer exist. At the time I was just thinking about the joy of being paid for reading something you want to read anyway. I still feel that same pleasure. Sometimes I feel like a bit of a reading freak, as opposed to a speed freak, but then I remind myself that that's what we do in this business—we read as much as we can, and we write as much as we can, and we live as much as we can.

WINGFIELD:

How has American fiction changed since you started reviewing?

CHEUSE:

I don't think it's changed that much. Of course, it's more difficult to see the greatness among one's contemporaries, if it's there, than it is to see the greatness of one's predecessors. So I read the work of our predecessors and ancestors like the case histories of trials that have ended, and the work of our contemporaries as trials where the jury's still out. But I don't see any tremendous difference. People are still striving to be as good as they can possibly be. We live in a time when there are dozens and dozens and dozens of really wonderful writers. Without doing a close study of, say, Paris in 1872, to see if there was a comparable number of really terrific writers, as well as the major figures we're aware of, I would say there are more writers, better writers working now than lived before in this age of book commerce.

WINGFIELD:

So you think the publishing industry has influenced fiction in a positive way?

CHEUSE:

Oh, no, the publishing industry is always doing its best to work against the great writers, but people somehow persevere. Look at William Kennedy, who had to get a letter from Saul Bellow to get published by Viking. Viking rejected his first novel, and nearly twenty publishers later Bellow said, "I'll give you a letter to try and influence Viking to publish you." And that finally worked. But how long does someone like Bill Kennedy have to go begging for people to see that a lot of publishers don't know their own taste? They have to be told what's good and what's not. I think that's always been the case. André Gide rejected Proust at Gallimard, when he was an editor there.

WINGFIELD:

When you say book commerce has increased the number of good writers, then, what do you mean?

CHEUSE:

All of today's good writers have emerged in the age of commercial publishing. So obviously there's some effect that commercial publishing has had that's beneficial. The necessity to publish more books for as many readers as possible has meant that accidentally they've published some really good writers, as opposed to time-servers and the usual crap they turn out in order to appease an audience with no taste. So sometimes they even do good things—inadvertently.

WINGFIELD:

Do you think the rise of writing programs has played any role in shaping the fiction of the last twenty years?

CHEUSE:

Some people complain about the "workshop story," but I don't really believe that. Or if it's true, it's not that unusual. When the pulp magazines were in their heyday, in the twenties, thirties, forties, and into the fifties, there was a kind of pulp magazine story that filled the pages of all these magazines—*Argosy*, *Saturday Evening Post*, and so forth. They were written by writers whose names we don't know anymore. We remember Faulkner, Hemingway, Fitzgerald, and a few others— the people whose stories were published alongside these space-fillers. So you could say there's a pulp magazine story that arose in the same way that there's an M.F.A. story that's arisen. But there's no law that says every writer is going to be a good writer or a great writer. There are a lot of writers, and among them appear some really fabulous writers who publish stories, coming out of the same background as the space-fillers. In recent times they probably wouldn't have appeared if it weren't for the M.F.A. programs. In the same way Faulkner, Fitzgerald, and Hemingway wouldn't have had a place to publish if it hadn't been for the pulp writers.

WINGFIELD:

How does teaching in an M.F.A. program fit into your writing life?

CHEUSE:

It's a good place to hang out and talk about what we do. Think of it as a blacksmith shop where we all stand around the fire and hammer out our horseshoes and talk about the quality of iron. It's a nice place to be, but it's not to everyone's taste. I tend to be a very private person, and so I don't answer a lot of questions about myself in the way other writers might, or that apprentice writers might want to know. But I'm still enough of a public person to enjoy the company. We're fortunate that the humanities departments have allowed us to stick around. In some ways, it's like apes teaching courses in the biology department. But if that's what they want, that's fine with us.

What we've done, in fact, over the last ten or fifteen years, is keep the humanist tradition alive with great force while these dull Platonists have tried to sell their boring little theories about literature. We're flying the flag for literature, we're showing people what literature can be about and should be about. So in that sense I think the literature departments need to have writers around.

WINGFIELD:

What do you think twentieth-century American fiction will be remembered for?

CHEUSE:

One hopes it will be remembered because of the way the best of it preserves the characteristic and beautiful music of the way that we speak about the world at this time, the way we describe the world. By "world" I mean both inner life and outer landscape.

WINGFIELD:

What are the prospects for literary fiction in this country as we begin the next century?

CHEUSE:

I don't think they're any better or worse than they were when the nineteenth century turned into the twentieth century. We're still wrapped in that same cloth. I think most of us writing today are a lot closer to Henry James and Mark Twain and Theodore Dreiser and Edith Wharton than we are to those who'll be writing in America in the year 3000. I don't think there's a tremendous difference, or will be a tremendous difference at least for the next twenty, thirty, forty years. I think that the means of conveyance of fiction may change. People are currently trying to sell us electronic books. But the means of conveyance of food has changed, too. We drink water from a cup instead of dipping our hands into the stream. I don't see electronic books changing the serious work that will come. It's just that it may arrive in a different sort of package. Stories have always been told in the human voice, and then later conveyed by words on the page. If our definition of what a page is changes, we'll still make the same high demands of the word.